D1563586

Refugees and the Transformation of Societies

STUDIES IN FORCED MIGRATION
General Editors: Stephen Castles and Dawn Chatty

Volume 1
A Tamil Asylum Diaspora: Sri Lankan Migration, Settlement and Politics in Switzerland
Christopher McDowell

Volume 2
Understanding Impoverishment: The Consequences of Development-Induced Displacement
Edited by Christopher McDowell

Volume 3
Losing Place: Refugee Populations and Rural Transformations in East Africa
Johnathan B. Bascom

Volume 4
The End of the Refugee Cycle? Refugee Repatriation and Reconstruction
Edited by Richard Black and Khalid Koser

Volume 5
Engendering Forced Migration: Theory and Practice
Edited by Doreen Indra

Volume 6
Refugee Policy in Sudan, 1967–1984
Ahmed Karadawi

Volume 7
Psychosocial Wellness of Refugees: Issues in Qualitative and Quantitative Research
Edited by Frederick L. Ahearn, Jr.

Volume 8
Fear in Bongoland: Burundi Refugees in Urban Tanzania
Marc Sommers

Volume 9
Whatever Happened to Asylum in Britain? A Tale of Two Walls
Louise Pirouet

Volume 10
Conservation and Mobile Indigenous Peoples: Displacement, Forced Settlement and Sustainable Development
Edited by Dawn Chatty and Marcus Colchester

Volume 11
Tibetans in Nepal: The Dynamics of International Assistance among a Community in Exile
Anne Frechette

Volume 12
Crossing the Aegean: An Appraisal of the 1923 Compulsory Population Exchange between Greece and Turkey
Edited by Renée Hirschon

Volume 13
Refugees and the Transformation of Societies: Agency, Policies, Ethics and Politics
Edited by Philomena Essed, Georg Frerks and Joke Schrijvers

Volume 14
Children and Youth on the Front Line: Ethnography, Armed Conflict and Displacement
Edited by Jo Boyden and Joanna de Berry

Volume 15
Religion and Nation: Iranian Local and Transnational Networks in Britain
Kathryn Spellman

Refugees and the Transformation of Societies

AGENCY, POLICIES, ETHICS AND POLITICS

Edited by
Philomena Essed, Georg Frerks and Joke Schrijvers

Berghahn Books
New York • Oxford

First published in 2004 by

Berghahn Books
www.berghahnbooks.com

Library of Congress Cataloging-in-Publication Data

Refugees and the transformation of societies : agency, policies, ethics, and
politics / [edited by] Philomena Essed, Georg Frerks, Joke Schrijvers.
p. cm.
Includes bibliographical references.
ISBN 1-57181-866-9 (hardback : alk. paper)
1. Refugees—Government policy. 2. Forced migration—Moral and
ethical aspects. 3. Social conflict. 4. Humanitarian assistance. 5. Refugee
camps. 6. Return migration. 7. Repatriation. I. Essed, Philomena, 1955–.
II. Frerks, Georg, 1961– III. Schrijvers, Joke.

HV640.R4185 2004
362.87—dc22

2003063588

British Library Cataloguing in Publication Data

A catalogue record for this book is available
from the British Library.

Printed in the United States on acid-free paper.

ISBN 1-57181-866-9 (hardback)

Contents

Acknowledgements   vii

List of Abbreviations   ix

Introduction: Refugees, Agency and Social Transformation
Philomena Essed, Georg Frerks and Joke Schrijvers   1

Part I: 'Refugeehood': Claiming Spaces and Responsibilities

  1 Refugeehood, Loss and Social Change: Eritrean Refugees
    and Returnees
    Gaim Kibreab   19

  2 Repatriation: Angolan Refugees or Migrating Villagers?
    Oliver Bakewell   31

  3 Space and Movement in the Sri Lankan Conflict
    Oivind Fuglerud   42

  4 Contested Refugee Status: Human Rights, Ethics and
    Social Responsibilities
    Philomena Essed and Rianne Wesenbeek   53

Part II: Redefining Identities and Social Relationships

  5 A Life Project out of Turmoil: Displacement and Gender
    in Colombia
    Donny Meertens   69

  6 Permanent Refugees: Female Camp Inhabitants in Bihar
    Kathinka Sinha-Kerkhoff   81

7 New Opportunities: Angry Young Men in a Tanzanian
Refugee Camp
Simon Turner 94

8 Identities and the Sense of Belonging: Iranian Women
Activists in Exile
Halleh Ghorashi 106

Part III: Discouraging Policies; Empowering Agency

9 A Community Empowered? The Bosnia Project in the U.K.
Lynnette Kelly 121

10 Refugee-generated Return: The Case of Guatemala
Anita Rapone and Charles Simpson 135

11 Between Victim and Agent: Women's Ambivalent
Empowerment in Displacement
Darini Rajasingham-Senanayake 151

Part IV: Challenging Dichotomies: Relief versus Development

12 Refugees between Relief and Development
Georg Frerks 167

13 Rethinking the Relation between Relief and Development:
'Villagisation' in Rwanda
Dorothea Hilhorst and Mathijs van Leeuwen 179

14 Dilemmas of Humanitarian Aid: Supporting Internal
Refugees in Sri Lanka
Joke Schrijvers 190

Bibliography 201

Notes on Contributors 215

Index 219

Acknowledgements

The original idea of producing this volume goes back to 1999, when we organised the conference 'Loss and Recovery: Refugees and the Transformation of Societies' (24–26 April, 1999, The Netherlands). The initiative for the conference and the way it got shaped up emerged from the 'Interdisciplinary Network for Researchers in the Netherlands Working on Refugee Issues'. Ellen Lammers, Brigitte Lammers and Maria Brons were excellent organisers in bringing together these researchers for regular network meetings. The conference 'Loss and Recovery' was a most stimulating event. It helped sharpen our focus as editors, as we found that many of the papers challenged established notions and discourses on refugees and refugeehood. We would like to thank Maria Brons, Antje Falkenberg, Cindy Horst, Brigitte Lammers and Ellen Lammers for co-organising the conference with us in such an efficient and very pleasant manner.

We made a selection from the papers and were happy to find that the authors were willing to make comprehensive revisions and updates.

The joint strengths of the members of the editorial team have made producing this volume a great adventure. Friendships have deepened over the tedious work that goes along with editing, overloaded agendas, meetings squeezed in between international travels, and at times difficult decisions about the direction of the volume. Maria Brons was with us in formulating a first draft for the outline of this volume and coparticipated in the first round of editing. We are grateful for her valuable contributions.

The Amsterdam Research Institute for Global Issues and Development Studies at the University of Amsterdam (the institutional home of Joke Schrijvers and Philomena Essed) and the section of Disaster Studies of Wageningen University, Georg Frerks' workplace, have generously provided us with the opportunity and space for editing this volume.

We have benefited greatly from the comments and suggestions of two anonymous reviewers for Berghahn Books, as a result of which we have been able to qualify our approach and arguments more consistently and explicitly.

We wish to express thanks to Jeroen de Zeeuw and Ellen Buijn who took care of word processing and organising the manuscript. Without their assistance and critical eyes, it would have been impossible to get the book ready in time. We also thank Peter Schregardus for producing the index and proof reading the text.

Last but not least and much to our delight, Berghahn kindly consulted us about the book cover. We are especially indebted to Eegje Schoo for generously making available to us her marvellous collection of Indian art work, and to Rekha Rodwittiya for allowing us to use one of her paintings titled, The Reprieve. It speaks to the paradoxes this volume is about: vulnerability and strength, misery and hope, death and survival, continuity and transformation.

Philomena Essed
Georg Frerks
Joke Schrijvers

List of Abbreviations

AEF	African Educational Foundation
AIDS	Acquired Immune Deficiency Syndrome
CNDD	Conseil National pour la Défense de la Démocratie
ELN	Ejército de Liberación Nacional
EPL	Ejército Popular de Liberación
FARC	Fuerzas Armadas Revolucionarias de Colombia
IDP	Internally Displaced Person
INTA	National Institute of Agrarian Transformation
LTTE	Liberation Tigers of Tamil Eelam
LWF	Lutheran World Federation
MP	Member of Parliament
MPLA	Movimento Popular de Libertação de Angola
NGO	Non-Governmental Organisation
NRC	National Registration Card
OECD	Organisation for Economic Cooperation and Development
Palipehutu	Parti pour la Libération du Peuple Hutu
QIP	Quick Impact Project
RIC	Refugee Identity Card
RPF	Rwandan Patriotic Front
Rs	Rupees
SLMC	Sri Lanka Muslim Congress
UN	United Nations
UNDP	United Nations Development Programme
UNHCR	United Nations High Commissioner for Refugees
UNITA	União Nacional para a Independência Total de Angola

Introduction: Refugees, Agency and Social Transformation

Philomena Essed, Georg Frerks and Joke Schrijvers

Refugees and the Transformation of Societies is about cultures and societies in change, in the process of producing, refusing or receiving refugees. It explores experiences, interpretations and practices of 'refugees', 'internally displaced' and 'returnees' in or emerging from societies in violent conflict. It also addresses ethics and politics of interventions by professionals and policy makers. Contributions elicit specific contexts, histories, conflicts and negotiations in which refugees take part in the course of their flight and resettlement. Authors highlight the extremely dynamic nature of situations where refugees, policy makers and practitioners interact in trying to construct new livelihoods in transforming societies.

The main aim of this volume is to present empirical realities and policy discourses, to challenge prevailing orthodoxies and to encourage new developments in refugee studies and practices. There is a need for reconceptualising notions of migration and refugees, presuppositions about actors and their identities, and the impact of migration on identities and practices of receiving societies. We have reason to believe that the notions of agency and social transformation, central to such an undertaking, contribute to a more adequate, strategic and dynamic understanding of how refugees succeed in remaking their livelihoods, or, for that matter, in surviving a camp environment.

Agency

The notion of agency centralises people, conceptualised as social actors who process their own experiences and those of others while acting upon these experiences. 'Agency implies both a certain knowledgeability, whereby experiences and desires are reflexively interpreted and internalised (consciously or otherwise), and the capability to command relevant skills, access to material and non-material resources and engage in particular organising practices' (Long 2001: 49). Moreover, agency forms a sharp contrast to the more established approaches where refugees are pictured as passive victims of violence and disaster, or as mere recipients of relief aid. Making agency central is helpful to avoid undue generalisations. There are regional, gender, age and other differences in experiences and there are differential responses to forced displacement. Some refugees do not recognise the (new) opportunities available to them, due to trauma and loss of resources. Others seem to fare better. Individual decisions, experiences and life courses have to be seen as part of a larger cultural, sociopolitical and environmental framework that holds advantages as well as constraints.

Agency does not only refer to refugees, however. In this volume we also highlight other social actors, notably politicians, bureaucrats, policy makers and practitioners. What they do or fail to do, in relation to refugees, does influence prevailing practices and discourses, and, hence, the actual life worlds of refugees. Our approach claims space for moral responsibility and accountability. Thereby, we are not only critical of things that have gone wrong, but we also highlight examples that address the need to rehumanise and transform existing structures and policies. How do policy makers and practitioners perceive of their work with respect to refugees and the internally displaced? What roles do they play in countries in conflict as well as in host societies? How do they relate to refugees and the internally displaced?

The concept of agency, as used in this volume, has four dimensions. Firstly, it allows for revisiting formal and legal concepts and categories of forced displacement used in the literature and in international conventions. Bureaucracies dealing with refugees are ill suited to accommodate the more dynamic and actor-focused image of reality that emerges from the case studies in this volume.

Secondly, the notion of agency is quite pertinent where issues of identity and social relationships are concerned. We want to draw attention to the fact that in the process of violent conflict and forced displacement existing relationships and identities are challenged and may be transformed as a result. Here, it is essential to understand agency in a gender-specific way, because perceptions of gender and gendered identities change in the process of being displaced or living in exile. Also age and religion, as some case studies elucidate, impact on the ways in which individuals and groups renegotiate and reconstruct notions of femininity and masculinity, of 'self' and 'other'.

A third dimension related to the notion of agency is the finding that flight and refugee camp life, apart from causing losses and traumas, can also have some gains. Case studies highlight the circumstances under which refugees and displaced people develop more sophisticated awareness of their social situation and grow assertive in negotiating social space. Escape from hegemonic political structures and the redefinition of gender identities in camp environments have, in a number of cases, demonstrably reinforced women's social, political and economic empowerment and emancipation. Often, these achievements become more permanent assets after return. One of the questions then is how one can give practical support to these and other transformations.

A fourth dimension of agency questions the way politicians, policy makers and practitioners in host societies react to state-imposed restrictions on the extent and nature of refugee support. Do they acknowledge and respect refugees as capable actors or are they operating on the basis of stereotyped images, and top-down procedures that lead to passivity and dependence? Policy makers and practitioners are often situated between, on the one hand, the realities and needs of the refugees and the attendant (inter) national agreements and conventions, and, on the other hand, bureaucratic regimes, reluctant and hostile environments, political restrictions, and shortages of material and personnel.

Social Transformation

Agency, in this volume concerning migrations and 'refugeeness', can be instrumental in forging social transformations. Since the beginning of human history, people have moved around searching for better or safer homes, sometimes willingly, but more often under pressure. Migration and flight have always formed part of sociopolitical and environmental change, and it is therefore crucial to acknowledge the historical dimensions of 'refugeeness' (cf. Lammers 1999: 16–18). This awareness helps us to do away with explicit and implicit images of 'displacement as an anomaly in the life of an otherwise "whole", stable, sedentary society' (Malkki 1995: 508). On the contrary, (forced) migration and social transformation throughout human history can be considered the 'normal' state of affairs. The notion of social transformation is therefore central to our analysis, and people's agency in our approach is directly linked to these processes of change and transformation.

There is not anything intrinsically new about the notion of social transformation. It is not unproblematic, however, as it can have very different meanings and connotations. In common usage it generally implies notions of social and cultural changes in response to processes such as neoliberal policies, economic growth, political unrest, violent conflict and war. It can refer to the 'great transformation' in Western societies brought about by industrialisation and modernisation, or to more recent changes in connection with processes of decolonisation, nation-state formation, economic change and globalisation. However, the notion of social trans-formation can also be used to analyse processes and movements that run counter to the force of globalisation. It 'can be seen as the *antithesis of glob-alisation* in the dialectical sense that it is both an integral part of globalisa-tion and a process that undermines its central ideologies' (Castles 2001: 15). Emphasising social transformation as a dialectical process is helpful, we feel, to understand the changing life worlds of refugees *as part of* the broader historical context in which the problems they face have been cre-ated. The present-day political construction of 'the refugee issue' tends to ignore this context, narrowing it down to simplistic cause-effect relations, thereby distorting the total problematic.

Although change and (forced) migration have always characterised human society, the global processes that have taken place during the last quarter of the twentieth century have brought about unprecedented change. Accompanied by major social transformations throughout the world in all areas of human life, globalisation has affected the political, economic, social, cultural, environmental and interpersonal domains of an increasing number of people. Because of this process, old dichotomies such as 'modern and traditional', 'developed and less-underdeveloped', 'East and West', 'the South and the North' have become less extreme. It has become increasingly difficult to understand local situations and national levels as separate from their global context (Castles 2001). Although this has created enormous technical, economic and commu-nicative possibilities for many, at the same time it has given rise to new forms of exclusion and polarisation. Violent conflict and civil war have become endemic in many societies. The number of intrastate conflicts has increased considerably. Many governments today are at war with their own civilians, who belong to ethnic or religious minorities that have taken up weapons to stand up against exclusion and discrimination. As a con-sequence, the nature of (forced) migration has changed. Never before have so many people in the whole world been forced to leave their homes and take refuge elsewhere, as 'internally displaced people' within their own countries or as 'refugees' or 'illegals' in other countries or continents.

All contributions to this volume explicitly or implicitly refer to funda-mental social transformation processes within the various countries and regions that are discussed. Whether it concerns Colombia, Guatemala, Tanzania, Eritrea, the Horn of Africa, The Netherlands, Sri Lanka, Great Britain, Rwanda, the region of the Great Lakes, or the U.S.A., (forced) migra-tion and resettlement are shown to be intrinsically part of historical processes and wider (inter)national political and economic power relations. These transformations have deeply affected established discourses and practices, in the countries of origin of the refugees as well as in their host societies. Seen in this broad context, social transformation in our volume has four concrete dimensions. In the first place, in line with our emphasis on social agency, it refers to the fundamental changes in the lives of refugees themselves, which are part and parcel of their displacement. Flight implies changes in the livelihoods, perceptions and identities, 'life projects' and futures, in short, all aspects of the refugees' existence. Secondly, the concept refers to the consequences and challenges for people in the communities and agencies that are receiving and dealing with refugees. The transformations that occur in recipient societies are not only an effect of the impact of the numbers of those seeking refuge, but also of the particular capacities and resources the refugees add to their host societies. Thirdly, transformations are shown to take place in perceptions and identities, with far-reaching consequences. As indicated above, the history of flight may impact on essential dimensions of identity, for instance the way people perceive gender-related notions and images of themselves and others. Fourthly, transformations occur after the return of peace – no matter how unstable this situation can often be. There is no way back to the status quo ex ante, to the 'certain certainties' of the past. The experience of war and displacement implies irretrievable changes, both painful and rewarding. These changes are likely to be perpetuated, if they have not already become permanent.

Reflections

The volume is organised to reflect four major themes. Part One, 'Refugee-hood': Claiming Spaces and Responsibilities, contests taken-for-granted meanings attached to, and policies developed on the basis of such notions as 'refugee', 'migration' and 'illegal'. Likewise, prevailing assumptions are challenged, for instance that there is a clear distinction between political and economic refugees, or that repatriation is by definition a desirable outcome. Central to Part Two, Redefining Identities and Social Relationships, is showing that gender, ethnic, national, regional, and other relevant dimensions of identities are strategically renegotiated and changed in the process of recreating a sense of home and meaningful life in new environments. Discouraging Policies, Empowering Agency, Part Three, combines a critique of pacifying national aid programmes with counterexamples of empowering self-initiatives among refugees. Across locations and crisis situations, women in particular are noted for transgressing previous gender restrictions in claiming new spaces and responsibilities. Finally, Part Four, Challenging Dichotomies: Relief versus Development, addresses fundamental questions relating violence to the nature of (modern) development and development interventions. Relief and development are not mutually exclusive approaches. Even in crisis situations relief-cum-development should be the aim.

Having categorised the articles in one particular order, we hasten to qualify this by saying that several of the articles speak to more than one of the above themes. In light of this, in introducing themes and authors below, we deviate from the more conventional way of providing chronological summaries of each of the four parts of the volume. When we discuss in more detail what the contributions are about, we highlight at the same time a number of crosscutting insights we want to call to readers' attention. The reflections are not meant to suggest completeness, but to identify crucial issues the contributors to this volume address.

Flight: One Variant of Migration

None of the authors would deny the exceptional nature and dramatic impact of flight and of refuge in a situation of crisis, but few if any would label refuge as inherently different from other migratory experiences. Flight, representing one variant of the more general phenomenon of migration, involves many of the considerations other migrants go through when physically disconnecting from home regions or countries. In one of the first articles in this volume, Oliver Bakewell challenges the widely accepted view that one should distinguish generically between migrants and refugees. His study concerns border crossing between Zambia and Angola, where settlement and repatriation must be placed in the wider socioeconomic context of the area with its long history of migration among the people of the upper Zambezi. Repatriating Angolan refugees in Zambia have similar motives and interests as others 'struggling to maintain their livelihoods'. Because these migrations take place for political, social and economic reasons, it is too narrow to define the situation as a refugee phenomenon only. The tenuous link between the state and the population, the low population density in the area, and the shared ethnic and historical patterns of movement between Zambians and Angolans have enabled the self-settled Angolan refugees to become fully integrated.

Bakewell is also critical of the prevailing mode to push for repatriation, where refugees are seen as constituting a humanitarian problem or even a threat to their host environments. If refuge is seen primarily as an aberration in a modern world of fixed nation states and nationalities, repatriation becomes the only available solution. In the case at hand, however, the labels of refugee and returnee are meaningless. Furthermore, for many Angolans and Zambians there is no such thing as a strong attachment to something called 'nationality'. As a result, one cannot speak of one 'event of repatriation', but only of a process of continuous migration back and forth across the border.

Gaim Kibreab, whose study on Eritrean refugees and returnees is discussed further below, agrees that to adopt a one-sided focus on refugees as problematic and marginal is to 'telescope otherwise protracted processes of social change and transformation'. The problematisation of refugees is not only a South phenomenon. As will be seen in the article by Philomena Essed and Rianne Wesenbeek, European immigration discourses, setting against each other 'pure' refugees versus (fake) others, relegate increasing numbers of people to the status of 'illegality', a highly problematic and irresponsible situation.

Oivind Fuglerud pushes the point even further. He states that it is misleading to focus only on the flight response to conflict. Both migration and nonmigration are part of the time-space strategies available to all social actors involved. Why should there be a need to explain reasons to the 'move away' from conflict when considerations to stay in spite of conflict are as relevant for understanding the way people concerned conceptualise space and their own communities within it? Fuglerud explores this question as applied to war-torn Sri Lanka, comparing responses among the Tamil population in the Northern Province of Sri Lanka to the Muslims in the Eastern Province. It appears that kinship and marriage, the prevailing political imagery of origin preserved through oral histories about the earliest Muslim settlements, tie them to their surroundings – even in the situation of war.

Empowering Agency versus Reductionist Labelling

To entertain stereotypical presuppositions about the way people and cultures relate to space and social environments is one thing. To act upon stereotypes, in particular in terms of (non)governmental aid interventions, can have disastrous consequences. Lynnette Kelly describes how, due to misconceptions about refugees, the British 'Bosnia Project' for the resettlement of Bosnian refugees ended up suppressing rather than encouraging refugee agency. Ironically, the programme intention was actually to empower refugees, but it was based on presuppositions about 'ethnic communities' that did not work for Bosnian refugees. The idea was to facilitate refugee settlement through their community organisations. But Bosnian refugees had neither a clear community identity nor a definite common 'political project' or future in the host society. The project promoted refugee access to housing and welfare, but ignored the need for employment. As a result, motivation and self-initiative among the refugees got undermined, while they became more dependent on aid. This increased their sense of powerlessness and isolation and further complicated the possibilities to create a constructive role for community associations. This case study sadly confirms that it is necessary to remain critical of (even well-intended) policy interventions and of the underlying assumptions: 'It is not enough that the intention is to empower, the outcome must also be empowerment.'

Implicitly or explicitly nearly all of the chapters substantiate the fact that empowerment is foremost due to refugees' own agency, often against the grain of denigrating labels and stereotypes. Various studies point out that the concept of social agency is particularly central to understanding gender differences that emerge in the process of empowerment and in new environments. Refugee women, often more so than men, are able to transgress culture and tradition in asserting themselves. A case in point is the contribution by Kathinka Sinha-Kerkhoff, who has done research among female inhabitants of the so-called Permanent Liability Camps in Bihar, India. These camps were set up to receive the Hindu migrants from East Pakistan. The authorities promised to 'rehabilitate' the inhabitants, but certain categories were designated as 'unrehabilitable', especially widows and female-headed households without a breadwinner or other male adult. Sinha-Kerkhoff's case studies and narratives reveal the dramatic life histories and struggles of the women, who managed to overcome many of the traditional social and ritual restrictions. They have become astutely aware of the unequal gender relations and treatment in the camps and gained self-confidence as a result. The label 'refugee' reduces them to only one part of their identity, supposedly overshadowing ethnic, class, gender and other dimensions. But they throw back that label at the authorities, claiming their very status as refugees in order to make demands as women. On the one hand, this means that they are successful in strategically maintaining and using their refugee status in negotiating their interests with authorities and local populations. On the other hand, the (artificial) primacy of refugee identity blurs common interests and identifications they share with millions of other widows and women heads of households in India.

It is true, as various of the studies point out that, in crises, women tend to overcome debilitating effects of disruptions in their lives by negotiating traditional gender expectations against new demands and responsibilities. As a result they have acquired stronger political, economic and social identities.

Anita Rapone and Charles Simpson illustrate the way in which Guatemalan women refugees in Mexico have managed to assert their autonomy and agency in the process of flight and reconstituting communities. But their goals and achievements were not restricted to themselves. They meant to serve the whole community, women, men and children. The case provides an example where refugees have successfully negotiated their own repatriation in a way that is liberating from hegemonic forces and oppressive state rules. Guatemalan refugees who fled the 'scorched-earth' campaign of the military in the early 1980s became settled in Mexican camps. They shared a community culture and common narrative of the repression during the period of massacre and flight from Guatemala. This master narrative came to represent their identity and a framework to understand social reality. Shared identities and stories deepened their insight in political struggle and social development as a mode for securing their rights. They transformed camp life in such a way that it could become the basis for the reconstruction of a new Guatemala. Education was key to this project. Whilst sustaining their own culture, refugees managed to get Mexican certificates as teachers, health and human rights promoters and technicians. In the end, their autonomy, agency and the community-oriented nature of the population were important determinants of their successful repatriation. The returnees forged ties with broader segments of Guatemalan society as well as with international observers they invited in order to guarantee their rights.

In the same vein, Gaim Kibreab, who writes about initiatives and competences of Eritrean refugees in Sudan, finds that displacement, though taxing, can be a rewarding experience as well. After repatriation there can be no return to the status quo ex ante, simply because the losses and transformations refugees have undergone in exile are irretrievable. But returnees bring resources, skills, networks and knowledge, which can constitute an asset rather than a liability under conditions of restored peace and in a constructive policy environment. In focusing on the relationship between refugee experience and social change Kibreab examines whether refuge constitutes stimuli or constraints on development. He points out that risk-taking behaviour others have found among Punjabi and Sikh refugees is also prevalent among Eritrean refugees on the Sudanese border. They have developed new and broader networks, occupations, skills and relationships, and added to the diversification of economic activities. Many of these outcomes are positive and beneficial in the long term, too. These changes and transformations, in fact brought about by the experience of earlier unsettlement, refuge and survival in dire circumstances, provide necessary development stimuli in the reconstitution of the country. But neither aid agencies nor planners tend to recognise this crucial link between displacement and renewal. They fail to see refugees as people with initiative and talent. Instead they assume a generalised inability of refugees to help themselves.

Halleh Ghorashi, quoting from poignant 'auto-narratives' by Iranian women in exile, illustrates in more detail how the self-confidence and agency of refugees gets to be undermined when they are not recognised as individuals with talents or professions, but labelled as 'others' who do not belong. In her cross-location comparative study she describes the formation of identity among Iranian women activists in exile in the Netherlands and in the United States. The 'myth of return' dominates the host society's view of the migrants in the Netherlands, who continue to be perceived as guests and, therefore, others. This process of 'othering' reinforces dominant stereotypical (ethnic and gender) perceptions of Iranian women as traditional, dependent and passive victims. In contrast, the large numbers of Iranians in Los Angeles have made it possible to recreate a 'little Iran', forging a sense of belonging. In fact, the Iranian women in Los Angeles feel part of American society and have been able to construct a hybrid identity productively bridging space and time. This has not happened to the same degree in the Netherlands due to rejection and ethnic discrimination.

Last but not least, the tendency in critical studies to prioritise the agency of refugees is highly relevant and understandable given the overwhelming evidence of situations where refugees are silenced and dehumanised. At the same time, as Essed and Wesenbeek point out, it is crucial to see that critical members of host societies too can claim counteragency in defying unfair government policies. In their article they discuss civil disobedience among health workers who refuse to turn down refugees in need who have no legal status.

Redefining Gender and Other Identities

Various contributions indicate that social identities change due to threats to one's life, the disruptions of flight and the insecurities of resettlement. But certain identities are more adaptive than others. The Colombian and Burundian case studies in this volume bring into focus the pressures displacement puts on erstwhile gender and age configurations and identities. Whereas both men and women experience flight as a serious disruption in their lives, as a result of which familiar securities crumble, women tend to show more resilience in adapting to new environments. Donny Meertens' contribution about internal refugees in Colombia indicates that violence and destruction have disfigured rural women's access to informal networks of close kin and neighbours. On the other hand displacement has hurt men especially in their political identity, the loss of formal power networks they had access to and their institutionalised participation in society. Both men and women suffer under the lack of dignity and housing, but women are more successful than men in developing what the author calls alternative 'life projects', in the urban environments of their refuge. She concludes that it is exactly because of their gender identities that women get rooted sooner in the new surroundings. The fact that they were less invested in formal institutional and political power structures enables women to show more resilience than men, to take up familiar family responsibilities, no matter how difficult the circumstances, and to look forward rather than only backwards.

The theme of displacement and subsequent deprivation of power attached to masculine positioning and identities is elaborated upon eloquently in the contribution about camp life in Tanzania. Simon Turner describes how life in a refugee camp affects gender and age relations among Burundian refugees in Tanzania and how relief operations challenge older hierarchies of authority. Men especially are affected in their role as fathers, husbands, protectors and providers. Women no longer respect men for their capacities to provide economic and social security as partners and heads of the family. Now that international relief is available, the UNHCR seems like a 'better husband', a metaphor frequently referred to. For young men the suspension of traditional structures is not only a matter of deprivation. It may also facilitate positive change. Mobile and educated, some of them have taken up leadership roles in the camp and have learned 'not to be shy'. Others managed to get jobs with relief agencies and are now strategic intermediaries. Yet others get involved in politics or start a business. Young men have thus created new spaces for themselves, thereby adding new dimensions to their identities. These changes may well turn out to be persistent after return. Turner concludes that these young men in fact reassert the male identities the UNHCR had taken away from them.

Gender ideologies and practices are being transformed as new spaces and discourses for agency emerge as a consequence of conflict. For women who have lost husbands and sons to the violence of war there is no way back to the (gender) status quo of familiar, older ways of life. Darini Rajasingham-Senanayake describes how conflict and displacement in Sri Lanka transform gender ideologies and practices by exploring emergent spaces and discourses for women's agency and leadership. Violence affects both men and women differently according to religion, class and caste, but women also face certain common experiences, such as gendered forms of violence through rape, sexual violence and body searches. Yet, the 'victim discourse' of women's double burden in wartime, of restrictive caste ideology or of patriarchy obscures other realities and transformations, and the complexity of women's agency. Women, in fact, have taken up many new, nontraditional roles and responsibilities in situations of crisis. Female heads of households in refugee camps have managed to get employment and are in control of their situation. Young Tamil widows recast widowhood by refusing to accept the prescribed role of widow as a polluting and inauspicious state of being. Camp life and poverty, moreover, has eroded caste hierarchies by the difficulty observing caste inhibitions and maintaining spatial segregation. As these changes are not recognised in the settlement and land distribution schemes for the displaced, women struggle to legitimise and sustain these new roles beyond the victim ideology pervading relief and health interventions, in order to prevent a return to the prewar gender status quo. For these women there can be no simple return to the past, Rajasingham-Senanayake argues: peace constitutes a 'creative remaking of cultural meanings and agency – a third space between a familiar, often romanticised past and the traumatic present where conflict has remade culture'. She suggests this to be a situation of 'ambivalent empowerment'.

As we have pointed out, war and displacement have also led to growing political and social awareness and assertiveness in the Guatemala case. Likewise, Kibreab has shown that unsettlement and poverty provide a stimulus for creativity and adaptation. All these studies imply that identities evolve and transform in response to the experience of displacement and resettlement and that these changes may very well be maintained after return or in the process of peace. Gender and age characteristics are important determinants of traditional patterns and hierarchies, but they are also constitutive of innovations in the new environment. Women and young people, in particular, welcome those changes that liberate them from previous subordinations. But some caution is needed here. One should be careful not to celebrate too uncritically the transformative potential of flight and displacement. New identities, increased capacities, awareness and assertiveness come with a price: these changes are born in trauma, bereavement, loss, exclusion, and the pain of not belonging, due to attributed 'otherness'.

Addressing Moral Dilemmas

Dealing with issues of migration, and in particular with refuge, means operating in politically charged contexts with mutually contradictory interests, modes of operation and policy discourses. As Schrijvers indicates this type of work is not innocent and unavoidably implies 'dirtying your hands' and 'dining with the devil'. Yet, these moral dilemmas have to be faced and brought in to the open, which is also the position Philomena Essed and Rianne Wesenbeek urge when they discuss the negative impact of Dutch immigration policy on the human rights of refugees. The state bureaucracy has created criteria to distinguish 'genuine' refugees from the rest, considered fakes, thus administratively manufacturing the status of 'illegality'. Dutch policies exclude illegal immigrants from access to social and health care benefits except in a number of narrowly defined serious conditions. These policies deny those rendered 'illegal' their human rights, while shifting responsibility to deal with the health consequences to individual professionals. Health practitioners face an unhealthy choice: do they look the other way, or do they violate the law, thus engaging in civil disobedience? The authors present cases, illustrating how organisations and individual professionals struggle with the tensions between political pressures from the government, insufficient budgets and peer group loyalty on the one hand, and, on the other, their desire to be inclusive to all patients based on professional ethics and personal conscience.

It is common among international agencies to disconnect relief, that is interventions in case of emergency, from development, that is the human right to live under humane circumstances. Joke Schrijvers, who discusses dilemmas of humanitarian aid in relation to internal refugees in Sri Lanka, is clear about the need to link relief and development. Too often resettlement programmes boil down to settling refugees in areas where they are most likely to be killed or forced to flee, while the alternative offer is pure relief – i.e. semidetention camps controlled by army and government bureaucrats. Morally speaking, those options are equally reprehensible. The author suggests a less top-down and more participatory approach towards people where listening to their stories has central focus. The listener, however, can never be innocent, as sooner or later politics come in explicitly. Claims to neutrality are naive in the context of war and violent conflict and may very well support the powerful, rather than the needs of politically vulnerable groups. Neutrality is morally problematic because it tends to be tolerant of violations of the basic human right to development – participation, self-reliance and equity.

The Need to Bridge the Gap between Relief and Development

The problems arising when relief and development are seen as separate approaches are also exemplified in the case of the Rwandan government *Imidugudu* villagisation project. According to Dorothea Hilhorst and Mathijs van Leeuwen, this project started at first as a settlement plan for returning refugees. Later it came to cover the whole rural population in addressing issues of land use, service delivery, settlement, integration and security. There were questions and doubts about the programme, but many international donors came forward in support of a long-term compulsory development and housing programme, more than four years after the war. Their claim that the country was still in an 'emergency' situation eventually enabled relief organisations to continue their presence and to accept a blueprint approach for the whole country, apparently without bothering about the political implications. The question remains why such a top-down, authoritarian and generalised programme was internationally supported despite the well-known limitations of such planned development interventions? The authors suggest that the straightforward narrative and line of action fitted the ambiguities of the situation and the pressure to act. At the same time, the political dimensions of the programme remained hidden behind the technical terminology of planned development, only to be exposed when they surfaced locally.

Several authors show convincingly that there are serious limitations to pure relief aid. Kelly and Schrijvers discuss the 'disempowering' effects of philanthropic philosophies and welfare orientations. Rajasingham-Senanayake observes that relief might extend the trauma of the very people it is supposed to assist. She recommends cultural empowerment beyond 'the victim ideology that pervades relief and rehabilitation as well as health and trauma interventions'. Georg Frerks questions why the idea of linking relief and development has been implemented so scarcely and why there are so few salient results so far. He reviews the debate on 'linking relief and development' and evaluates the pro and contra arguments. Recently the simplistic notion of a 'continuum' between relief and development has been discarded and more complex modes of linking have come to the forefront. But it seems that similar conceptual, political and institutional problems emerge. Apparently, linking relief and development can only take place within a concrete time- and place-bound setting characterised by specific economic, social and cultural relationships. And this is exactly what refugees are lacking! Due to the specific situation and legal status they find themselves in there are a whole series of discontinuities that enormously complicate the possibility of linking relief and development. As most agencies tend to limit their discussions to the policy level, it is easy to underrate the practical difficulties that are involved in the linking exercise. The author argues that these situations can be beneficially analysed from the perspective of an actor-oriented approach, especially by limiting focus to those interfaces that normally constitute the most crucial interactions in interventions.

Critical Deconstructions of Policy Discourses

Lived experiences are often difficult to reconcile with predefined and sometimes stereotyped notions used in the international refugee regime and within the bureaucracies and aid agencies dealing with refugees. The case studies focusing on refugees in respectively Zambia, Sri Lanka and India, for example, are situated in widely differing geographical contexts and conflict histories, but each of these studies questions such taken-for-granted notions as 'refugee', 'displaced person', 'migration' and 'repatriation'. The specific connotations attached to these words and concepts are contextualised, determined not only by immediate events triggering decisions about flight, but, more fundamentally, by wider historical and socioeconomic patterns and deep-seated perceptions, meanings and discourses that structure actors' understandings of their life worlds.

Several contributions in this book are critical of dominant policy discourses. Discourses are defined as an ensemble of ideas, concepts and categories through which meaning is given to phenomena (Gasper and Apthorpe 1996: 2). In reality there is always a complex interplay between multiple discourses. Some may achieve dominance while others function as counterdiscourses, such as the debates referred to by Schrijvers on neutral emergency relief versus the integration of relief and development indicate (see also Schrijvers 1999 on the interplay of established and new discourses on masculinity and femininity in the context of violent conflict in Sri Lanka). The study of policy discourses may be rewarding, as such discourses tend to inform, and thus explain, the practices of governments and international agencies. Stereotypical references depicting refugees as passive and dependent do not reflect the way most refugees experience their situation. Often, bureaucratic categories and notions employed by refugee regimes hardly correspond to the experienced reality, as indicated, among others, by Bakewell. Indeed, relief workers, international agencies and host governments still evince top-down and patronising attitudes. Often they operate on the basis of dubious assumptions and questionable labels inducing passivity and dependency instead of promoting empowerment. Kelly shows how the 'Bosnia Project' was premised on the basis of a wrong perception of 'community'. Essed and Wesenbeek expose the arbitrary nature and unrealistic idea that one can totally exclude those labelled as 'illegal' from even the most basic human rights. Hilhorst and van Leeuwen describe how a top-down, authoritarian and blueprint programme received international support even when the limitations of such interventions were quite obvious. But certain narratives, the use of particular technical parlance, overemphasis on the urgency of the emergency situation can be quite convincing to donors. Schrijvers shows the dangers involved in a position where the concept of 'neutrality' has obtained positive value among those engaged in emergency relief. Frerks mentions how linear, 'developmentalist' approaches fail to come to terms with complex political emergencies. These examples all point to the need to critically unravel policy discourses and to study how particular discourses have become powerful in framing those actors' notions (Hilhorst 2000: 20).

Agendas and Approaches for Future Research

The above conclusions and insights have implications for future research approaches to be adopted. First of all, existing concepts and notions may not represent a lived-through reality and definitely should not be taken for granted. Moreover experiences of refuge, displacement and repatriation have to be understood in the contexts of constructed identities and discourses and with reference to the wider socioeconomic environments. Decisions and considerations of refugees may not be very dissimilar to those of other (migrant) groups in society. This implies that such decisions cannot be explained only with reference to traumatic experiences in the immediate past or with simplistic choice models. There is a need for longer-term historical approaches to account for social and political frameworks of perceptions and life worlds. In a spatial sense research needs to cover both rural and urban settings in view of the fact that most displaced peoples end up in urban conglomerations. All these arguments highlight the need for contextualised analysis. The prevailing multiplicity of experiences and differential responses must be grasped conceptually. This requires more emphasis on agency, in particular the agency of refugees and of other critical actors – an actor-oriented approach. It is relevant to perceive experiences of flight and repatriation in terms of individual and group characteristics, material as well as immaterial, and to identify differential patterns of knowledge and power. The emphasis on agency also calls for participatory research approaches in order to support those involved who want to voice their insights and needs regarding their own situations.

The contributions to this volume make a strong case for gender-specific analyses of the nature of violence and the responses to it. Making agency central opens up ways to qualify local transformations, as it becomes possible to identify the consequences of lost resources, and to seek the relevant conditions to create and benefit from new opportunities.

There is ample evidence in this volume to show the advantages of holistic and interdisciplinary approaches and of historical and comparative analysis. There is a need to account for one's own values and for political and moral dilemmas encountered while doing research or in the course of day-to-day engagement with refugees. Contributions have criticised policies, agencies and bureaucrats for lacking sufficient understanding of the real life worlds and experiences of refugees, and for reinforcing distorted images of refugees as passive, helpless or cunning. It has been shown that the implementation of ill-designed policies leaves researchers and practitioners with moral dilemmas. We see it as a challenging task for researchers to remain vigilant and critical, while deconstructing dominant policy discourses and thinking through their implications for the livelihoods, identities and rights of refugees and displaced people.

Part I

'Refugeehood': Claiming Spaces and Responsibilities

1

Refugeehood, Loss and Social Change: Eritrean Refugees and Returnees

Gaim Kibreab

The chapter discusses the losses experienced by Eritrean refugees; analyses the processes of social change; and examines whether such changes constitute stimuli or constraints on development.

Involuntary Displacement and Losses

Refugees are people who flee against their will because of fear for their lives. They are pushed from their social, cultural and economic moorings by conditions that are or are perceived to be potentially or imminently threatening to their physical safety, security, dignity, liberty and property. An actual or a perceived threat to these central tenets of human existence renders the place of abode hazardous and consequently makes the need to seek safe haven and succour in a neighbouring country or elsewhere imperative.

Though hitherto the main focus of outside interventions in refugee situations has been invariably on material losses, the nonmaterial losses experienced by refugees are equally important. Some of these include loss of national citizenship; social relationships through which memberships are formed, maintained and changed encompassing familial relations, kinship ties, friendships, neighbourhood networks; identities; informal institutions that regulate interactions; statuses; trust; traditional authority; and organisation (Hansen 1979, 1982; Baker 1981; Harrell-Bond 1986; Kibreab 1987, 1996a, 1996b, 2000; Krulfeld 1992, 1994; Zetter 1994, 1999). It is important to realise that the distinction between the material and nonmaterial losses suffered by refugees is analytical rather than real because in most developing societies access to, and control over, productive resources (land, pasture, water, forest produce, etc) and other forms of sources of livelihoods such as the right to participate in formal and informal labour markets, to obtain a business licence for engaging in off-farm economic activities are secured through membership in national citizenship or a community inhabiting spatially bounded social spaces.

As Baker observes, a person is held in position in her/his culture by diverse links of relationships to other people, organisations and social structures. These relationships do not only provide the 'webs' within which 'the individual is confirmed, but also through which boundaries, structures and social support functions are provided' (Baker 1981). When refugees flee their areas or their countries of origin and cross into other countries in search of succour and safe haven, they become uprooted from their social and cultural moorings with the consequence of being stripped of what Baker calls 'webs of relationships'. The loss of relationships is said to represent an enormous threat and challenge to the individual's coping and adaptive capacities (Baker 1981) in the new environment. It is often assumed therefore that the burden of losses of the 'webs' of relationships becomes too taxing to bear and results in a breakdown of the old social order and way of life. As I have argued elsewhere (see Kibreab 1995), urban refugees adapt to such dramatic changes in gender-specific ways. Whilst men react to the changes in a confused, defeatist and chaotic manner, the need to meet the daily bread of their family members forces women to waste no time and consequently engage in menial economic activities without being constrained by their previous economic or social statuses.

The important question that arises in connection with this is how relevant this conceptual framework is in the description of refugee experiences and in the explanation of post-flight outcomes. If the phenomenon of 'social breakdown' exists, how does it affect refugees' capability to cope in adversity? Refugees are not homogeneous masses of people. They differ in terms of their socioeconomic background, occupation, geographical origin (urban-rural), ethnicity, status, etc. They differ in terms of their experiences associated with the conditions that prompt flight. Some flee after being subjected to horrendous treatments whilst others flee in anticipation of an impending danger (Kunz 1981). Their flight experiences are also different. Some flee individually because of fear or threat of persecution or a whole community flees because of the threat to their collective safety and security (Kibreab 1987). Some flights are also less dangerous than others are. Refugee experiences also differ in terms of destination. Among some rural refugees, flight tends to take place from rural to rural areas. Urban refugees often flee to urban areas, but some are forced against their will to stay in rural camps where the environment is unfamiliar and threatening (Kibreab 1996c). There are also refugees of rural origin who due to lack of sources of livelihoods are forced to drift to urban areas without having lived in such settings before (Karadawi 1983; Kibreab 1996c). Some refugees also flee to familiar places where they have either been before or where their clan members or members of their ethnic groups live (Hansen 1982). In such situations, there may be little or no differences between the physical and social worlds of their areas of origin and destination. Consequently the extent of adaptational change required may be minimal. Not only do all these conditions mitigate or exacerbate the extent and consequences of the losses suffered by refugees but they are also likely to have discernible impact on the process of recovery and repair.

Displacement and Social Change

Though understanding of the losses refugees experience during and after flight is important, from a development perspective, an understanding of the effects of such losses on refugees' adaptational responses is more crucial. It is thus important to ask how refugees respond to their losses and to the challenges posed by exile. Refugees' responses to such challenges are mediated by different sets of variables, including structural similarities or dissimilarities between themselves and receiving societies, availability and accessibility of resources and income-generating opportunities, availability and nature of assistance at the initial stage, host government policies and practices, attitudes of nationals towards refugees, etc. For urban refugees, availability of training opportunities, credit facilities and rights of access to business licences are crucial.

The relationship between refugee experiences and social change is a complex one and this complexity is exacerbated by lack of empirical data. One of the consequences of this paucity of data has been a lack of consensus not only among aid agencies, but also among academics. For example, whether refugees become more dependent, or more predisposed to change or become more conservative as a result of the experiences they undergo in connection with social and economic 'uprooting' is controversial. Research on these issues is still thin. These issues are crucial because whether refugees are perceived as a burden or a resource and consequently how aid agencies, donor and host governments respond to emergency and development needs of refugees is partly determined by their preconceived ideas concerning the impact of uprooting on refugee behaviour. If international responses to refugee situations are predicated on the assumption that refugees are traumatised, immobilised and deskilled, the emphasis of international interventions is most likely to be on care and maintenance as is often the case. This is because refugees are assumed to be unable to assess their situation critically, to take initiatives and to devise solutions to their problems. Since outsiders' responses are often shaped by expectations, adequate knowledge on the impact of refugee experiences on social change and the expected outcome of such changes are crucial.

One of the most elaborate attempts to examine the link between uprooting and social change was made by Keller (1975) among the Punjab Hindus and Sikhs who were displaced by the act of partition of India in 1947. By studying the psychological trauma experienced by these two groups of refugees and the symptoms they exhibited, he studied whether they helped or impeded India's push for economic development and growth. Keller identified three stages in the refugee experience. The first is the period of arrival in which the refugee may be benumbed and seized by grief. This period is quite short. The second stage is marked by a feeling of guilt for having survived whilst others have died. These feelings of guilt prompt refugees to ask themselves why they survive when others could not. This engenders a feeling of being special and more deserving than others are. In the third phase, the refugee becomes aggressive. (Though Keller did not differentiate between men's and women's reactions, it is not a moot point to suggest that aggression is a typical male rather than female reaction and hence the last element in his model may not apply to female refugees.)

This sometimes leads to physical violence and sometimes to economic and political risk taking. Keller attributes this willingness to take risks to the refugee experience that generates a sense of 'invulnerability'. One of his interviewees, for example, told him:

> [W]e have gone through so much; what more can happen to us? No one can do anything to us that can be more terrible than has already occurred. Why should we be afraid? Once everything was taken from us and we have come back from our pennilessness to prosperity. If we lose it all again we could do it once more. (Keller 1975: 116)

It is these feelings and sentiments which predisposed these refugees to take risks which in many developing countries are *sine qua non* for economic growth and social development. In many of the rural areas of the developing world, where production decisions tend to be risk-averse to maximise subsistence security (Scott 1976; Kibreab 1996b), risk taking is a scarce resource. One of the greatest assets the Punjabi and Sikhs refugees brought into Eastern Punjab was therefore the quality of risk taking and the determination to start afresh not only to regain a lost economic position and social status, but also to discover new and previously unknown frontiers of opportunities.

Whenever I asked those Eritrean refugees and returnees who were involved in risky income-generating activities, their usual answer was 'kabti zihalefnayo zikefi'i yelen' – 'Nothing is worse than what we have been through.' Sudan being an Islamic state is ruled by Sharia law, which, inter alia, prohibits drinking and selling of alcohol. Noncompliance is a criminal act punishable by long imprisonment and flogging in public. Yet there were a number of refugees who made a living by smuggling alcoholic drinks from Eritrea to Khartoum. There were also many refugees who were involved in cross-border trade and took goods from Sudan up to the Eritrean cities and brought the same to Sudan from Eritrea during the war. A few of the refugees were also involved in dangerous activities such as forging of documents, including passports. Many of these paid heavily if detected but they were not deterred from pursuing such activities. Asked why they took such dangerous risks, most of them said, 'We have seen the worst and there is no suffering we cannot endure.' In the 1980s, a considerable number of Eritrean refugees from the Gulf States and Western Europe also invested their savings in trucks in Sudan. In view of the political instability that characterises post-independence Sudan and in view of the marginalised position of the refugees, these were indeed risky undertakings. During the late 1980s, the trucking industry was dominated by Eritrean refugees. This enabled Sudan to overcome a major bottleneck in its national economy (Kibreab 1996a). At the time of the fieldwork (1997–98), the border between Eritrea and Sudan was closed. Some areas were even heavily mined. In spite of the potential danger, I met a number of returnees who continued pursuing cross-border trade. In March 1998, a landmine blasted off injuring a lorry driver and some of the traders. Two days after, I met one of the traders who was injured in the blast in Tessenei. I asked him whether he had learned his lesson not to take such risks. He replied, 'I have already been back to Sudan twice since the incident. Where there is risk, there is big money.'

Keller's study in India and the findings of my own studies on Eritrean refugees and returnees show that the breakdown of the old way of life instead of constraining development and change provides a stimulus for creativity and innovative adaptation. These changes in combination with severe deprivation and poverty seem to set refugees free from the manacles of tradition, culturally prescribed roles, as well as from the dominant value systems and norms. The reason why creative and innovative adaptation is entwined with displacement is that when a familiar universe of associations and sanctions is distorted or destroyed, the need for reorganisation becomes indispensable (Taggart 1918, quoted in Mabogunje 1974; Barnett 1953). Drawing on Taggart and Barnett, Mabogunje, for example, points out that 'unsettlement irrespective of its cause has a tendency to create a fluid situation in which the old values are no longer operative' (Mabogunje 1974–75: 52). He further states: '... with the old sanctions and compulsion gone or of doubtful validity, the way is open for the creation and the acceptance of new interpretations' (ibid.: 52). Poverty and deprivation are also often the motive forces of innovative change and adaptation. As Wilkinson perceptively states: 'Development comes out of poverty, not out of plenty, as many economic theories would lead one to suppose. Poverty stimulates the search for additional resources of income and makes people willing to do things they may previously have avoided' (1973: 5). Eritrean refugees and returnees are definitely doing things which they previously avoided or even dreaded doing.

The link between the breakdown of the old way of life and structures, and openness to innovative change is rarely appreciated by either aid agencies or planners. Not only is this crucial link disregarded, but aid agencies and planners often interpret the breakdown of the old organisational structures as being synonymous with loss of capacity to think and to work out solutions to immediate and long-term problems. That is the reason why relief agencies instead of enabling refugees to build on their capability, do for them the things which refugees previously did for themselves. The consequence of this is that agencies fail to recognise refugee initiatives and capabilities. 'For them' as Mister argues 'it becomes necessary to bring in western concepts and structures without being aware that these might be alien to those that already exist' (Mister 1982). The dominant view of refugee relief assistance workers is lucidly summarised by Harrell-Bond. She states:

> It is usually assumed ... refugees are generally not only physically too weak to take responsibility for themselves but mentally too disoriented as well. Whether this assumption is made explicit or not, most relief workers operate on this basis. At the outset of an emergency, refugees are treated like patients being admitted to hospital ... (Harrell-Bond 1982: 1–12)

One of the major assumptions underlying outside intervention in refugee situations is, therefore, the assumption of generalised inability of refugees to help themselves. This generalised helplessness is said to be developed in response to loss of home, work, role, status, lifestyle, self-esteem, self-worth, personal identity, trust in the self and others (Baker 1981).

The corpus of knowledge on refugees and refugee assistance programmes is permeated by such assumptions (for critiques see Kibreab 1993). What follows is an analysis of the responses of Eritrean refugees to some of the challenges posed by displacement in Sudan.

Making up for the Losses: Eritrean Refugees in Sudan

Though this may not be true in every case, studies on the responses of Eritrean refugees in Sudan show that they responded to their losses and to the challenges by developing new and broader forms of social networks, occupations, skills, survival strategies, relationships, divisions of labour, and social organisations. In a chapter of this size it is not possible to discuss the diverse income-generating activities in which the refugees engaged to make ends meet and to expand the scope of their coping strategies. Nevertheless, it is important to point out that at the heart of this lay diversification of economic activities, which, inter alia, enabled the refugees to spread risks and to ensure stable supply of minimum subsistence needs. As Krulfeld and Camino (1994: ix) state: 'The refugee experience is a complex process characterised by loss and regeneration.' In most social situations, whenever there is a disruption or breakdown, there is always a process of construction but seldom reconstruction.

Though the construction process may involve utilisation of some of the constituent elements of the broken-down social order and informal social institutions, the outcome is rarely a replica of what existed before. Studies conducted by the author among Eritrean refugees in Sudan over a period of nearly two decades show that a particular way of life, social relations, social networks, informal social institutions and social organisations that break down due to involuntary displacement and exile are not reconstructed. They are replaced by new forms of social relations, networks, social organisations and institutions. Though some of these new forms provide threads of continuity with the past, it is more appropriate to conceive them as being embodiments of change and transformation. The new forms of transethnic and transreligious social organisations, networks, occupations, practices and ways of life that have developed during the last three decades among Eritrean refugees in Sudan and the way the former refugees are tapping into this social capital to construct their communities and livelihoods in the areas of return in Eritrea, suggest that a return to the past is either not possible or most probably undesirable.

Data elicited from key informants representing a cross-section of the refugee and returnee populations show that a return to the past is seen as highly undesirable. Though some of the problems that faced the refugees were familiar, the circumstances under which they occurred were radically different from the past. This necessarily required new approaches, alliances and solutions (Kibreab 2000). Thus, the raison d'être of postflight construction efforts is to overcome problems that arise in the unfamiliar social and physical environment. The post-flight situation of Eritrean refugees in Sudan seems to fit Krulfeld and Camino's eloquent description, namely,

> For refugees, these experiences are attended by liminality, in which they are caught in positions of transition from a more orderly and predictable past to a new and as yet unpredictable future. Refugees tend to be marginalised in their new societies; that is, to suffer from feelings of alienation and, more often than not, lower status than they had in their countries of origin. In such positions of liminality and marginality, all aspects of their lives are called into question, including ethnic and national identity, gender roles, social relationships, and socio-economic status. (Krulfeld and Camino 1994: xi)

In the case of Eritrean refugees, and this may be true elsewhere, it is these experiences that telescoped the otherwise protracted processes of social change and transformation. For example, prior to their displacement, the large majority of the refugees were either pastoralists or agropastoralists. In Sudan, all have become sedentarised. Without suggesting that sedentarisation is a good or a bad thing, this undoubtedly constitutes a dramatic social change in such a short time. Prior to their displacement, very few of the refugees were involved in cash crop production (Kibreab 1987, 1990). This is no longer the case in exile. In the six refugee settlements in Qala en Nahal, for example, up to 50 percent of the refugees' hawashas (plots) were planted with the cash crop – sesame – every season (Kibreab 1987, 1996b). After the dramatic reduction in productive capability of the renewable resources in the settlements – particularly arable land due to unsustainable land use practices precipitated by misconceived government policy which kept the refugees in a state of confinement (see Kibreab 1996b) – the majority of the refugees have been deriving their major sources of livelihoods from wage labour by working in the large mechanised rain-fed schemes in the Gedaref region. A large number of men, women and children also migrated to the irrigation schemes of Semsem, New Halfa and El Rahad to pick cotton during the dry season (Kibreab 1987, 1990). Of those who are settled in the three villages of Es Suki (Fatah el Rahman, Kilo 7 and Awad es Sid), particularly women and children participate in weeding and clearing of the cotton fields as well as in cotton picking. In the preflight period, only a small proportion of the households participated in wage labour (Kibreab 1990).

In the early 1980s, when the productivity of the land was adequate and when there was supplementary provision of food aid, only a few women participated in agricultural production (Kibreab 1987). By the second half of the 1990s, the productive capability of the land in the settlements decreased substantially (Kibreab 1996b). This led to a dramatic increase of women's participation in agricultural production. During the peak seasons, most of the male spouses were absent working in the rain-fed mechanised schemes. During their absence, women assumed responsibility for the family farms. This was even true among those ethnic groups in which the division of labour was gendered and women prohibited from taking part in farm work. The prescription of the gender ideology notwithstanding, not only did women work in their own farms, but during the dry season, most poor women also migrated to work as wage labourers. These are considerable measures of social change precipitated by forced migration and subsistence insecurity.

In the case of Eritrean refugees, forced migration, the losses that accompanied it, the state of liminality in which they found themselves, abject poverty, the stigma attached to being a *laji'i* (a refugee), the discrimination in the labour markets and elsewhere, the lack of freedom of movement and residence, and the process of 'othering' have functioned as catalysts of relatively rapid social change and transformation. For example, the refugees in Sudan and the returnees in Eritrea refer to exile as a 'difficult experience' but more importantly as a 'school'. Asked whether after more than two decades' exposure to tractor use, they would revert to traditional methods of cultivation upon return, a refugee elder in Salmin (Sudan), for example, told the author: 'In spite of the hardship and suffering displacement entailed, exile has opened our eyes and we have no intention of closing them ever again. We shall only move forward and never backward.' Reverting to hand or ox plough was considered as backwardness.

Data elicited from Eritrean refugees and returnees, therefore, suggest that whilst forcible and sudden departure from one's own sociocultural moorings and consequently the inability to exercise freedom of choice reflected in the right to stay in one's place of origin and country in security and dignity may have some detrimental consequences, however, on balance, for those who survive the violence, the trauma and poverty, the overall medium-term outcome can be positive and beneficial.

Return and Recovery: the Case of Eritrean Returnees

There is also still a dearth of data on repatriation. This is, inter alia, because of the predominant assumption that voluntary repatriation is considered to be a straightforward and problem-free solution in which refugees return to their former communities and recoup their losses and consequently are able to reassume the roles they played before becoming refugees. The jargons used in the repatriation discourse such as 'reintegration', 'rehabilitation', 'reconstruction', 'readjustment', 'readaptation', 'reassimilation', 'reestablishment', etc. clearly indicate that once the factors that prompt flight are removed, refugees return home and once they are at home, their roots will be reestablished utilising preexisting social networks, kinship ties, old skills, property rights, etc. Not only does this presuppose a society whose institutions and actors have remained in stasis; but also assumes a willingness to return to the status quo ante.

This belief applies equally to those who stay behind – namely internally displaced persons (or IDPs), local residents, demobilised soldiers and ex-combatants. It takes little account of the changes experienced by all actors and fails to consider them other than as a mass of homogeneous groups of people all sharing the same aspirations and goals (for more on this see Kibreab 1998a). The reason why repatriation is not a straightforward or a problem-free solution is, inter alia, due to the irretrievable nature of the losses and transformation refugees undergo in connection with involuntary displacement and exile. Return after a prolonged period in exile can be as traumatising as flight itself (Ghai 1993; Allen and Morsink 1994; Rogge 1994). Both social relations, socioeconomic and political life at 'home' are most likely to be radically different from what they used to be in the past. Thus, repatriation instead of being characterised by harmony and placidity could be characterised by tension and intense conflicts. Between 1989 and 1998, nearly 180,000 Eritrean refugees returned from Sudan.

The Eritrean refugees in Sudan had undergone some fundamental socioeconomic transformations during the 1960s, 1970s and early 1980s (Kibreab 1996a, 1996b, 1996c, 1999, 2000). The extent of the transformation experienced by the refugees has been so profound that many of the returnees, i.e. those who lived in the rural areas as farmers or agropastoralists prior to their displacement did not consider it worthwhile to recover the houses and other property they left behind when they fled two or three decades ago.[1] This is because very few have returned to their preflight way of life. The overwhelming majority has settled in the border towns notwithstanding the fact that their places of origin were elsewhere. It is interesting to note that for the overwhelming majority of the returning refugees, regaining of national citizenship has been more important than regaining their original homes (*restitutio ad integrum*) from which they were originally uprooted. In fact the large majority of the returnees does not consider their preflight kinship ties, friendships, neighbourhood networks as relevant to their present situation. As Elizabeth Colson states, 'When kinsmen move apart and no longer interact, eventually they cease to be kinsmen. Dispersal is therefore a threat to the integrity of lineages and to their relationships ...' (Colson 1972: 76). The returnees claim that though their relationship with the stayees are nonconflictual, their outlooks about life in general and towards work in particular are quite different. They also claim that they are more generous, more polite, more hardworking and more open to new ideas and new social relationships. The stayee populations also have the same perception of the returnees. A stayee shopkeeper in Barentu, for example, told the author: 'The refugees [returnees] are hardworking, friendly, polite, reliable and they are often together laughing or joking about their experiences.' For the large majority of returnees, the transethnic and transreligious social networks, friendships and social relations forged in exile are more important than the ones they left behind two or three decades ago. The results of a survey conducted among self-repatriates in Tessenei, Goluj, Barentu (Gash Barka region), Hagaz (Anseba region), and Ginda (Northern Red Sea Region), for example, shows that 82 percent of the sample heads of households have settled in areas outside their previous places of origin or habitual residence (Kibreab 1998b). Among those who returned under the government repatriation project, only 7 percent have returned to their places of origin.

The decision concerning choice of place of destination was determined by economic and service availability considerations. The factors that were most important in the decision of choice of destination among the returnees from the PROFERI programme – Program for the Reintegration and Rehabilitation of Resettlement Areas in Eritrea – were (in order of importance) access to education for children, cultivable land, employment opportunities, desire to join returnee friends, neighbours and relatives, greater opportunities for self-employment and greater rainfall.

Asked why they have opted to settle outside their 'homes', a group of systematically selected returnees comprising members of different ethnic, religious and age groups, unanimously said 'this is our home. Eritrea is our home.' Each respondent also gave the same answer when interviewed in a setting where others were not present. The same answer was also given by a group of female focus groups collectively and individually.

Conclusion

For Eritrean refugees in Sudan, displacement has been both a taxing and a rewarding experience. Though they incurred substantial losses, it was the determination to make up for the losses that constituted the motive force for change and transformation reflected in development of new skills, occupations, social relationships, networks and organisations. The changes the refugees underwent in exile are manifested in the manner in which the returnees are constructing their communities and livelihoods in the areas of return. They have brought with them skills, knowledge, savings, work ethic and dense social networks, which are proving indispensable in the process of construction of their communities and livelihoods.

Before their arrival, the border towns such as Tessenei, Um Hajer, Telata Asher, Goluj, Ali Gidir, Haikota, Barentu, etc were ghost towns. Since the arrival of the returnees, these towns have grown from stagnant and insignificant sites to thriving regional markets. This experience suggests that under conditions of restored peace and a conducive policy environment, returnees constitute a resource rather than a liability to receiving communities and areas of return. This case amply demonstrates that a key in the construction of communities and viable livelihoods in war-affected societies is the presence of a well-functioning state. This state does not necessarily have to be democratic in the conventional sense of the term but rather a strong state that is able to protect life and property, whose administration is transparent, able to deliver services and to establish institutions which promote and enhance social and economic interaction by reducing uncertainty and insecurity.

Notes

1. This is only true of housing and property left in the rural areas. Most refugees who left housing and property in urban areas had either recovered or were in the process of recovering housing and property they left behind in the Eritrean cities.

2

Repatriation: Angolan Refugees or Migrating Villagers?

Oliver Bakewell

The Refugee Problem and Repatriation

Repatriation is often presented as the optimum durable solution to the refugee problem in Africa and it is taken for granted that the return of peace to a country will entail the return of the refugees who fled the war. This chapter questions this assumption by looking at the movement of self-settled refugees from Zambia to Angola as a process of migration rather than the end of the refugee cycle.

Before considering voluntary repatriation as a solution, it is worth considering in greater detail the nature of the refugee problem it is expected to solve. It has three aspects that can be clearly identified. Firstly, at the start of any refugee emergency is a humanitarian problem as refugees flee their homes, families are separated and they arrive in a neighbouring country exhausted and with very few possessions. Aid operations may be essential to help refugees through these critical times. After the crisis when refugees have been able either to settle temporarily among local communities or in settlements, it is still assumed that there is chronic suffering caused by exile.

Secondly, refugees are perceived as posing a threat to the local society, economy and environment where they settle, particularly in the case of mass movements of refugees in Africa (Chambers 1986). A large and sudden increase of population clearly causes stress on the affected area and initially the resources are likely to be severely stretched. Nevertheless, the longer-term impact depends on the availability of productive resources and the contribution refugees are allowed to make to the local economy.

Finally, the presence of refugees constitutes an aberration in the modern world, which is neatly partitioned into nation states and everybody has a nationality or, failing that, a country of 'habitual residence' where they belong. Movement from one country to another is governed by immigration procedures which either allow temporary residence or a change of nationality but only with the agreement of the state to which a person moves. Refugees are an exception, and states which are signatory to the UN Refugee Convention of 1951 are obliged to receive them. For this world of nation states, refugees constitute a problem because they do not fit and the international regime for dealing with refugees is concerned with temporary measures to be taken until such time as they can fit once more (Malkki 1995; Hathaway 1997).

Voluntary repatriation can be seen as an ideal solution to the refugee problem as it restores refugees to their homes, it relieves the burden on the host society, and it brings them back under the protection of the state. This assumes that the conditions which caused them to flee have substantially changed, that their idea of home remains related to a particular place even a generation or more after leaving, and that their presence has continued to be a burden to the host society. All these assumptions are open to question (UNRISD 1993; Bascom 1994; Warner 1994; Zetter 1994; Stein et al. 1995).

The range of studies of repatriation over the last decade has grown (for example, Allen and Morsink 1994; Allen 1996; Black and Koser 1999) but often the primary concern has been with questions of how refugees return home, rather than *why* they should do so. It is widely assumed that:

> Once the root causes that prompt population movements are eliminated the affected population "vote with their feet" homewards in order to re-establish themselves in their former areas of origin or habitual residence. Thus, since repatriation is expected to happen automatically in response to changed political and social conditions in countries of origin, research into the factors that influence refugees' decisions concerning repatriation has not been considered worthwhile. (Kibreab 1996: 6)

The rest of this chapter presents a summary of a study which analyses decision making about repatriation in the case of self-settled Angolan refugees in Zambia by looking at the process through the lens of voluntary migration (Bakewell 1999). Rather than attempting to identify refugees and then ask them about repatriation, the study enquired about all villagers' (refugee and nonrefugee) interests in Angola and observed cross-border movements.

Fieldwork was carried out between November 1996 and October 1997 at a time when the Lusaka peace process was still in place in Angola and UNHCR was planning formal repatriation from official settlements. The study focused on a group of villages within the area of the Lunda senior chief Kanongesha in Mwinilunga District of Zambia's North-Western Province. The situation in Angola deteriorated rapidly in 1998 after the fieldwork and any hopes of repatriation were abandoned. With the end of hostilities in 2001, the prospects for a permanent peace have dramatically improved. In June 2002 UNHCR stated that it expected to restart a formal repatriation operation during 2003 if the situation in Angola remained stable (see UNHCR website www.unhcr.ch). There are no signs that the approach will be very different from that adopted in the 1990s and the same issues discussed here will be encountered in this new operation.

Self-settled Angolan Refugees in Zambia: Finding Their Own Solution

The Angolan revolution against the Portuguese colonial regime began in 1961. As a new eastern front opened in 1966, refugees started to flow into Zambia's Western and North-Western provinces (Hansen 1979). As war continued after independence the numbers of people fleeing to Zambia rose steadily with a large increase in the mid 1980s as the conflict between the MPLA and UNITA escalated. Since 1986 Zambia has hosted over 100,000 Angolan refugees and it was still at that level at the time of the research in 1997. There were further large influxes of refugees from the end of 1999 to the beginning of 2001. By the end of 2001 there were estimated to be a total of 220,000 Angolan refugees in Zambia, of which over 100,000 were self-settled.

Although the extreme violence, scale and speed of refugee movements since the 1960s may have been new, the practice of moving to escape violence was not. The people followed patterns of migration from earlier generations and many came into Zambia and joined their kin who had arrived before. The majority of refugees were of the Lunda, Luvale, Chokwe, Mbunda and Luchazi people of the upper Zambezi, who have a long history of movement from the north and west into present day Zambia. All these groups trace their origins to the kingdom of Mwanta Yavwa in Congo (Kinshasa) and recount their migration through Angola into Zambia. In the nineteenth century there was further migration as people tried to escape the reach of the Atlantic slave traders, and later in search of ivory, beeswax and rubber in the remoter forests of Zambia (von Oppen 1995). In the first half of the twentieth century people crossed the border in both directions, either to avoid British taxes in Zambia or Portuguese forced labour in Angola. Further migration was caused provided by the labour needs of the mines of Katanga in Congo and the Zambian Copperbelt from the 1930s.

Not only there is a long history of migration among the people of the upper Zambezi but also mobility is an essential element of the local society (White 1960; von Oppen 1995). In the past whole villages would relocate if the headman died, or if there were a number of other deaths or illnesses. Access to better land or disputes between families and neighbours' feuds may also cause villages to shift. Individuals, especially women, also shift residence frequently throughout their lives. On marriage a woman will move to join her husband in his village and on divorce or the death of the husband, she will move back to her mother's village. The children of the marriage 'belong' to the mother's side and often they will go to spend long periods with their maternal uncles as they grow up.

This social and historical practice of migration enabled refugees who fled from Angola to make new homes among the Zambian villagers and today they are completely integrated. Those arrived as refugees were welcomed within Kanongesha and very rapidly built new villages, planted fields and established new livelihoods. Although many people would describe themselves or their neighbours as refugees with the past tense, since they stopped receiving aid and refused to go the official settlements, they no longer use the term. This was strongly reinforced by the late senior chief who decreed that nobody should be referred to as a refugee in his area; they are all simply (his) people.

The rejection of the label was reflected in the social, economic and local political context of the villages. Those who came as refugees lived intermingled with others and there was no refugee quarter. Intermarriage was common and was entered into without consideration of the potential spouse's background as a refugee. Social networks and friendships did not respect any differences between refugees and nonrefugees and everybody regardless of their origins was present at social gatherings such as circumcision, girls' coming of age, funerals, weddings or village meetings.

Within the villages there was no clear distinction between refugees and nonrefugees standard of living or their wealth. For most people the constraint on their production was labour power and access to markets. Land is abundant in Kanongesha and villagers could use as much as they could cultivate. Those who arrived as refugees were just as likely to own livestock and poultry and the quality of their housing was the same. The only man in the village to have a house with a roof of metal sheets had arrived as a refugee in the 1980s and set up one of the two village shops. Living standards varied much more strongly with the gender of the household head or the length of time that people had lived in the area (as it took a few years to build up good houses and fields) than with their origins from Angola.

In this remote area of Zambia the major direct contact with the state is through schools, clinics and agricultural extension staff. These services were available in the villages at the same (low) level for all villagers. The local school kept no figures for enrolment of refugees or Zambians but teachers estimated that the families of about 40 percent of pupils in the local secondary school were from Angola. The increase in population caused by the arrival of refugees was seen locally as beneficial as it made the provision of schools and clinics viable. Any potential depopulation caused by repatriation was regarded with concern, as it would undermine the case for maintaining the services.

The only discrimination suffered by those who came as refugees occurred in formal contact with the authorities that required the production of a Zambian National Registration Card (NRC). A government infrastructure project to rebuild roads using local labour only employed those who could produce an NRC. Travelling to the provincial capital, Solwezi, or the Copperbelt proved difficult, as there were identity checks along the way. Many of those who arrived as refugees (40 percent of those interviewed) had managed to obtain NRCs and their children receive them as a matter of course at the same age as others. Only 15 percent of those who fled Angola claimed to have a Refugee Identity Card (RIC) which was issued by the government through UNHCR when aid was being given to refugees. A sizeable minority (14 percent) of all villagers claimed to have no papers at all.

The papers that people hold do not necessarily correspond with the views they express of their nationality. There are those who describe themselves as Angolan who have only Zambian papers. In contrast there is a larger group of people describing themselves as Zambian who have no Zambian papers. For many their attachment to a nationality is loose and they will claim the most appropriate nationality in different contexts. When they go to town, some claim to be Zambian to avoid any of the harassment they may receive as Angolans there. When UNHCR was distributing food aid for Angolan refugees in Kanongesha, some Zambians presented themselves as Angolans and received the assistance. Angolan young men claimed to be Zambian to avoid conscription by UNITA in Cazombo in 1997. At other times Zambians in Angola may declare themselves Angolan to get access to the meat, fish and honey there. I would describe them as having a handheld idea of nationality.

In contrast staff in the local council, immigration office, the national registration office and the office of the government commissioner for refugees have a *heartfelt* idea of nationality; they expected a person's nationality to be part of their personal identity and immutable. This was reflected in the support for the current Zambia law that has no mechanism for refugees to become citizens. Some argued that if Angolan refugees are granted citizenship (i.e. green NRCs) they will still leave when Angola is peaceful and then reject their new Zambian nationality to become Angolan again. When Congolese refugees who had obtained papers with the assistance of village headmen, returned to their country from Kanongesha in the 1980s, they pinned their NRCs to trees at the border. While the people of the border areas see this lack of respect for their nationality as normal, for officialdom it is a reason not to grant it to them.

The social category of refugee, which may have been very useful when people first fled into Zambian villages, has now dissolved and serves little purpose. In 1990 Hansen concluded 'it was wrong to still categorise these self-settled people as "refugees"' (Hansen 1990: 35, emphasis added) and in Kanongesha at least it is *meaningless* today to categorise people as refugees. The level of integration is such that there are no grounds for reliably distinguishing a refugee from a Zambian on the basis of any verifiable information. Any exercise to identify and register refugees has to rely on the cooperation of the villagers which past experience suggests is unlikely to be forthcoming (Freund and Kalumba 1986). To a large extent those who wish to portray themselves as refugees can do so, and others can portray themselves as Zambian.

In the area studied self-settled Angolan refugees and their Zambian hosts have effectively found a local solution to all three aspects of the refugee problem. The refugees have made new homes among their kinsfolk following social and historical precedents. Far from being a burden on their hosts they are perceived as boosting local production and maintaining services. As they acquire official papers they are even becoming de facto citizens despite the protests of state officials. There still remain the wider problems of being in a very remote area of Zambia bordering a country at war.

Official Settlements and Repatriation Plans

In contrast to this picture of complete integration of refugees in the border villages, in the official refugee settlements, Meheba and Mayukwayukwa, the refugee label has been maintained and reproduced in new generations. Under Zambia's Refugee (Control) Act 1970, a person who enters Zambia as a refugee remains a refugee, and the status is passed down the generations. All refugees should reside in official settlements unless they have permission to stay elsewhere from the Zambian Government Commissioner for Refugees.

Meheba Refugee Settlement is the largest of the two settlements for refugees in Zambia. In 1997 it housed approximately 26,000 Angolans,[1] some of whom have been there since it opened in 1971. Meheba is defined by the authorities as a 'settlement', rather than a 'camp': the key difference being that in the former refugees are expected to be self-sufficient in food. Each refugee household is allocated a plot of land (2.5 hectares) for their house and fields. The settlement is under the overall control of the Commissioner for Refugees' office, which has extensive powers over what happens within its boundaries. School, clinics and agricultural extension services are operated by line ministries, which are assisted by UNHCR and international aid agencies. Lutheran World Federation

(LWF) was the main implementing partner in 1997 and it played a very large role in the management of the settlement. Meheba is regarded as a great success in agricultural production and sizeable surpluses of sweet potatoes, vegetables and other crops are marketed in the provincial capital Solwezi. For those unable to produce their own food such as the elderly or chronically sick, there is a safety net of rations distributed by LWF.

Refugees in the settlement complained of the lack of food, their struggle to sell their crops, or the injustice of paying school fees, which they interpreted as reflection of their refugee status. However, they conceded that they had better access to market, better services such as health and education resulting in better livelihoods (cf. Hansen 1990). For these material benefits and better opportunities, particularly in education or chances of a job, the refugees pay a price in the restrictions on their behaviour. They are allowed to leave Meheba only with permission from the refugee officer and there are limits on their freedom of association. Perhaps more importantly they have to accept the status of refugee and relinquish any chance of integration. They are geographically isolated from Zambians and this restricts social interaction. Their children will also be refugees and as long as they live within the settlement they have no permanent home in Zambia. They remain ready to move when UNHCR and the government decide that repatriation should start.

Plans for their repatriation were made and continually revised between 1995 and 1998. The programme aimed to provide transport for refugees from the settlements back to Angola. It was anticipated that self-settled refugees would make their own way across the border once the conditions were appropriate and there was no assistance planned for them on the Zambian side of the border. Once back in Angola, all returning refugees, whether self-repatriated or transported from the settlements, were to be provided with resettlement assistance including such elements as food aid, kitchen sets, seeds and tools. Another element of the programme was the general rehabilitation of the areas to which refugees would return with the implementation of quick impact projects (QIPs) reestablishing infrastructure such as clinics and schools.

The preparation for repatriation was at an advanced state in September 1997 and departure areas had been prepared in Meheba and a road reconstructed from the Zambian border to the Angolan town of Cazombo. QIPs were being undertaken around Cazombo and the distribution of resettlement packages to returning refugees had started to the 20,000 people who made there own way to register as returned refugees. In the border villages, the progress of repatriation plans in Meheba was followed very closely as the transport of refugees was awaited as a mark of the international community's faith in the Angolan peace process. However, as the security situation worsened in Angola and the country reverted to full-scale war, the programme was called off in June 1998.[2]

Cross-border Movement from the Villages

In the border villages, given the very high level of integration and the widespread access to Zambian nationality papers, it might be expected that there would be limited interest in repatriation. However, the opposite was true. In the focus village nearly 30 percent of adults interviewed anticipated settling in Angola, when there is a stable peace, and almost as many said that they would be making visits. Any movement to Angola will not be restricted to those who left because of the war and over 20 percent of those planning to settle there have never lived there before. At the opposite extreme over 20 percent of those who fled the war in Angola expressed no interest in going back there, even to visit, and wanted to remain permanently in Zambia. In other border areas, people talked in the same terms and some residents expressed concern that their villages would be left empty and revert to forest. From the perspective of the Zambian villages Angola was widely regarded as an attractive place blighted by war.

The most commonly cited reason for wanting to go to Angola, particularly among men, was its abundance of natural resources. The underpopulated forests of Angola still harbour game animals, which have long disappeared from the Zambian bush (outside game parks). Many men cross from Mwinilunga and other border areas to hunt. The thicker forest provides richer supplies of honey, caterpillars and mushrooms and there are larger rivers for fishing. All of these natural resources provide valuable supplements to the local diet and can generate more cash than the local agricultural production based on cassava, maize and sweet potatoes. Another source of income was trading to supply commodities such as clothes, soap, salt, bicycle spares and other basic manufactured goods to eastern Angola. Much of the trade was conducted through barter, traders returning with meat and fish. Others were attracted to Angola in anticipation of job opportunities in education, health or construction, as the country lacks qualified staff. The interest in Angola is not limited to farmers alone.

Women frequently cited reasons for going to Angola based on kinship. Married women spoke of following their husbands; others were concerned to be with their parents, uncles or brothers. Some explicitly said that they would go to be with their matrilineal kin with or without their husbands. Women living alone were keen to join their relatives in Angola in order to get support, particularly from male relatives for building houses or clearing fields.

Less than a third of people who wanted to move to Angola expressed their reasons in terms of going home, but it was still a significant motivation. They made comments such as 'it is my country' or 'it is where I was born from' and did not cite any other reason for moving. It is worth noting that among this group some described themselves as having Zambian nationality and one man had never even lived there before.

Migration to Angola is a process rather than an event. People were going back and forth across the border continuously. Some are described as having 'one foot in Zambia and the other in Angola' and their weight shifts constantly from foot to foot. There is no clearly defined time when their migration finishes. For households this can be drawn out over months or years as different members move and others follow.

Thus it appears that any repatriation of self-settled refugees from Zambia to Angola will be mixed with and largely indistinguishable from the 'normal' movement of Lunda people across their land. When peace eventually comes to Angola, people will move from Zambia but at their own pace. Those who were actually moving in 1997 stressed their interest in seeing Angola being completely peaceful but expressed very little interest in the aid effort being made there, except as an indicator of international faith in the peace process. They were more concerned about the state of the country's services and infrastructure, especially clinics, schools and roads, compared to Zambia. Nobody cited the receipt of aid as a likely factor in any decision to move or its timing, but no doubt many will take advantage of any supplies offered.

Conclusion

The government and UNHCR plans for repatriation assumed that, when the war in Angola came to an end, a group of people could be identified as refugees who would repatriate and need aid in doing so. Their motivation for moving to Angola was not relevant; it was sufficient explanation to say that they were refugees. Assistance was only offered to those who could show themselves to be 'genuine' returned refugees, rather than economic migrants or internally displaced people. This reflects the institutional framework in which UNHCR's mandate is to assist refugees, and the need to justify its interventions by reference to the number of refugees involved.

This perspective failed to recognise the local solution to the 'refugee problem' which occurred in the border villages. While the situation in the villages has moved on from the initial emergency when refugees first came, to a complete solution to the problem, the official view of refugees has remained static; those who entered Zambia as refugees are locked into that status until such time as they return to their country. This is explicit in Zambian law, which offers no avenue for change of status, and it is implicit in the attitude of aid agencies which work with an essentialised view of the refugees as people out of place and waiting to go 'home', regardless of the local situation.

A result of this static view of refugees was the development of aid interventions that were inappropriate. By establishing a system of targeted food aid and individual household resettlement packs, UNHCR created a rod for its own back. It must distinguish returning refugees from 'economic migrants' (or internally displaced people); as noted above there are no criteria that can make this distinction. Since the category of refugee does not reflect the realities of people's lives, aid is delivered to those who could jump through the bureaucratic hoops, rather than on the basis of need. Transporting food, kitchen sets and other commodities is very expensive and logistically complex and in Cazombo UNHCR was failing to deliver sufficient quantities to meet its own targets.

The Zambian government's concern appeared to be on facilitating repatriation rather than looking at the impact on the border areas of Zambia more broadly. Peace in Angola will have profound effects on the west of Zambia, opening up new trading patterns and other economic opportunities as well as closing others down. In particular, Zambian villagers were anticipating a large migration of people into Angola, reducing the productive capacity of the border area, which is already the least densely populated region of Zambia and very poor.

As noted above, aid was marginal to people's decisions about moving to Angola, as they would only go when they expected to secure their own livelihoods and did not want to rely on aid. Rather than enticing people to move into Angola with aid packages for individual households, resources could be put into the rehabilitation of infrastructure. It is more appropriate to see the objective of aid as enabling people to repopulate Angola instead of aiming to repatriate refugees.

For the people who live in the villages on both sides of the border, the focus on the 'refugee problem' deflects attention from the difficulties which they share with all residents of this isolated area of Africa. For the most part, people's major worries are not special problems for refugees but problems shared by all. Repatriation programmes offer little to bring solutions to these issues which will continue to dominate people's lives here. They may even create more problems as they hasten the depopulation of western Zambia.

This study of cross-border movement as migration shows how the process needs to be understood within the wider historical and socioeconomic context of the area rather than as a refugee phenomenon. The tenuous link between the state and Angolans and Zambians living near the border, their shared ethnicity and patterns of movement, and the very low population density in the area, are all factors which have enabled

Angolans to be fully integrated. Those choosing to move will do so as voluntarily as any other migration decision made by people struggling to maintain their livelihoods in rural Africa.

Although the particular findings from this case do not necessarily lend themselves to wider generalisation, the study illustrates the different perspectives revealed by looking at repatriation through the lens of migration. Many refugees may want to maintain their national identity and attachment to their country of origin by remaining marked out with special status and treatment. Nevertheless, there are also likely to be many, like the self-settled Angolans in Zambia, who wish to establish new lives as 'normal' people among those with whom they settle. For such people, assuming that there is a 'refugee problem' for which repatriation is the best solution may undermine whatever progress they have made in rebuilding their lives. Taking a migration approach sets the issue of postwar movement in a wider context and brings greater understanding of the perspectives of those most concerned.

Notes

1. Since 1999 this has increased with new refugees, arriving taking the total over 40,000 by the end of 2001.
2. A new repatriation operation is expected to start in 2003 if the current peace continues.

3

Space and Movement in the Sri Lankan Conflict

Oivind Fuglerud

Introduction

Based upon fieldwork among Tamil refugees from Sri Lanka's Northern Province living in Norway and among Muslims in Sri Lanka's Eastern Province, I will in the following discuss migration and nonmigration as related to social practices and political imagery in Sri Lanka. Available data suggest that we find very different responses to the situation of war among the Tamil population in the Northern Province and the Muslim population in the Eastern Province.

The questions of when and for what particular reasons people decide to flee from conflict situations have been of interest to refugee research since its inception (Kunz 1973). In this chapter I argue that in dealing with these questions we need to take into consideration broader issues and more deep-seated traditions than the immediate trigger mechanisms that make people break up and leave. In particular we need to understand how the people concerned conceptualise space and their own communities within it. To grasp the social dynamics behind processes of displacement we need to realise that individuals and communities do not respond in an equal manner to situations of conflict and violence. This is a fact that is often bypassed in refugee research. Stein's understanding is that research should focus on 'refugees everywhere from a broad historical perspective that views them as recurring phenomena with identifiable and often identical patterns of behaviour and sets of causalities' (Stein 1981: 321). One 'set of causalities' is that the refugee, as opposed to the immigrant, '... is not pulled out; he is pushed out. Given the choice he would stay' (Stein 1981: 322).

This portrait is a simplification. It neglects the fact that the reasons why particular persons end up as refugees may be complex. When a person leaves his or her home country in a situation of war, this is often the result of a process where family and friends have contributed, expecting in return future assistance in their own migration. Involuntary migration often involves making priorities and decisions similar to those found in other forms of migration and should be seen as one aspect of larger cultural and sociopolitical processes. To the extent that our interest is in response mechanisms and social dynamics, we need to move beyond legal definitions and conduct in-depth studies of the way possibilities are perceived and acted upon in situations of violence.

Geography of War

The population of Sri Lanka is divided into a complex arrangement of social and ethnic groups, of which, according to the 1981 census, the largest are the Sinhalese (74 percent), the Sri Lanka-Tamil (11 percent), the Indian Tamil (7 percent), and the Muslim (7 percent). Since the early 1980s the country has been in a state of civil war, mainly fought between the Sinhalese army and armed representatives of the Sri Lankan-Tamil minority. While the northern part of the country is predominantly Tamil, the east has a mixed population of Tamils, Muslims and Sinhalese. The Muslim minority in Sri Lanka consists of communities living dispersed among the numerically stronger groups.

From its early days in the mid 1970s, the armed Tamil liberation movement comprised a number of separate groups. In 1986 one of these groups, the Liberation Tigers of Tamil Eelam (LTTE), through a number of surprise attacks on its rivals (Hoole et al. 1988), emerged as the stronger. However, as a consequence of the accord signed by the governments of India and Sri Lanka in 1987, some of these rivals gained political influence backed by Indian military forces. From the autumn of 1987 until the spring of 1990 around 90,000 Indian soldiers, assisted by these local handymen, struggled to control the forces of the LTTE without success. When they finally withdrew, this was a combined result of military failure and a mounting pressure from the Sri Lankan government, which by then was accused by their Sinhalese voters of allowing India to rule its domestic politics.

The Indian withdrawal brought death to towns and villages in the Tamil areas. In Jaffna the LTTE were after fierce fighting able to establish control and to build an administration, which remained in place until the end of 1995. In the Eastern Province the organisation took control over local police stations. After having surrendered, many policemen were taken away never to be seen again. One officer, who escaped with injuries,

later told the papers that he and 113 of his colleagues from the police sta-
tion in Kalmunai had been lined up by the LTTE and shot (UTHR 1990).
These kinds of actions were not limited to the LTTE however. In one of its
reports Amnesty International estimated that 3,000 Tamil people had 'disappeared' or been killed by government forces in Amparai, the district
south of Batticaloa, between July and October 1990 (Amnesty
International 1991). In Batticaloa Town, more than 1,500 people were registered as 'disappeared' between June and December by the local Peace
Committee (ibid.).

The Muslim population was part of this apocalypse. In the Eastern
Province tensions had existed between Tamils and Muslims at least since
the mid 1980s. In the LTTE's actions against police stations, Muslim officers were grouped with Sinhalese and taken away while most of the
Tamils were allowed to go. On 3 August 1990 around 30 members of the
LTTE, in two groups, simultaneously attacked the Meera Jumma and the
Hussainiya mosques in Kattankudy during prayer, killing 128 civilians,
including a number of children. One week later Eravur, a Muslim town
north of Batticaloa, was hit. Entering the town from both sides in the early
hours of the morning, LTTE soldiers raided houses along Main Street, and
121 sleeping men, women, and children were slaughtered. The massacre
was followed by the killing of twenty-one Tamils in what is locally known
as the 'border area', the overlapping area between Eravur itself and the
neighbouring Tamil town of Chenkaladi, an area which at that time had
an ethnically mixed population. Muslim 'home guards' from Eravur carried out these retaliatory killings. The violence led to the vacating of the
border area by both parties.

Movement and Space

By this brief presentation I hope to have established that the violence that
has engulfed Sri Lanka during the last twenty years has also affected the
eastern part of the country. Indeed, while the armed Tamil liberation
movement first originated in northern Sri Lanka, the Eastern Province has
become an increasingly important area for all parties to the conflict for
asserting their military capacity.

Against this backdrop the difference in the population's responses to
the continuous violence in various regions of Sri Lanka is quite striking.
At a press conference in Colombo in December 1995 president
Kumaratunga suggested that out of a prewar population of 950,000 in the
Northern Province, the one predominantly Tamil province in Sri Lanka,
approximately 400,000 had at that point settled outside the country. While
as a group their relationship with different national immigration authorities has by no means been smooth, these Tamil refugees have individual-

ly been able to secure legal residence in countries from Finland to South Africa and on continents from Europe to Australia. Indeed, to someone who has worked among Tamil refugees outside Sri Lanka it seems clear that Paris, London, and Toronto today are as much parts of Tamil geography as Jaffna, Trincomalee or Colombo.

Among the Muslims in the Eastern Province, on the other hand, an opposite dynamic seems to be working. There is no international refugee flow and no internal displacement to Colombo or other areas outside the war zone. Rather than people moving out, Muslim towns have themselves become destinations for Muslims displaced from rural areas. In 1990, as the Indian troops withdrew, the LTTE took control over the territory on the western side of the Batticaloa lagoon, a position they have since defended successfully. This area, a very fertile agricultural zone, was an area of mixed Tamil and Muslim landholdings and cattle farming. When the LTTE took control, the Muslim families were driven out and today most of them live in refugee settlements in Eravur and in Muslim towns along the coast south of Batticaloa. The land- and cattle owners living in Eravur and Kattankudy at the same time lost their property, being deprived of much of their traditional economic basis. Despite these difficulties, however, people clung on, and my leading questions to informants concerning planned mobility were largely met with incomprehension. 'Refugee' as a legal concept was not known to anyone I met, and the idea of being allowed to settle permanently in another country because their lives might be in danger seemed to most almost absurd. The scenario of moving to Colombo, on the other hand, was clearly not a tempting one; most people travelling beyond Polonnaruwa, 75 kilometres away, seemed to carry the connotation of going to velinatu, a foreign land. Even members of the small class of people having been educated outside the region, gave answers like 'I belong here', 'we have nowhere to go', 'this is my village, how can I leave?' when asked if they had any plans to move out of the war-zone.

The Importance of Marriage

The most important explanation for the relative success of Tamils in securing emigration and protection as refugees in Western countries has been the previous existence of family members outside Sri Lanka. In the post–independence period Tamils started migrating to find work when Sinhala politicians in the 1950s consciously sought ways of reducing Tamil entry into the public sector in Sri Lanka (Daniel and Thangaraj 1995). When the war started and Western countries tightened their immigration and asylum controls, these early emigrants became instrumental in assisting relatives in need of a safe haven. To Tamils, going abroad to settle often involves the use of professional 'agents'. The cost of a full-service package to bring a Sri Lankan to Canada was in 1997 estimated to be between $22,000 and $26,000 (DIRB 1997). To go to Norway most Tamils pay $10,000–$15,000. The only people with access to this amount of money are those with relatives already in the West.

The argument that kinship ties are important to the process of migration would probably qualify as a truism. Since the 1960s analysts have been interested in the importance of social networks for processes of chain migration and the role of family and friends in settling new immigrants in receiving countries (Boyd 1989). The important point here is that Tamil kinship and social practices have attained a spatial form that today structures a perception of their own community in transnational terms. Through the practice of arranged marriages Tamils become part of transnational networks, incorporating new members into the grid of Dravidian classificatory kinship semantics. Classificatory kinship not only groups relatives together in a limited number of categories, but also defines modes of action and bonds of solidarity on the basis of such categories. The most important aspect of Dravidian kinship is that it indicates an ideal of bilateral cross-cousin marriage (Trautman 1981), an ideal still found in Jaffna. The ideal marriage is with the closest possible kin, and in theory one can imagine two male cross-cousins exchanging sisters down through generations, so that mother's brother's daughter and father's sister's daughter will be the same person.

In the Jaffna-Tamil case this centripetal dynamic is, however, counter-balanced by the practice of hypergamy through dowered marriages (Fuglerud 1999). It is within this socioeconomic context that we must explore the importance of migration to the Jaffna society. There are strong indications that under present conditions where obtaining refugee protection in Western countries is becoming increasingly difficult to obtain, dowries among Jaffna Tamils are subject to hyperinflation. To a male refugee a sizeable dowry is one way of recovering part of the cost of going abroad. To parents and brothers securing a daughter's or sister's marriage to an émigré is worth paying for, and the particular nationality of the groom's passport is an important variable in dowry negotiations. The migration situation thereby drastically alters the role and function of dowry. Instead of one dowry helping to finance another, floating as capital within the system of family networks, the cost of transport and settlement papers now siphons off this capital to greedy 'agents'. Among my informants in Norway dowries of $50,000–$100,000 are not unusual, a substantial part often going into arranging the very meeting of the two parties. As I have noted elsewhere (Fuglerud 1999: 152), this is one curious consequence of the increasingly strict immigration regulations in the West; because of the extremely high costs of circumventing them, migration has retained its aura of social mobility into the era of full-fledged civil war. While this situation means bending the former ideal of marriage within the family, there is no sign that the fundamental structure of caste is breaking down. By combining cultural values rooted in the sedentary society of South Asia with the economic bargaining power obtained through migratory careers, Tamil marriages can be seen as what Olwig terms 'cultural sites'; institutions created through an interplay between dwelling and travelling, presence and absence, localising and globalising (Olwig 1997: 35). To women themselves the consequences of this changing pattern are predominantly negative. On the one hand marriage outside the family, and in particular to men settled abroad, weakens the possibility of support from relatives in daily chores and in situations of difficulty. On the other hand male migration and rising dowries create a situation where many women are not able to marry at all. According to a survey conducted by the Northern District administration, in Jaffna women in 1994 outnumbered men six to one (Associated Press 29.04.94). There is reason to speculate that the difficulties of establishing a meaningful family life help to explain the large number of women recruited into the armed liberation movement.

One way of presenting the eastern Muslim situation with respect to kinship ties is simply to say that their marriages are not, or at least to a much lesser degree, characterised by hypergamy and inflation in dowries. According to McGilvray (1989: 199), in eastern Sri Lanka kinship categories are embedded in marriage alliances between partners of equal standing. In a footnote McGilvray points out that '(f)ieldwork by Hiatt (1973) and McGilvray (1974) has found no empirical evidence of the pattern of hypergamous marriage between matriclans ...'. While there is no need here to go into the intricacies of matrilineal kinship, we may note that McGilvray emphasises that: 'For everyone ... the matriclan system is a significant constraint upon marriage choice ...' (McGilvray 1989: 200). In other words, the eastern population so far adheres to the ideals contained in kinship semantics. De Munck (1996) has reported the same situation from Moneragala. He found that in the Muslim village of Kutali, 61 percent of the marriages entered into during his fieldwork were marriages between first cross-cousins; 'percentages ... significantly higher than those recorded for other South Asian and Sri Lankan communities' (ibid.: 706). While money may be of interest also to the Muslim population, marriage outside the kindred is not an important mechanism for converting economic remittances into social status.

Also among Muslims social relations have a spatial dimension. The main difference from the situation prevailing among Tamil migrants from the Northern Province seems to be that while among the latter dowry is today increasingly provided in cash, Muslims in the east still hold that the essential core of a woman's dowry is land and a house, the absolute minimum being only a house. 'Without it, or without at least a firm pledge that it will be built, a marriage is usually impossible' (McGilvray 1989: 201). The typical pattern is that the mother's dowry house, that is the house where the couple has lived after their marriage, is given to the eldest daughters as her dowry while the parents and the rest of the family move to another house nearby. Daughters are expected to marry in strict order of age, and the process will be repeated until they are all settled in independent households. Ideally this results in a clustering of the extended family around daughters' houses.

McGilvrays's observations, which were made in the town of Akkaraipattu, are confirmed by my own observations in Eravur. While there is in fact an inflow of money to the Muslim settlements in the east, stemming from short-term work migration to the Middle East, this so far seems not to have changed the conception of what a dowry should be in the way that is the case among Tamil refugees. Rather than externally earned money resulting in a monetarisation of the marriage sphere, houses are bought which enter this sphere as capital in the traditional way. Thereby money from abroad strengthens the uxorilocal practice and the localising tendency rather than the opposite.

Perspectives and Politics

The differently structured networks discussed above are reinforced by different political imagery within the two groups. On the Tamil side a debate on contemporary politics must centre on the Liberation Tigers of Tamil Eelam (LTTE). This organisation is the Sri Lankan government's military adversary in Sri Lanka. Its power, and in fact also its organisation, is diffused throughout the Tamil diaspora: its main office in London, its development branch in Australia, its Internet news server in Oslo. As one Tamil journalist complained to me who was trying to work out an agreement on news distribution with the LTTE, and had come from Colombo to Oslo for that purpose: 'now you have to travel around the world to do what you could earlier accomplish in two hours at the Jaffna *katchcheri*' (the office of the Government Agent).

Again, among the eastern Muslims we see another dynamic at work. Rather than viewing Eelam from globalised positions, the localising strategy of the Muslim population entails a particular perspective on Sri Lanka from the inside. The defensive withdrawal into their own patrolled areas must be understood as alienation not only from their Tamil surroundings but from the elite representatives of the larger Sri Lankan Muslim community.

So far not much substantial work has been done on the political identity of the Muslim minority in Sri Lanka. However, Ismail (1995) points out that in Sri Lanka the construction of a Muslim national identity could only take place within the terms and boundaries determined by the more assertive forces of Sinhala and Tamil nationalism. For the community's elite this construction has involved a double problematic. On the one hand to represent their origin and character as distinct from those of the Tamil, on the other, in its capacity as a separate minority, to find ways of representing itself as accommodating vis-à-vis an increasingly chauvinistic Sinhala state machinery. The ways in which this challenge has been met have varied with the terms in which the Sinhala and Tamil nationalisms have been expressed. As long as these communities argued their own cases in terms of 'race', Muslim leaders grounded their own ethnicity in geographical origin and 'Arab blood'. As language replaced race in the postcolonial discourse on identity, efforts were made to ground Muslim ethnic identity in the Arabic language. The need for members of the Muslim elite to distinguish themselves from the Tamil must be seen as part of a strategic response to the growing Sinhala chauvinism surrounding them. In 1915 Muslims were the first community victimised by ethnic abuse in Sri Lanka. In Kandy, Colombo and other towns in the south, organised groups of Sinhalese men destroyed mosques and burnt Muslim property. During the colonial era the Colombo-based Muslim elite sought protection from the British against these attitudes. When independence was imminent, however, they not only accommodated themselves to the Sinhala state, but also built a public image on this accommodation. The Muslims have portrayed themselves as a community (*one* community) that, contrary to the Tamil, has been successful *because* of its cooperation with the Sinhala state.

This legacy of Muslim elite self-representation is directly relevant to the question at hand here. Historically, one consequence of the dispersal of the population has been the tendency for the elite based in and around the capital of Colombo to publicly represent the community on a part-for-whole basis. Since 1983 there exists one party claiming to represent the Eastern Muslims, the Sri Lanka Muslim Congress (SLMC), which from 1994 has been part of the coalition government led by the Sri Lanka Freedom Party, a party with a history of Sinhala chauvinism. Increasingly, however, the SLMC seems to be perceived as a new elite replacing the old one based in Colombo. Mainly drawing its support from the Amparai District within the Eastern Province where the Muslim population is the larger ethnic group, it is seen as neglecting the situation of the Muslim minority settlements located in Tamil majority areas like Batticaloa District. In particular, the SLMC's policy of promoting a separate Muslim South-Eastern Province finds little resonance outside the Muslim majority areas. In Batticaloa District there is a feeling that this objective, rather than solving their problems, may aggravate their relationship to the Tamil population in general and to the LTTE in particular. It is symptomatic that when the SLMC's fifteenth annual congress was held in May 1998,

Muslim shops in Batticaloa District were closed and black and white flags were flown in protest.

Place and Ethnicity

This opinion on the policy of the SLMC reflects more deep-lying cultural conceptions. In Eravur, the town I am most familiar with in eastern Sri Lanka, there is no question that their language is Tamil, not Arabic, and that they share cultural traditions with their social surroundings. In their own understanding, what separates them from their Tamil neighbours are not linguistic or cultural diacritics but these neighbours' recent betrayal of the common history of the two communities.

In the different Muslim settlements in eastern Sri Lanka one finds stories explaining their separate origin. These oral histories articulate models of the relationship between a particular settlement and its surroundings. In Eravur the origin story tells that a group of Pathan warriors from today's border area between Afghanistan and Pakistan, came by boat to the eastern parts of Sri Lanka in the fifteenth century and sought shelter from storms in Batticaloa harbour. In those days men of Thimilar caste from Batticaloa every year used to come to Eravur, which was a Mukkuvar caste area, during harvest time to rob gold and women. The people in Eravur asked the Pathan warriors to come and protect the village. The Pathans came and drove the Thimilars to Vakarai, a place north of Eravur. In reward the Pathans were given a choice between land, gold or women. They chose women because, as it is said, no amount of material worth comes up against the importance of blood relations. The Mukkuvar then chose women from their seven main *kutis* and gave these to the Pathans in marriage. The Pathans settled and had Hindu service castes serving them.

Two aspects of this story seem significant. One is that, even as it is told today, the story reflects no ethnic or territorial antagonism between Tamils (or Hindus) and Muslims. The conflict that moves the story is internal to the Hindus. While the Hindus were on location first, the Muslims were invited as harbingers of peace and order. This invitation, and the events which follow, establish Eravur as a 'territorial place', opposed to the outside geographical surroundings. It is the land, and in particular the land where people live, which is significant, not any wider social, ethnic, or religious loyalties. Second, the marriages between Muslim men and Mukkuvar women from all main sections provide the descendants of these unions with a double origin. At the same time, however, they establish a subtle difference in social status between the Muslim and the Hindu. The tradition of male dominance found in the Tamil areas, including the Muslim settlements, provides wife takers a somewhat superior position to wife givers. The fact that Pathan men married women from *all* main sections of the local Mukkuvar society may be understood as a statement to the effect that in matters of rank the Muslim will always be superior.

This claim must be understood in its proper context however. Today, speaking in a 'reality mode', people deny any common occurrence of marriages between members of different communities. Where this happens, like with the present Member of Parliament from Eravur, this is noted as an exception. While people readily admit to following typical Hindu-Tamil traditions, like the tying of *Thali* and the transfer of dowry at marriage (Fuglerud 1994; 1999), and in conversations may say things like 'at heart we are all Tamil', ethnic boundaries are socially reproduced on the basis of religion. What the origin story expresses, being set in a society characterised by feudal dynamics, is that Muslims see themselves as providers and protectors of the territorial community as a whole. It is told with pride that in Hindu temples in the Tamil settlements surrounding Eravur offerings are still made in gratitude to the Muslim Pathans. Eravur farmers claim that until 1990 the Muslims owning land on the west side of the lagoon were in general more prosperous than their Tamil neighbours. They explain how they used to help Tamil farmers with seeds and fertiliser, and how they ploughed the fields of Tamil neighbours with their own tractors. 'We (Tamil) have rice, you (Muslim) have plates' is by Muslim landowners quoted as a Tamil saying, expressing the close interconnection between the two communities. It does not mean that Muslims do not grow rice but that while the local Tamil population worked and lived on the land, Muslims were regarded as land-owning town people with access to markets, money, and products of the 'modern' world.

Concluding Remarks

In approaching the different responses to the engulfing violence above I avoided framing this question in terms of 'migration choice'. From an anthropologist's point of view the application of choice models in migration research has provided limited insights. We should, I believe, in analyses of displacement and migration put less emphasis on causal connections and more on the knowledge and discourses that organise actors' understanding of their own actions. As demonstrated by studies of the relationship between internal migration and suicide (Kearney and Miller 1987; Daniel 1989), in Sri Lanka the issues of migration and displacement cannot be separated from the larger theme of discursively constructed identities.

In this chapter I have outlined two responses to a situation of prevailing violence in Sri Lanka; the Tamil migration as refugees to Western countries and a Muslim community's withdrawal into its own defended territory. In my understanding this difference illustrates the point made by Hägerstrand (1969) thirty years ago, that migration – except for the most extreme cases of forced migration – is one out of several 'time-space strategies' available to social actors, the others including staying, commuting, circulating etc. Instead of considering staying as the expected outcome of time-embedded processes, and moving the phenomenon always to be explained, one point of entry into the study of migration, 'forced' or not, is to identify determinants of the different time-space strategies which people choose. This process of identification should include not only economic goals and constraints but the perceptions and meanings through which actors understand the various elements in their life world and related to which they strive to secure a livelihood.

4

Contested Refugee Status: Human Rights, Ethics and Social Responsibilities

Philomena Essed and Rianne Wesenbeek

Introduction

The question of who counts as 'refugee' in the enactment of international human rights is a continuous source of struggle among governments, state bureaucracies and critical movements (Lauren 1998). Individuals who leave behind home and country in the hope of surviving elsewhere and who subsequently knock on Dutch (or other European Union) doors may find that their primary agency, the definition of their own reality, throws dice in a political casino – the passing test. Eligibility for asylum depends on whether the home country situation is taken to produce refugees and whether the individual applicant has a plausible story to fit certain bureaucratic criteria. But the different bureaucratic categorisations and procedures are unable to catch the variegated realities of flight, a global condition shaping the lives of millions of people. As a result those who get to be rejected after a period of waiting for the outcome of the decision-making process might go underground to join the 40,000–100,000 undocumented immigrants – a relatively new category consisting of immigrants who entered on a tourist visa and then decided to stay, those who crossed the border illegally, and those who became illegal when they were refused refugee status (Leun et al. 1998).

More than anything the construction of the category 'illegal' symbolises the bankruptcy of the notion of 'refugee' in the Human Rights Declaration, in an era of global capitalism, environmental disasters, internal wars, massive mobilisations and continuous movements of people. At the same time, the concept of 'illegality' gives new meaning to old problems of exclusion and inequalities, not only between countries (who determines the direction of globalisation, who benefits and who does not) but also within countries (who belongs and who does not belong in a nation state that has also become a multi-ethnic society). The common-sense reaction among the population at large is to exaggerate the issue of immigration and to criminalise refugees in particular. Basic concerns about human rights and dignity are pushed aside, while politicians and policy makers reinforce the myth that only people who are formally recognised as such are refugees. The linking of different administrative database systems suggests that the real issue is not (only) the number of people without legal status, but to make sure that *only* legal residents have access to education, health care and other resources. Those who do not fit the criteria are just irregular immigrants who, because they lack legal status, have no rights at all.

Human rights, according to Zygmunt Bauman (1989) are the building blocks of all moral behavior. The denial of human rights in the name of European and Dutch policy highlights the problematic relation between immigrant policy and moral behaviour. There are few areas where the contradiction between policies and moral principles is negotiated more critically than in healthcare for people without legal status. Why health-care? Among the pressing needs immigrants experience when entering a country are housing, income and good health. Those who cannot apply legally for state provisions are usually very creative in finding a place to stay. Furthermore, some employers are keen to hire nonregistered work-ers, because they can get away with paying them lower wages. Nonregistered people are often also successful in finding alternative sources of income, through ethnic communities, other networks or infor-mal entrepreneurship, selling goods or playing music in the streets.

Health is a different matter. There are situations where there is no other option for someone without legal status but to seek professional medical help. Healthcare professionals are aware of this necessity too, but Dutch policy excludes the undocumented from access to social and healthcare benefits. Their applying for medical service confronts healthcare profes-sionals with the choice between civil obedience and professional ethics. We discuss this problem using cases exemplifying the way hospitals and individual professionals deal with this dilemma. Some take over social responsibility where policy makers fail, others do not. With our focus on professionals in the receiving society we intend to broaden the debate on agency and empowerment to *include* those critical members of so-called hosting societies who actively denounce repressive state policies (Hollands 1998). We intend to show that state policies and the nature of bureaucracies undermine some of the fundamental human rights of peo-ple without legal status, including those who consider themselves refugee. At the same time Dutch national and local governments are lenient when organisations intervene on behalf of immigrants without legal status (Engbersen and Burgers 2000). This implies that state obligations to enforce basic human rights are reduced to a matter of personal responsibility. By way of introduction we first make a few general remarks about the nature of human rights and about Dutch and European immigration policies.

Rights, Responsibilities and the Manufacture of Illegality

According to the first and second articles of the Universal Declaration of Human Rights of 1948, everyone is born free and equal in dignity and rights and entitled to all rights and freedoms mentioned in the Declaration 'without distinction of any kind such as race, colour, sex, language, religion, political or other opinion, national or social origin, property, birth or status' (Lauren 1998: 300). The Declaration encompasses all human beings, but that does not mean that all individuals or groups enjoy these rights equally. Some have or are able to take more freedoms than others according to power and depending on gender, ethnicity, nationality, age, social or economic circumstances. The violation of human rights often occurs as a function of inequalities between categories of people who are perceived as different from the prevailing normative standards.

At the heart of the Universal Declaration of Human Rights is the right of individual freedom specified in a range of principles, including protection against discrimination, freedom of self-determination, freedom of movement and residence, the right to work, the right to leave any country, including one's own, and the right to asylum in another country by way of protection against political persecution. While critical of making 'the individual' central, our purpose is not to question the nature of universal human rights as such, but their relation to notions of citizenship and the production of a status of 'illegality'.

The opening sentence of the Declaration reads: 'Everyone is entitled to all the rights and freedoms ... without distinction of any kind.' This indicates that human rights are at odds with inequality and discrimination in access to the rights and freedoms to which one is entitled. At the same time, the predominance of the classical freedom rights, that is, individual political and civil rights sustains social inequality (Richters 1994). Historically, elites more so than populations at large have been able to appeal to the classical freedom rights. Along the same lines the idea has developed that the enactment of indivisibility of human rights and human equality is subject to internal national politics. In international arenas the principle of non-interference, that is, autonomy in national affairs, predominates.

Throughout the 1980s and 1990s, the northwestern European countries became distinct destinations for refugees from all over the world, the number of asylum applications averaging from 200,000–300,000 per year. Germany has long been the most important country of destination, but numbers have increased as well for other countries, including the Netherlands (Havinga and Böcker 1999). Hosting global refugees represents the tail end of a longer period of steady migration to the Netherlands after the Second World War. Over time, and as a function of global developments, the nature of immigration has changed, from labour migrants and population shifts in the context of decolonisation in the 1960s and 1970s, to refugee arrivals in the late 1980s and the 1990s. Today over 10 percent of the Dutch population consists of ethnic minorities, the majority of whom live in the larger cities (Veenman 1996). Numbers vary from a low of 15 percent, to almost 40 percent in the city of Amsterdam.

Like most other Western European countries the attitude of the Dutch state has been ambivalent, varying between a discourse of tolerance and one of immigration control. Policies ranged from laissez-faire in the 1960s and early 1970s, when the economy needed unskilled workers, towards severe control of 'unwanted migration', in particular from Eastern Europe and from developing countries, especially from the 1980s onwards (Essed 1996). A central concept in the discourse legitimising restrictive policies has been the idea of 'limits'. Even when human rights are recognised as important and acceptable guidelines for policy, acting accordingly is defined as a function of the successful enforcement of 'limits' in the area of immigration policy. Accordingly, it is assumed that immigration policy entails managing choices between competing societal interests (Sciortino 2000): 'Holland is already overcrowded.' Humanitarian acceptance, so the argument goes, can only be guaranteed to a limited number of refugees, because both the socio-cultural strength of Dutch citizens and the financial power of this country have their limits: lodging refugees and asylum seekers simply costs money (Meloen et al. 1998; Lakeman 1999). Our concern here is not that governments pursue certain regulations in the area of immigration. It should be mentioned that underlying sentiments of limitation and discouragement, in state circles as well as among the public at large, are often predicated on an image of cultural threat, a trend Martin Barker had already identified in the early 1980s in his study of *The New Racism* (Barker 1981). What these perceived threats entail is ambiguous, depending on the economic, political and cultural context. One commonsense presupposition is that there is a distinction between economic and political refugees, where the first category threatens the human rights of the 'real refugees' (Hollands 1998). In this perception the Dutch population is the neutral bystander concerned about the refugees themselves turning into a threat for each other. Another commonsense argument is that the human rights of the 'real' refugees, as well of the Dutch population, are jeopardised due to overcrowding and high costs.

Little if any attention is paid to the fact that immigration services are an industry in themselves, a large, if not the major, proportion of which goes directly to the salaries of Dutch government employees and a range of subsidised organisations involved in the hosting and policing of refugees. Also real-estate businesses, supermarkets and other shops around centres for asylum seekers profit from immigration. The official discourse, however, emphasises one-sidedly that the number of immigrants must be controlled and regulated within the context of the nation and preferably within the context of so-called European harmonization policies (Hughes and Liebaut 1999; Schans and Buuren 1999). The political sustainability of the latter is being called into question, given the fact that countries such as Italy are giving increasing voice to the need for more immigration in order to finance current and future generations of pensioners.

In order to honour human rights guidelines, while at the same time justifying the policy of discouragement, the applications for asylum are legally *assessed*. Two sets of criteria are used for this. The first is inferred from the 1951 Convention relating to the status of refugees. Here, what is of supreme importance is the definition of the 'genuine refugee'. Only the applicant who conforms to this definition receives a permit to stay. Another set of criteria applies universal human rights to specific individual cases, which can result in admission on humanitarian grounds. In line with the policy of discouragement, however, since the 1990s assessment procedures have been regularly tightened up and bureaucratic attitudes with them. Asylum seekers are perceived as suspects charged with fraudulent inclinations unless officials feel the refugee story is plausible according to their own interpretation.

Control and discouragement of immigration has forged a division between groups of people based on legal status: indigenous Dutch, legal migrants and refugees with citizen status on the one hand, and 'illegal' people on the other. Considering the severe consequences of the administrative elimination of individuals, it is worth noticing that the construction of the idea of the 'genuine' refugee places unprecedented powers with bureaucratic officials. All the ingredients for a balanced assessment are to be gathered at this level. However, the increasing national and European political pressure on immigration laws, and consequentially the numbers of refugees who appeal to correct the assessment of their situation according to human rights principles, have made immigration laws complex and opaque. As a result, the assessments of asylum applications risk becoming (and are increasingly perceived as) more or less arbitrary decisions about who can stay and who will be sent back. The fact that asylum-seeking individuals are in politically insecure and sensitive situations make arbitrariness even more problematic.

The principle that refugee stories are assessed for plausibility implies that applications for protection and residence are honoured or refused according to rules and regulations into which the refugee has no input. In other words, he or she has to play the game according to imposed rules. Once the Dutch official considers the 'flight story' to lack sufficient plausibility, the applicant is branded a 'pseudo'. His or her name is eliminated from the application procedure and the 'subject' turns administratively into an 'illegal' and thus 'undesirable' individual. The individual involved dies a bureaucratic death. No papers, and thus, no existence. We call this process from assessment to rejection 'the manufacture of illegality'. One crucial problem in the assessment process has to do with the nature of administration itself. During the last decade both the assessment and the sheltering of asylum seekers have become highly institutionalised and bureaucratised, including the rent of lodgings, salaries of personnel, and overhead. The expansive growth of institutions for asylum seekers and refugees has revealed a number of problems which actually have little to do with asylum seekers themselves, but which can nevertheless adversely influence their interests (Dekker and Senstius 1997). Shortages of personnel and failing management created a backlog in the handling of refugee files at the Immigration and Naturalisation Service (IND), that has triggered public criticisms. Other problems have to do with the definition of the refugee in relation to the situation of traumatised people in general, women and children in particular (Spijkerboer, 1994b; Ghidei Biidu 1995; Evenhuis 1996). The 1951 Convention on the Status of the Refugee acknowledges exclusively as refugees individuals seeking refuge from political persecution in the narrow sense: state violence and deprivation of civil and political rights. This may sound gender neutral, but it has been found that gender is a relevant factor in determining the possibility of successful application for refugee status. First of all, it is more difficult for women and children to flee to the West. Secondly, women (and children) tend to flee because of exposure to specific forms of violence that are not regarded as political. For example, rape is perceived predominantly as domestic violence and not as a gender-specific form of oppression. Children conceived through rape as a crime of war represent the mother's 'embodied pain' (Wieringa 1997).

The plausibility of the flight story as a criterion for entry is a controversial instrument. Traumatised victims are not unlikely to have inconsistent stories, because of the sheer fact of trauma. Women find it hard to speak about experiences of rape because they feel shame, fear, rejection or other negative judgements. Sometimes the assessors' questions cause confusion (Wieringa 1997). Children's stories have to fit adult standards, regardless of age and their state of psychological development (Thomeer-Bouwens and Smit 1998; Morelli and Braat 1999). Officials, suspicious about the age of child refugees, often expose youngsters to so-called 'bone tests', a normative medical assessment of the child's age according to the development of his or her bone structure. Few if any officials are proper-

ly trained and prepared to deal effectively and respectfully with traumatised people, with the shame of women and with the shock of children
(Jong 2000).

Another problem has to do with the fact that the refugee status of a
spouse usually depends on that of the primary applicant, often the husband. In case of divorce within three years of arrival, for instance due to
domestic violence, the woman risks losing her legal status (Kommitee
Zelfstandig Verblijfsrecht Migrantenvrouwen 1999). Thus she may end up
having to choose between the devil and the deep blue sea; accepting
domestic violence or plunging into the insecurities of social violence, that
is, the hazards of life in illegality. This situation is particularly unfair also
because refugee families are often prone to internal disruptions as a function of political prosecution, flight, and the building of a new life in a different environment. In the end, women bear the greater burden if internal
tensions lead to divorce. If a dependent parent, usually the mother, 'dis-
appears' into illegality, accompanying children 'disappear' as well
because of their dependent status. As we write this article, a new law is
being devised to grant more independence to divorced women.

Since the introduction in the Netherlands of the so-called 'Koppelingswet' (Bill of Connection, 1998) linking immigration files and citizen status
to social security files, those construed as illegal have lost legitimate
access to public services, health and welfare provisions, Theirs is a life
without basic rights. There are some exceptions to the Bill of Connection.
The government is careful to take into account the ill effects of medical
exclusion in the case of infectious diseases, such as tuberculosis and AIDS.
For this reason specific community healthcare organisations get public
funding for the services they offer to 'illegals'. Another exception is more
general and applicable to all organisations and professionals in healthcare. Access to medical treatment is still permitted in the case of 'really
serious' conditions, including the following:

- Life-threatening conditions, for the subjects or for third parties
  involved;
- Situations where the acute malfunctioning of essential organs can
  cause chronic disabilities;
- All situations demanding care for 'illegally residing children', including prenatal care, delivery and postnatal care.

The policy rationale behind these exceptions is that neglect can be more
costly for society than timely intervention. But there are also other reasons
to intervene. As professionals with an ethical obligation to support those
in need, social workers, nurses and doctors feel an obligation to offer professional service. If they accept nonregistered patients, thus ignoring the
limitations of the law, it means that political responsibilities are trans-

ferred to the semi-private domains of the professional and personal consciousness.

Healthcare

Before proceeding with concrete cases of ethical dilemmas and civil disobedience in healthcare, it is perhaps helpful to say something more general about the nature of healthcare in the Netherlands and its conduciveness to inclusion. Professional welfare and healthcare is rooted in what used to be called charity. For ages, helping the poor and the ill was a religious and social mission for those who had the financial means and expertise. According to Abraham de Swaan, the development of collective social and medical provisions and the rise of the social and medical professional elite relate closely to the development of the state and the industrialisation of Western societies (Swaan 1996). In his analyses of the process of collectivity formation and the development of care as a profession, he points out that the idea of 'giving help' is foremost a question of self-interest. In Western cultures and according to dominant perspectives of the human sciences and professional practices, self-interest, as distinguished from altruism, is seen as a 'normal' human feature (Monroe 1996). The concept of self-interest links people who are in need of help to people who can offer help. At the same time, it is believed that the expectations of neutrality and scientific objectivity, dominant in the professional domain, are instrumental in regulating the balance between the self-interest of the professional and the needs of the client. Professional training and professional autonomy are supposed to socialise professionals into this mode of professionalism.

The ethical ground underlying health and care, captured in professional codes, reflects some of the basic principles of universal human rights. For instance, in the mission statement of the International Nursing Association, it is mentioned explicitly that nurses should protect individual human rights 'not only in times of conflict but also in daily practice' (Nationale Raad voor de Geestelijke Volksgezondheid 1995). The code of secrecy, guaranteeing the privacy of the client, qualifies the unique position of the professional. At the same time discretion provides a basis in professional care for openness in relation to clients in regard to their illegal status.

After the Second World War, there was an explosive growth in the domain of social and healthcare. The growing army of professionals, representing highly specialised social and medical disciplines, has been increasingly organised into mega-bureaucratic institutions. Health institutions are ruled by new managerial elites, assisted by experts in policy and research. Organisational interests and the protection of professional knowledge are integrated into the dynamics of the relation between the client and the professional (Meurs 1997). Michael Lipsky has exposed the dangers of what he calls street-level bureaucracies:

> Ideally, and by training, street-level bureaucrats respond to individual needs or characteristics of the people they serve or confront. In practice they must deal with clients on a mass basis, since work requirements prohibit individualised service ... At best, street level bureaucrats invent benign modes of mass processing that more or less permit them to deal with the public fairly, appropriately, and successfully. At worst, they give in to favouritism, stereotyping and routinising – all of which serve private or agency purposes. (Lipsky 1980: xii)

The history of healthcare shows that professionalism and ethics do not always guarantee care 'for everyone ... without distinction'. Professional organisations as social institutions manifest the usual attributes social relations entail, such as inequality in power, chances and opportunities (Fernando 1995). Over the years the growing assertiveness among clients, patients and particularly among women has contributed to demystifying the 'almighty' and 'objective' status of the professional, shedding full light on ongoing inhuman and discriminatory practices (Richters 1991).

We do not mean to suggest that discrimination is always intentional. The acute dilemma emerging from the questions 'should or should we not give treatment to patients without legal status?' highlights the existence of other problems in the healthcare system. The more systemic the problems, the less easy it is to deal with new problems. Mounting pressures throughout the past ten years include shortage of personnel, budgetary cuts, assertive, sometimes aggressive patients, stressful working conditions, mismanagement, and increasing demand for hospitalisation among the elderly and patients with chronic diseases. Professionals suffer from feelings of insecurity, fear of failure, and anxiety that they will be unable to live up to the image of the 'know-it-all', professionally as well as socially. Racial, gender and other stereotypes contribute to discriminatory practice in health institutions (Wesenbeek 1996).

From an ethical and human-rights perspective, equal care should be provided to everyone without distinction, but national politics create differences between categories of people on the basis of citizenship. The professional has to deal with a potential conflict between politics and ethics in deciding how to interpret 'necessary care' in assessing whether exceptions can be made for an individual 'illegal' who applies for treatment. There is, for instance, no clear demarcation between necessary care and desirable care. In the case of 'illegals' the distinction becomes a question of restriction and assessment. Take, for example, the case of pneumonia. Assessing when care is necessary or desirable, or when lack of care is life-threatening, is not purely a medical matter but also depends upon the patient's social and economic circumstances. Poverty, physical harshness and the stresses of life in illegality create extra health risks. Apart from the purely medical assessment, organisational factors also impact on medical evaluation and decision making. 'Illegals' are seen as a financial risk because they have no medical insurance. Moreover, communication with them often takes more time because of language problems and cultural differences. Furthermore, the most vital skill that is needed – flexible and creative problem solving – is a scarce resource within modern institutions, where the rules of the game dictate routines within fixed parameters in order to run health companies as ordinary competitive businesses.

How are these dilemmas dealt with in everyday life? We present a number of cases, illustrating how professionals negotiate among rules, personal ethics and responsibility with respect to clients with an illegal status. The cases are part of an ongoing exploratory project, 'Refugees, Citizenship and Healthcare: Ethical Dilemmas and Solutions', for the purpose of which we are interviewing professionals in health and social care. Many of the professionals we included expressed relief that they were being given the chance to discuss this subject. They experience there 'helping people without legal status' as a public secret, a taboo, the mentioning of which may trigger negative opinions, sentiments often mixed with commonsense racism, blaming the victim, or xenophobia (Essed 1991).

We have selected four cases to illustrate some of the tensions indicating that organisations struggle with the ethical implications of political and financial pressures to exclude 'illegals'. Is it ethical to question the principle of inclusion of all patients, irrespective of legal status, when organisations are understaffed and health professionals feel structurally overworked? Is it fair to the staff to risk financial retaliation from the government for ignoring the law against accepting patients without legal status? The dilemmas on an organisational level are acted out too in daily interactions between colleagues. Individual professionals feel torn between the unbearable moral weight of rejecting a person in need, on the one hand, and on the other hand, peer opinion that 'illegals' add too much burden to the overall workload.

Case 1: Business before Ethics: the Rejection of Patients without Legal Status

Public hospital X is located in an area characterised by a sharp income division among its inhabitants: one segment is extremely rich, another very poor. For many years the hospital staff managed to work relatively autonomously according to their own mission statement and professional interests. But according to national policy makers, hospitals all over the country are overspending. They demand more transparency and a new approach to patients: no pay, no treatment. The list of exceptions – emergency interventions allowed regardless of the legal status of the patient –

has been narrowed, redefined more strictly and precisely, leaving little room for flexible interpretation. Through the tightening of rules, management aims to increase control over its 'product' and over the behaviour of their staff. The hospital management demands that each and every staff member sticks to the rules in order to retain his or her job, arguing that tolerance of service to illegal patients will threaten the very existence of the hospital, and hence the jobs of hundreds of other colleagues.

Case 2: Ethics Do Not Undermine Effective Management of Budgets

Hospital Y, located in a multicultural neighbourhood, tries to save overhead costs by offering private services. The profits can be used to finance medical services for the poor, mostly for people who live in illegality, who cannot guarantee payment for treatment. Emphasising the fact that professional ethics generate obligations, the management claims professional autonomy in catering to the needs of their clients. As a result, they can remain supportive of their staff as well. Because the management takes responsibility, individual professionals are protected against the stress involved when feeling torn between human compassion and government policy.

Case 3: Loyalty and Tension among Team Members

One mental hospital has assigned a team to work exclusively with homeless people. Gradually they also started to include 'illegals' who live in extremely poor and isolated circumstances. The treatment of these patients regularly forms the cause of arguments among team members who are concerned about how far mental healthcare can stretch its limits in order to remain inclusive of all patients. Illegal patients often take more time and tend to be more distrustful – which of course is a survival strategy – which makes it even harder to establish a professional relationship with them. Their chances of recovery are poor; they have little, if any, future possibilities and few, if any, networks on which to rely. Time is a scarce resource and staff members have many other patients too. The decision to continue or to discontinue their services to patients without legal status is pending.

Case 4: Taking Individual Responsibility

The decision to remain faithful to one's professional sense of ethics, to respect the humanity of all patients, can weigh heavily on the individual professional who does not get any support from management and colleagues. This situation is extremely common.

A social health worker from a community-care organisation has told us that she is in touch with one woman without a residence permit. This woman has two children, the younger still a baby. The woman is depressed and can hardly take care of herself, let alone her children. The health worker, the only person taking any care of this family at all, worries a lot about the children. The neighbourhood where the woman hides out is known for traffic in children, often for purposes of child prostitution. The thought haunting her is 'will this naive and vulnerable young mother sell her children too? How can I protect her and the children?' Thus, the desperation of this illegal family filters through into the life of this professional care worker, who thereby suffers from a sense of powerlessness. She feels extremely alone in this – her organisation has no clear policy that might offer guidance. She knows that most of her colleagues disapprove of her contact with this family, because they do not fit the patient profile. They feel that another institution should take care of the mother and her children, but no one knows which one.

The above examples show that organisations as well as individual professionals are struggling with the tensions between political pressures from the government, insufficient budgets and collegial loyalty, on the one hand, and wanting to be inclusive in their policy to patients, on the other hand. We suspect that local and government bodies are not unaware of the situation. Turning a blind eye gets them off the hook of taking responsibility themselves, which is a larger European problem. In the meantime, tolerance of civil disobedience contributes to keeping open the possibilities for people with illegal status to gain at least some access to healthcare.

It has been pointed out that opinions and political loyalties over immigration issues cut across the distinction between conservative and progressive (Sciortino 2000). Likewise, whether or not individual health workers accept patients without legal status becomes a function of personal consciousness. As citizens, some professionals are opposed to people 'going illegal' when entry has been denied, but they extend services regardless of personal political convictions and the restrictive policies of their organisations. Because the burden of work is not equally spread, the professionals who honour their ethical values in accepting patients without legal status risk overwork and subsequent burnout. They navigate among complex political and ethical dilemmas, weighing responsibilities and possibilities against each other. Many become part of the 'silent' network of volunteers from all sectors of society, who offer skills, time and money in order to relieve the burden of illegality. Cutting through and transcending the boundaries of institutionalised care, the networks bring together representatives of different kinds of disciplines and organisations who would otherwise not meet in the everyday practice of their profession.

Summary and Conclusions

'Illegality' is one of the most complex urban problems of today. Solutions are not likely to be found in grand suggestions like 'fully open borders'. But, it is equally irresponsible and simplistic to maintain national preoccupations with criteria to distinguish between 'pure' refugees and 'polluted' immigrants. Global economic inequalities, the worldwide overproduction of weapons, local conflicts rooted in colonial pasts, to name just a few conditions eventually contributing to 'flight', cannot be solved by laws only. The production of illegality as an instrument of (perceived) national protection is problematic both as a creation and in its consequences. First, it divides and discriminates against people. The reformulating of social (public) responsibility as something limited to only legal citizens strips the 'humanity' from a substantial number of individuals. Second, the preoccupation with 'illegal' immigrants rather than with ways to address the historical and global causes of flight feeds populism. The shunning of responsibility for the consequences of immigration is politically 'safe' because no mainstream consensus will be threatened by declaring public services closed to 'illegals'. Accordingly, the question of responsibility ends up in the street, in neighbourhoods, among social and health workers who are confronted with the unacceptable consequences, from a human perspective, of refusing services to those in need.

There is also another side to the construction of the category of illegality. It magnifies the weak spots of international human rights. At the same time it highlights in microcosm old and new injustices of the declining welfare state. In that sense it can have transformative potential. In everyday life individual professionals struggle with discrepancies between ideals and reality, and, specifically in the case of extending service to people who live in illegality, with situations that have to remain hidden from view. The words and practices of responsible professionals thus disappear in illegality, much as papers and identities do. Openness is necessary in order to reveal the ethical and social dilemmas they are exposed to. The responsibilities now borne almost exclusively by healthcare professionals ought to be borne by society as a whole. Sooner or later these oppositional practitioners will seek more openness. This cannot but challenge the Dutch government and those of other rich societies to reconsider the ethics and durability of their response to the global problem of flight in search for justice.

Part II
Redefining Identities and Social Relationships

5

A Life Project out of Turmoil: Displacement and Gender in Colombia

Donny Meertens

The continuous escalation of the armed conflict among guerrillas, paramilitaries and the regular army in Colombia has caused an enormous humanitarian crisis. One of the most visible and disrupting effects of this crisis is the internal displacement of more than one and a half million people during the last two decades. This chapter explores the gender-differentiated ways in which women and men negotiate their identities during the process of displacement and the rebuilding of their daily lives and social networks. Women, in contrast to men, tend to gain some autonomy and visualise new horizons for their life projects in the urban environment. The argument draws on 150 testimonies, life histories and open interviews collected by the author in Bogotá and provincial capitals between 1994 and 1999.[1]

The Context: Dynamics of Violence and Displacement in Colombia

To understand the complex dynamics of Colombia's armed conflict, several elements are crucial: a history of fragmentation of the state and of national and political identities; the increasing importance of territorial, instead of ideological, dominance in the dynamics of political conflict; guerrilla practices such as kidnapping and extortion as mechanisms for obtaining financial support, and vengeance as a permanent spiral of reproduction of violence, not only at the political but also at the private level of rural (and increasingly urban) family life. Violence has been considered an endemic feature of Colombian history. Today, it involves a conjunction of political violence perpetrated by guerrilla forces, the regular army and paramilitary groups, mixed with drug-related violence, the presence of mercenaries and all kinds of so-called 'ordinary criminality'. During the 1990s, the annual number of violent deaths oscillated between 25,000 and 28,000, which represents a national rate of about 85 per 100,000 inhabitants (Deas and Gaitán Daza 1995: 223–31).

The history of Colombia's guerrillas goes back to the 1950s and 1960s, a period called La Violencia, which was a contest for political hegemony between Liberals and Conservatives, fought by the peasants on behalf of their party elite. During that time, the rural civil population became highly involved both as actors and victims, and entire peasant families belonging to the opposite political party were massacred. At the end of that period, the Moscow-oriented *Fuerzas Armadas Revolucionarias de Colombia* (FARC) was formed, followed by the Castro-oriented *Ejército de Liberación Nacional* (ELN), the Maoist *Ejército Popular de Liberación* (EPL) and, in the 1970s, several smaller groups. During the 1980s, most of these groups agreed to reintegrate into civil society and legal politics, with the exception of the FARC, the ELN and part of the EPL. During the last ten years, the guerrillas have moved from their traditional strongholds in poor and isolated colonisation areas to richer municipalities, especially those where unbridled capitalist accumulation has fostered social exclusion and popular discontent on one hand, and a potential for kidnapping and extortion on the other. From the 1980s onward, guerrilla actions have been counteracted by paramilitary groups, who are sponsored by big landowners and drug traffickers and frequently operate with the compliance of the Colombian militaries. The frequent shifts in power holding on the local level and the permanent risk of raids or reconquest by competing groups heavily influence the relationships between those in power and the civil population in the disputed territories. Mostly, for the armed groups no time is left for providing effective protection or building trust towards the local civilians. Therefore, increasingly all armed actors replace protection by *terror* as the most easily available mechanism for obtaining popular support, or rather, submission (Pécaut 1999). For many people, the only escape out of this turmoil is to flee to the cities.

Following the irregular patterns of regional conquest, reconquest and terror, the flows and dynamics of displacement of rural populations are also unstable, disperse and highly individualised. There are no camps for reception, except for the town of Turbo, near the Atlantic coast. Therefore, rural families flee silently, arrive in a drip in the cities and look for refuge, each on its own. Since the 1980s, the flows of displaced people have dramatically increased and their geographical origins enormously extended. By the end of 1999 a commonly accepted figure is 1,500,000 displaced persons over the last decade (CODHES 1999: 462), which represents over 2.5 percent of Colombia's total population (about forty million).

The Uprooting of Gendered Identities

In all armed conflict identity processes are at stake, not only power and material resources (Cockburn 1998: 8–9). For our analysis of gender differences along the displacement process, we found it useful to adopt Malkki's definition, in which identities are not seen as static or given, but as dynamic, complex and relational processes: '... partly self-construction, partly categorization by others, partly a condition, a status, a label, a weapon, a shield, a fund of memories ...' (Malkki 1992: 37; see also Schrijvers 1999: 308). We have analysed the differential identity effects of gender along the whole process of displacement, according to two main phases: the one pertaining to the destruction of lives, goods and social relationships, the uprooting and the flight; and the one comprising the *reconstruction* of daily life, social networks and projects for the future at the place of arrival. While displaced persons are moving through these phases, the influence of gender becomes visible in the strategies they undertake or the possibilities that are open to them to renegotiate their changing identities.

Before the uprooting itself, rural people's lives were already heavily influenced by the conditions of violence and war. The most devastating effects have come from the acts of terror: their arbitrariness causes the confusion and even the negation of social identities. Normally, even in the politically fragmented history of Colombia, the public domain, in which individuals find their place and through which they define part of their being-in-the-world, has been sustained by a certain measure of trust between neighbours, members of the same community, the same political or civic organisation or among family members. Under the erratic and arbitrary exercise of power by means of terror, however, nearly all bonds of solidarity, even those of the private domain, are eroded by mistrust. Primordial attachments like kinship and family membership become extremely confused as they are overruled by successively imposed group loyalties: guerrillas, paramilitaries, official militaries. Only 58 percent of our interviewees reported communal relationships *before* displacement based on trust and solidarity; the remaining 42 percent expressed mixed feelings, mistrust or even the absence of social relationships apart from nearest kin (Meertens and Segura-Escobar 1999: 87). Their narratives of violence are entangled in a labyrinth of rumours and accusations, where the boundaries between what is real and imagined tend to dissolve.

> When they killed my brother, people first said it had been the guerrillas because he was a friend of 'the others', then they said it had been the paras because he refused to join them ... (Interview with a displaced man in Bogotá, March 1999)

Most of the interviewees expressed this kind of confusion, very similar to the description given by Daniel and Knudsen of mistrust as an 'agitated state of awareness, of restlessness in reaction to a surrounding of extreme uncertainty and unpredictability' (Daniel and Knudsen 1995: 2). For those who lived under the shifting rule of first guerrillas and then paramilitaries – or vice versa –, distinctions between good and bad guys became floating, or even irrelevant as all actors represented evil: their camouflage uniforms seemed so very much the same, their motives so completely mixed up. In those cases everybody may have become their victim, because innocence does not matter, as the following quote underlines:

> When somebody knocked on the door, we immediately used to think 'they have come to kill,' because that was the way they killed many people over there ... like the woman who lived in the same house as we did: they knocked and she opened the door and she was shot ... and she was just a woman! She did not owe anything to anybody ... (Displaced woman interviewed in Bucaramanga, November 1998)

Representations of gender are explicitly played out at the scenarios of terror. In most rural areas, men participate more than women in political and communal organisations, in spite of increasing female leadership in peasant and civic organisations (see Meertens 2001). Therefore, men are accused of being helpers (in the economic or political sense) of one or the other armed group; women are accused of raising new enemies or hiding their children to avoid recruitment. Rural school teachers, mostly women, are particularly vulnerable because of their visible and politically sensitive role in educating new generations. Displaced women teachers constituted a mere 5 percent of our interviewees, but nevertheless may be an important segment of the displaced population, too ashamed or too scared because of persecution, to register as such. However, the most frequent accusation for women, especially young ones, is that of being *lovers* or having a flirt with 'the others'. There are many examples to illustrate this statement. For instance, that of the guerrilla force, which once bombed two peasant girls and their monkey, because their lovers were policemen. Or the case of the paramilitaries who killed a young girl, accused of having an affair with a guerrillero, after a public trial in the plaza of the village where she had been tied to a tree (interview with a displaced woman in Bogotá, 1998).

Gender differences also become manifest in the ways uprooting from community life is experienced. Two elements of personal history play an important role in this differentiation. In Colombian traditional rural society, opportunities for geographical and social mobility, and access to public participation and information are deeply gender-biased. For most rural women, mobility used to be more restricted than for men: only 18 percent of the interviewed women had had 'mobile lives' (that is, they had lived in three or more different places before displacement), against 34 percent of the men (Meertens and Segura-Escobar 1999: 52). Most women had a childhood and adolescence characterised by geographical and social isolation. Even if women had moved to another place, this was mainly due to their fathers' or husbands' jobs as hired agricultural labourers. The limits of the world, the contacts with society were all given by the male heads of household: first the father and then the husband. Only few women managed to escape from the confinement of the home by means of independent migration to new land-settlement areas or to the cities as domestic servants.

The second aspect of rural women's confinement was their low participation in civic or communal *organisations* that used to be a predominantly male domain, and, on the other hand, their high participation in close, informal networks of neighbours and kin. In our research, more than half of the women did not participate in any organisation, not even a religious one – traditionally a woman's domain – compared to only 30 percent of the men (Meertens and Segura-Escobar 1999: 58). Frequently, husbands discouraged participation of women, because they did not like their involvement and preferred them staying at home. As a consequence, for many rural women, the confrontation with violence was much more of a surprise. Most of them had no precise knowledge of the dynamics of conflict in their region and relied upon the idea that there was no reason for violence to knock at their door (like the woman who saw her neighbour being shot). Testimonies that widows gave about the first years of massacres are remarkably dramatic, precisely because of this lack of forewarning and the suddenness with which they had to leave. The destruction of their intimate worlds and the rupture of social texture at the level of the family and the community produced the sensation of being completely adrift, as one of the displaced women expressed her feelings: 'like a ship without a bay'.

These traditional gender arrangements have several consequences for the identity processes involved when men and women become uprooted and have to rebuild their lives in the cities. The withdrawal from formal, public, social and political organisations, as well as from more opaque, but nevertheless public, clientelistic bonds came first. It used to be a gradual retirement that affected mostly men in their *political identity*. Men were foremostly affected in their institutionalised forms of participation, in their clientelistic ties and even in their political discourse, particularly in relation to the state. Then, violence encroached upon informal social networks and eroded solidarity, creating mistrust between neighbours, friends and kin – a world of both men and women, but for the latter usually their *only world*. The uprooting from this intimate world of social bonds in which *women* were so much embedded meant the destruction of *social identity* to a much higher degree for them than for men. These gender differences also become visible during the next phase of the displacement process: the reconstruction of daily life and life projects in the city.

Life Projects in the Urban Setting: Strategies for Gendered Identity Reconstruction

The experiences and representations of men and women in the political and social spheres, before uprooting, gave them different vulnerabilities and abilities to rebuild life, once in the city. The traditions of mobility, as we saw more common among men, helped them to create resilience at the moment of uprooting, but did not stimulate their ability to build new social networks. On the other hand, women's experience of participating in social support networks in an informal way, less associated with 'politics', gave *them* more resilience in their new urban environment. We will elaborate upon this argument in the next paragraphs.

Upon arrival in the cities, the displaced do not only need material conditions (work, income, housing) in order to survive and rebuild their lives; they must also give meaning to their past experiences and their present situation in order to connect these in a realistic way to their hopes for the future. In effect, this articulation of experience, identity, self-perceptions and proposals is what we may call the reconstruction of a *life project* (Sobernigo 1990: 46–47). A life project provides new directions and references for social inclusions that are *not only rooted in the past*. However, the unpredictable character of terror makes these processes of meaning giving and refinding of identity extremely difficult. Men and women show some similarities, but above all substantial differences in the processes of reconstruction they undertake, both in the sense of 'doing' – concrete daily activities for survival and the taking of small initiatives for a new future – and that of 'being' – overcoming the subjective experience of being literally and symbolically out-of-place (see the definition of human capabilities in these terms by Amartya Sen, 1989). The differential weight of 'the political' and 'the social' in their gendered life experiences is of crucial importance.

As to similarities, displaced women and men have much in common in their ways to escape from war. Invariably, they look for close relatives, former neighbours or *paisanos* (people born in the same region) when they arrive in a city. Sometimes they have chosen this city because their relatives live there. At other times they have had no time to make a choice: they just run off, take a bus and end up in a city 'because the bus stops there', as one of the displaced women explained. From the moment they arrive in the city onwards, however, survival strategies, time paths and urban routes start to diverge. The time they spend with close relatives or *paisanos* before getting a place to live; the time it takes them to get a job or some street selling in order to survive, depend on multiple factors. These constitute the *baggage* of personal characteristics and experiences they took with them on the route of displacement and rebuilding. Some parts of this baggage may work in a double sense: they alleviate or aggravate the transition to urban life. A former good social and economic position, for instance, may bring about a greater sense of *loss*, but it can also foster confidence and facilitate the building of new social relationships. Social conditions, both those of the displaced families before migration and of their relatives or friends in the city, are undoubtedly an important factor for differentiation. We found that the former waged worker at a banana farm or the schoolteacher had more supporting structures due to their labour bonds, than the traditional peasant family or the landless labourer without social security. However, even in case of formal labour relations of the male head of household before displacement, when they were killed their widows remained completely unprotected.

Another important factor, as mentioned before, is the degree of *suddenness* of the act of violence and the subsequent need for displacement, because this is related not only to the degree of trauma suffered, but also to the assets a family can mobilise on arrival in the city. A couple of days to prepare for leaving provide more emotional resilience and therefore more energy to set out a strategy for displacement. Less than half of the interviewees (41 percent) managed to anticipate the displacement, mostly motivated by fear and general threat to the civil population (Meertens and Segura-Escobar 1999: 69). They could collect a small capital through the selling of some animals, furniture or part of the crop, all of which helped mitigate the first period of survival in the city. On the other hand, widows with small children who suddenly had to break with their homes and previous lives after the murder of their husbands, needed much more time to overcome despair and find their way to the institutions, to a job and to education for their children, than families with both parents who had had some time to prepare for migration.

A strong contrast between men and women originates in the opportunities that both have to join the labour market and assure their survival in one way or another. An enormous increase of unemployment among men has been found after the displacement takes place, in comparison with a much more moderate increase in the case of women heads of household (see for comparison of statistical data Meertens and Segura-Escobar 1996). Men worked previously with agriculture and livestock, which are not very useful occupations in their new urban environments. Women, in contrast, worked before and after the displacement in the same activities, that is, *domestic labour*. This gave some continuity to their work experience, whereas the fact that they sell their labour now to others, opened new – all be it precarious – opportunities for them. Finally, most women agreed upon a positive change of status within the household, as they have now become the main providers of means of subsistence for the family.

A further gender contrast is to be found in the ways women and men link themselves to governmental institutions. During the first days of arrival, family networks, friends and *paisanos* are of equal importance for men and women. However, their support generally is of short duration, as they also belong to the urban poor. Most displaced, then, find their way to the church, the international institutions and the government for some money and food: the International Red Cross, the Ministry of Internal Affairs, the Ombudsman, the Presidential Solidarity Network charged with institutional coordination of assistance to displaced people. Although every step requires much patience, queuing, coming-back-another-day and arbitrary treatment, some support is delivered and most displaced men and women benefit from it. After three months, however, emergency aid stops and things change radically. No clear policies for reintegration and development support have been traced, institutions have run out of money, employees have become even more disinterested, actions lack any coherence. To be put on a list for resettlement, to get a ticket for return to the countryside or apply for an income-generating project, has become an endless struggle with a completely unpredictable outcome. At that point, most women quit. They do not want to lose time with inefficient bureaucracies unwilling to help, nor do they think obsessively about returning or resettling. They are too busy with daily survival, which requires a lot of personal networking: for whom she is going to work that day, which neighbour will look after the children, who can she ask for some food or a loan.

> Look, I went to the Red Cross and they said: come back next day… this way they kept me going for a week and you know, señora, each day I lose, each day I do not work, my kids have nothing to eat … (displaced woman in Bogotá, December 1998)

Men tend to hold on. From time to time they organise desperate protest actions (CODHES 1999: 358), like the occupation of the International Red Cross offices in Bogotá in November 1999. In all these actions, women participated although rarely have they been protagonists. However, most frequently, displaced men try to establish personal-bonds-as-usual with civil servants. They tend to become permanent visitors of government offices waiting for help, dreaming of returning or resettling, walking many miles daily in order to visit more and more institutions, or always the same ones, going across the city with no money for local transport and without assimilating to the urban environment. Some of our interviewees became caught up in a web of institutional dependency. This contrast between – to put it in stereotypes – *working women* and *institutionally dependent men* brings along different outlooks for their life projects. We found that many women became rooted sooner than men, precisely because of their responsibilities in daily survival (cf. Schrijvers 1997, who found this also in Sri Lanka). When asked which of the officially sponsored options for the future they would prefer, even more women than men wanted to stay in the city. So we may conclude that women's life projects tend to be more firmly urban-oriented than men's.

A life project is more than the satisfaction of immediate needs, it comprises also the reconstruction of social relations, autonomy and self-esteem, all related to the social identity of the displaced, and therefore, to the meaning they give to their existence. However, the displaced women and men we interviewed told us that giving meaning to their existence in the city is at least as hazardous as physically surviving.

Women and Men on the Move: Representations of 'Being Displaced'

Before 1995, the term 'displaced' did not officially exist in Colombia, in spite of its history of forced migrations. The term circulated only among the nongovernmental organisations devoted to the defence of human rights and among grassroots movements. Finally, in September 1995, one year after the first publication of relevant data by the Episcopal Conference, the status of 'displaced person' was officially recognised, as the Colombian government formally adopted a policy (CONPES 2804 1995) for protecting those who, forced by violence, had abandoned their home and work and had fled to the cities. In subsequent years, this policy statement, with some modifications, became Law (No. 387, 1997). However, in the official assistance programmes, the emphasis has been placed on emergency aid, in the first place, and on the subsequent (voluntary) return or resettlement in rural areas, in spite of the rather unrealistic prospects of achieving this. Whereas war goes on, return often equals a risk of death. What is more, the government institutions have got a very low capacity to work out resettlement solutions, since they often depend on uncertain juridical procedures such as confiscation of properties of drug traffickers. The official recognition that displaced people basically constitute an *urban* problem has still to be made.

The internally displaced in Colombia, unlike the international refugees, do not receive any 'refuge' in the legal sense of the word. Each family must obtain a certificate of 'displacedness' to access emergency assistance on its own, which makes it difficult to undertake collective action. Moreover, they constitute a very heterogeneous group whose common status as displaced is not derived from any shared characteristic (for example, ethnicity or political affiliation). Theirs is a circumstantial character: being inhabitants of a region where armed conflict is taking place.

Consequently, they cannot oppose the collective discrimination to which they are submitted, by having a countervailing *common* claim of recognition and justice. In public opinion, being uprooted and displaced tends to be associated with belonging to one of the armed groups, and, at the same time, having lost one's culture. Therefore, as the French sociologist Pécaut states, the uprooted, in Colombia like elsewhere, suffer a loss of moral rights to citizenship, or their pertinence to a *moral community* (Pécaut 1999; Malkki 1992: 32).

Forced to flee by violence, they are also different from *economic migrants*. They share nostalgia with the economic migrants but at the same time such feelings have become more abstract and distant. The *before* was not so idyllic at the moment they had to leave, it was already damaged by the war, stained by the blood of their neighbours and close relatives. With the displaced families, it was difficult to talk about their memories, which nevertheless constitute such an important part of their social identity. They expressed the way that their memories had become traumatic and that the immediate past was not worth being named any longer.

The urban social imagination about the displaced, attributes several common characteristics to them, generally in two negative senses, which are associated with the idea of 'lost morality'. On one hand, the prevailing popular opinion is that, if they have been displaced, 'it must have been for a reason' (*por algo será*), implying political distrust. On the other hand, there is the notion that they are all poor and rootless people and therefore 'natural thieves, robbers and malefactors', implying social distrust.

The displaced themselves showed themselves to have a flexible image with respect to their proper status, sometimes unfolded towards the public sphere and sometimes towards the private one. In public, they presented themselves as victims of violence before the social aid entities, but maintained anonymity in other places, out of fear of social stigma, discrimination and political persecution by one of the armed actors, who also operate in the cities. They tried to hide their condition from neighbours and employers. It is a fact that even in the city (and particularly in the smallest cities closest to the armed conflict), the displaced are usually associated with one of the armed actors ('if he is displaced by the paras he must be a guerrillero' and vice versa). It was impossible for them to maintain a neutral status of 'civil population not involved in the conflict'. Again, given the gender-differentiated representations of involvement in the conflict, women suffered less from persecution. Both women and men suffered from stigmatisation, but women used to overcome this in an easier way by weaving practical social relationships of reciprocity at the neighbourhood level.

In the private sphere, 'feeling displaced' is in the first place related to an *ambiguous nostalgia*, experienced because of traumatic memories.

Women and men equally feel that their social identity has been disrupted and even after many years in the city (we interviewed people who had been displaced from one month up to five years ago), nearly all (84 percent) told us they still felt *not in place*. In the second place, it is linked to a lack of *dignity* – a feeling stressed above all by men, and linked to their suffering from unemployment (very shocking, as we saw, for male peasants, associated with loss of status as economic providers for the family). Thirdly, it is linked to a lack of housing, that can be seen as a concrete expression of the need for belonging to a place, and as a basic need for replacing, in a minimal way, the old links to land, animals and primary relationships. A house or a shack of one's own is also an expression of the sense of belonging to a place and therefore part of a life project in its non-material sense as well. Finally, feeling displaced is linked to perceptions of the *future*. One of the greatest dilemmas displacement poses is precisely the condition defined as transitory by all those involved (displaced persons, the state, communities of arrival). It is not clear at all to which final destination the period of transition should lead. Before the disjunctive of returning to the place of expulsion or staying in the city of arrival, attitudes expressed at a national level clearly show a favourable trend towards staying. Fear and ongoing armed conflict make return an unrealistic option for many. Women are even less interested in returning than men. We probably find an explanation for these attitudes in the *own experience* that women develop in the urban setting. In spite of multiple difficulties, suffering and enormous responsibilities, becoming part of the urban labour market as domestic servants or street sellers has given a guarantee of survival to many women, no matter how precarious, which men lack. Moreover, their participation in communal organisations and networks provides them with new elements for the reconstruction of their identities, sociability and perceptions of new horizons for their life projects that did not exist for them in the countryside.

Concluding Remarks

Do the displaced – women and men – succeed in constructing new *life projects* in the urban environment? What are the differences? We mentioned several elements that have an influence on the ways identities are continuously negotiated among the displaced. These 'gendered identity trajectories' are related to differential experiences of mobility, participation and work.

For *both* men and women being a *displaced person* is a persistent sentiment, very difficult to eradicate from their experience. In spite of diminishing stigmatisation over time, the displaced continue to perceive themselves as *people without a place* in their new urban environment. They do so, in their own words, because of an overwhelming nostalgia. In contrast to economic migrants they know they cannot go back. This knowledge, paradoxically, makes the displaced attached to the past, in a much stronger sense than any other migrant. The past, therefore, remains a burden to the present and, together with material restrictions on surviving, limits the emotional capabilities to reconstruct a life project as a coherent proposal for the future. Men mostly dream of returning and trying to recover their political discourse. They demand solutions from the state, but paradoxically become sometimes dependent on public institutions. Women often develop more autonomous behaviour and become rooted sooner than men, precisely because of their survival responsibilities. Thus, the *gender balance* of the displacement process refers to traditional dichotomies of the public and the private, the political and the social, but these become redressed with new meaning in the daily construction of the future.

Notes

1. Fieldwork was carried out with funding from the Colombian Institute for the Promotion of Academic Research, Colciencias, and the National University of Colombia. Academic support for the preparation of this publication was provided by the Amsterdam School for Global Research and Devlopment Studies, AGIDS/INDRA, University of Amsterdam. Some parts of this article have also been used in Donny Meertens, 'The Nostalgic Future: Terror, Displacement and Gender in Colombia', In Victims, Perpetrators or Actors, Caroline Moser and Fiona Clark, eds. London, Zed Books, 2001: 133–48.

6

Permanent Refugees: Female Camp Inhabitants in Bihar¹

Kathinka Sinha-Kerkhoff

Introduction

This chapter concerns forced migrants who hitherto have been completely ignored by scholars. It focuses on (widowed) women now living in two
so-called permanent liability camps in Bihar, a state known as one of the
poorest, most populous and underdeveloped states of India. These
women belong to a small section of the linguistic and historic minority of
Bengali-speaking Hindus who migrated from East Pakistan to the State of
Bihar in India during the aftermath of the 'Partition'. At the juncture of
the British withdrawal in 1947, British India was divided into India and
(East and West) Pakistan. This division is commonly referred to as 'the
Partition'. It was associated with extreme violence and massive transfers
of populations. No one knows how many were killed during the Partition
violence. No one knows how many were displaced and dispossessed.
What we know is that, between 1946 and 1951, nearly nine million
Hindus and Sikhs came to India and about six million Muslims went to
Pakistan. According to the newspaper *Hindu* (3-1-2002), of the said nine
million, five million came from what became West Pakistan, and four million from East Pakistan. Most left their place of birth due to a sense of
insecurity. Many had experienced extreme violence during Hindu-
Muslim communal riots, others had suffered discrimination and again
others severe economic deprivation.

Unlike those from West Pakistan, where the flow of refugees was huge
but of short duration, refugees from East Pakistan started arriving in
West Bengal even before the Partition (*Telegraph* 21-11-2001). Already in
1957, the government of India felt however that the state of West Bengal
was almost saturated and that the 'burden' of accommodating the

Bengali Hindu refugees should be shared by other states of the Indian Union. As a result, many refugees who crossed the international border during the late 1950s and early 1960s were told to leave West Bengal and settle in states such as Bihar, Assam, Tripura, Orissa, Meghalaya and Madhya Pradesh where they were promised proper rehabilitation. Though their problems are far from solved (see Mukherjee 2001: 130–55), most of the erstwhile Bengali refugees in Bihar are now rehabilitated in the sense that they received a plot of land or a house and some cash. They now live in so-called colonies and many, though not all (see Sinha-Kerkhoff 2000: 74–93), have stopped identifying as refugees.

Apart from large-scale dislocation, mass widowhood was another result of the massive flows of population accompanied by extreme violence. As a result, the Indian government perceived it was its duty to look after 'the rehabilitation of what it called "unattached" women' (Menon and Bhasin 1998b: 398–99). Most women discussed in this chapter were decreed 'not rehabilitable' however and accommodated in one of the permanent liability camps. They had therefore become 'permanent refugees' in the eyes of the government. Increasingly however, the government of India sought to get rid of this 'burden' and is now seeking to abolish all these camps. Interestingly however, many women as well as their family members consider it their right to remain in these camps and have no intention to leave them. They cling to their identity as refugees as the permanent liability camps provide refuge to these widows, otherwise severely marginalised in all respects (see Chen 1998). The main argument in this paper is therefore that living in these camps generated gender awareness and even created a 'culture of resistance' (Chen 1998: 51) among these widows and other female inhabitants of the camps.

'Unrehabilitable Refugees'

Reporting on the stream of Hindu migrants from East Pakistan, the Indian government normally employed the term 'displaced persons' (Ministry of Rehabilitation 1955–56: 86–87). Nevertheless, those displaced persons who took refuge in relief or transit camps were registered as 'refugees' (Ministry of Rehabilitation 1955–56: 87). Allegedly due to lack of land, both the Central as well as the West Bengal state government argued that the 'burden' of resettling and rehabilitating these refugees had to be shared (Pakrasi 1971: 23). In 1956, it was therefore agreed that further camps should be located outside West Bengal (Ministry of Rehabilitation 1956–57: 4). Bihar was one of the states selected to 'share the burden' (Roy Chaudhury 1960: 87). Officially, the Bihar government had three rehabilitation policies: i.e. for agriculturists, for nonagriculturists and for businessmen (Ministry of Rehabilitation 1965–66: 37). After staying for some time in camps, the displaced were rehabilitated in so-called refugee colonies (Ministry of Rehabilitation 1955–56: 15). Officially thereafter, they were not labelled as refugees any longer. Yet, there remained one category of displaced who were considered 'unrehabilitable'. The Annual Report of 1959–60 mentioned:

> There are families who are no longer 'rehabilitable' in the usual sense of the term because of either the death or the debility of the bread-earner and the absence of any other male adult member in the family to support it. (Ministry of Rehabilitation 1959–60: 25)

Special camps were established and 'the objectification of these refugees as helpless victims and recipients of aid was almost caricatured in the designation of these camps as "Permanent Liability Camps" which captures the mixture of pity and anxiety that the government felt for them' (Menon and Bhasin 1998a: 131–67). In the Annual Report of 1964–65 (Ministry of Rehabilitation 1964–65: 6) it was however complained that the number of families in these camps was disproportionate. Systematic examination with a view to weeding out persons who did not properly belong to the category was therefore carried out. Moreover, various subcategories were enumerated: able-bodied middle-aged women who can become employable; able-bodied young women who can undergo training and education; grown-up children who can get vocational and technical training; women and men aged over 55 and 60 respectively; infirm who cannot do any work; and finally aged who can do light work. In fact, the Central government initially considered these refugees as 'liabilities'. It acknowledged that it had a moral debt and legal responsibility towards the refugees, but it considered them also as burdens hindering development.

All these people were encouraged to stay with relations if available and some even survived on usual doles. By educating them the government hoped to 'discharge them from camps with rehabilitation benefits', make them 'useful citizens' and 'enable them to stand on their own legs' (Ministry of Rehabilitation 1964–65: 4, 7). In the long run the government thought the camps could be closed and, therefore, that its duty would be finished. Yet, in Bihar many families refused to leave the camps and therefore remained 'burdens' of the state. There had been permanent liability camps in Gaya, Darbhanga, Deoghar, Ranchi and Monghyr. Though many inmates of the Brahmbey camp in Ranchi settled themselves elsewhere, some 'unattached' women, their children as well as 'aged and infirm displaced persons' were sent to Deoghar after closure of the former. Afterwards and quite recently, the Deoghar camp was converted into a 'normal' colony and some inmates were again relocated in the Khanjarpur permanent liability camp in Bhagalpur District. In 1999, only twenty families (around a hundred people) remained whereas in 1997 eighty families were staying here. The Hazari transit camp in Bettiah (Champaran District) was only later converted into a permanent camp. Around 40 percent of the inhabitants have been rehabilitated but 60 percent (around 400 people) are still in the camp. In 1999, Hazari and Khanjarpur were the sole remaining permanent liability camps in Bihar.

The narratives of these widows, their at times married daughters or granddaughters who still dwell in one of these two remaining camps make interesting empirical data providing 'other stories or other silences' (Butalia 1998: 224). They cast light on women's agency in situations that have hitherto only been described in terms of victimisation, i.e. non-agency. This chapter shows that Partition indeed implied enormous 'losses' for these women. Yet, it is simultaneously claimed that there was 'recovery' too.

The State: Step-parents of the Orphans

Inmates of the permanent liability camps, who were generally placed there during the early 1960s, had faced extreme disruption. Not only had they lost their relatives; they also had to cope with a new non-Bengali-speaking environment. A typical example is that of Indrabala Burman. She and her husband left East Pakistan along with her brother-in-law but the latter had been issued with a separate migration card. While staying in a transit camp, Indrabala had lost her husband. Her brother-in-law also died and suddenly Indrabala was left with no one but her two little daughters. The government of India therefore sent her to the Hazari permanent liability camp. Indrabala married off her two daughters but the eldest died two years later leaving behind no children. Women like Indrabala not only experienced acute loneliness, but also lacked relatives to support them. These women looked upon state-based security as their last resort. It was indeed the state who started 'acting as custodian and guardian on behalf of missing men' (Menon and Bhasin 1998a: 162). Nityabala Das' husband, killed during communal riots, had been a well-to-do farmer. Yet, after his death all their cultivable land had been captured. Due to various diseases she had also lost four of her children while still in East Pakistan. At that juncture Nityabala recounted:

> Indira Gandhi appealed to us the minority Hindus. If you feel unsafe, she said, you can come over to India. In haste I made a plan to leave my house and along with my little daughter I crossed the border. My in-laws had severed relations immediately after my husband's death. The government entered Bihar in my migration card so I had to go there in order to receive help. Without the mercy of the Indian government I would not have survived but when Indira got murdered we were also finished.

From relative richness Snehalata Ghosh almost became a beggar but for the government's help. Some relatives had already settled in West Bengal, but Sneha and other family members proceeded for Ranchi in South Bihar. There they could afford to live in a rented house. Actually, Sneha said her family had explicitly rejected the idea of staying in a camp:

> We did not like to depend upon government's mercy. Yet, things worked out differently. Hardly settled in Ranchi my husband got a massive heart attack. Besides, two of my little sons died. My brother-in-law struck my name from the migration card and all of a sudden I found myself poor and alone. One little son was the only thing left to me. At that point, the government came forwards and sent me first to the permanent liability camp in Ranchi and afterwards to Deoghar.
>
> At this point, Sneha was interrupted by her youngest son, now 45 years old: 'In Deoghar, the government provided training to my mother and she became a nurse. We were also allotted a quarter. Where would we have been without this help?' Another widow, Maroni Das, also decided to settle in a permanent liability camp. Though her parents had disliked her decision, she preferred the camp above 'burdening my father. Moreover, after his death what would have happened to me and to my children? At least we had somebody.'

The camps were known as 'orphan' camps. The government saw it as its moral and legal responsibility to help, posing as the 'mother and father of these orphans'. They thought it was their duty to provide a rich, warm, nurturing relationship (the mother-part) as well as paternal protection from the 'dangers of life' (the father-part) (see Menon and Bhasin 1998a: 153 and Menon and Bhasin 1998b: 399). These women were considered victims and agency was denied. Becoming 'refugee' did therefore imply vulnerability.

Few indeed expressed their dislike and hated the dependence that had come as a counterpart of 'being a refugee'. Unlike most others, Amya Bala Sarkar perceived the camp as an expression of power over her body and life system by others (see Asif 2000: 2005) and preferred to return to Bangladesh: 'My motherland, where we were free. Here we are depending on government's mercy.' Generally however, inhabitants had been happy with this newly established relation.

Withdrawal of Support: Becoming Orphans Again

In 1988 however, the government of India stopped funding the permanent liability camps in Bihar. Subsequently, the Bihar government also terminated all facilities. The above-mentioned Maroni Das described the change: 'We came to India when Jawaharlal Nehru was Prime Minister and he announced: our Hindu brothers and sisters, who have come without a single cloth, the government will help you. But increasingly, the government considered us burdens and finally they took no attention at all.'

The 'step-parents' were to be replaced by a son, government had ordained. After the latter would reach the age of eighteen, rehabilitation was promised. Indeed, a son often replaced the government. Again, Maroni Das' case is exemplary. Her husband's death after only four years of marriage had been followed by his elder brother's and since her father-in-law had died long before, the government 'advised' Maroni and her two small boys as well as her aged mother-in-law to go to the Bhagalpur camp. In that camp they were given one single room with a veranda and an outside toilet. Yet, though the government had increased the dole it was not enough to support four persons so Maroni had to start working as a maidservant. After losing two sons in such a short timespan, her mother-in-law had been too distressed to take up any job and it was her son Nishit Chandra Das who had started, still being a child, helping his mother to sustain this lower-caste family.

Instead of camp provisions, old age pensions and ration cards were promised but rarely given. In fact, even those with rehabilitation rights were driven to despair. Besides, though the central government had promised to provide vocational and other training, employment, housing, food and education and had assured the camp inmates safe refuge for the rest of their lives if necessary (see Menon and Bhasin 1998a: 162), the Bihar government did not heed these promises. Though plans had been announced, the inhabitants of the camps were rarely prepared for the labour market. Some children had indeed received basic education yet this was discontinued. In practice, the 'help' provided by the Bihar government had not extended beyond short term 'relief'. Only widows or couples with sons were promised rehabilitation. Moreover, many also stated they had no voting rights, did not receive their rightful pensions, ration cards or caste certificates. Almost none knew even about other government schemes designed especially for the poor and for widows. The government therefore showed 'a benign paternalism while simultaneously upholding patriarchal codes and practices'; ensuring the realisation of a few social rights but withholding civil and political rights (ibid.: 163).

Widows and their families would finally leave the camps, government predicted. In that case, the government would be relieved from its 'burdens'. Childless widows as well as aged and infirm men were thought to wither of their own accord. Daughters were supposed to get married and thereafter they also would leave the camp. Sons and their families would be rehabilitated in one of the colonies. In the long run therefore the camps would be empty and could be used for other purposes.

Admittedly, leaving the camp was a good alternative to remedy hardship preferred by some. Indeed, recently girls and boys have left for Delhi in search of work. They might not return. Yet, others decided to remain in the camps even though some officially had been offered rehabilitation. Most daughters of widows remained in the camps, often bringing their husbands and children along. Property, a one-room house, remains in their (mother's) name.

Though Sobharani had tried to get help from her brothers-in-law in West Bengal while her husband was still alive, nothing came:

> They did not take up their responsibilities as family members nor as human beings. They must have sensed that if my husband died, I myself as well as my three children would present burdens. Therefore, after six months, we decided to go back to the Hazari Camp in Bettiah.

After losing her husband there had been nobody to support Priyabala Das, her three little sons and two daughters. The government had therefore promised that if she went to Hazari camp, they would look after the family and rehabilitate her once her sons would be grown-ups. She went and while waiting for her sons' adulthood all her children received basic education and simultaneously she started working. Finally in 1989, the government gave four acres and twenty-five decimals of land yet the family had remained in the camp. Priyabala complained that the newly acquired land was useless: the soil was sandy, not at all cultivable and divided into small plots. Even the few crops cultivated on that land were stolen by 'antisocial elements'. Moreover, the land was far removed from urban areas and therefore also not suitable for business. She concluded: 'The Hazari refugee camp is nearer to town. We prefer to stay here.'

These refugees therefore have, to the dismay of the government, become permanent features in the landscape of Bihar. They remain identifying as refugees, refuse to leave the camps or even return to the camps after receiving (dissatisfactory) rehabilitation. They keep on fighting for proper rehabilitation, their rights as women and as (aged) widows. They consider the refugee status capital, which might empower them as refugees but also as (widowed) women. These women therefore resisted as refugees and as women.

Identifying Oneself as a Refugee: Female Protest

Though people staying in the permanent liability camps, men and women alike, do not face the restrictions normally associated with camps, living in them is often described as derogatory. One retired rehabilitation officer therefore believes the inmates in the Hazari permanent camp face a dark future and 'their children will die as foreigners'. Indeed, inhabitants sometimes explicitly stated they disliked not only the place but also the ascribed status that goes along with living in the camp. Nevertheless, and somewhat surprisingly, not only does labelling continue, so does self-labelling. Dr. Satish Mishra had once asked his late maid why she always kept identifying herself as a refugee. This Bengali widow who had been living in Bihar for over thirty years replied in *Hindi*: 'I am a refugee because there is nobody in front and no one at my back.' Ashok Kumar Roy, adopted son of a widowed aunt, also identified himself as a refugee since, 'the one who reared me was a refugee and I have no support from anywhere.'

While identifying as refugees these women do not refer to themselves as burdens depending on the state but generally emphasise the government's debt towards them. The above-mentioned officer verbalised this as follows: 'Even the youth identify as refugee. I feel they do that to remind the government they need proper rehabilitation.' Though the above-mentioned Kiranbala Burman perceived that after 1988 they had lost power: 'First we had power to reject things. The government listened to our demands and if things were inferior we would not accept it. Nowadays we are powerless.' Nevertheless, she reiterated 'I have always paid taxes and moreover my father had some property in East Pakistan so the government should give us either land or a house. They should also provide loans and instalments will not do.' His aunt had brought up Hara Krishna and the two of them had been settled in the Brahmbey permanent liability camp in Ranchi. According to Hara Krishna:

> The Chief Minister of Bihar thought it is better to divide the refugees otherwise we would unite and protest. So in 1954, many of the refugees of the Ranchi PLC were sent to Deoghar. I also went along with my widowed aunt and I received Rs 1000 loan and a house at the age of eighteen. This was our minimum right. The government owes us much more.

Just after the government's decision to stop funding, refugees had even become violent. Consequently, some rehabilitation officers had been put in jail. One of them remembered: 'The refugees caused sleepless nights to us.' Maroni Das defended: 'Some people say that I am a Bengali refugee and that in the future the government will throw me out from the country. I always reply that nobody has the power to kick us out. The government has helped us during forty to fifty years now. We are citizens of India. If something happens to us, the government is responsible. After saying this these locals, especially the Biharis keep mum.' Juthika Rani Dubay firmly stated 'if the government is going to close the camp, it will be its responsibility to look after us, since they settled us here.' Not leaving the place and identification as a refugee can indeed be understood as a way to contest government policies and lay claims as (widowed) women. Below, it will be described how, by remaining in the camps, these widows also tried to change kinship and gender relations and in this way coped with, if not combated, certain patriarchal relations.

Building up New Relations

The permanent liability camps do therefore not only reflect disruption. Their inhabitants also succeeded in establishing new support systems and relations. Quite a number of widowed mothers received their daughters with open arms after the latter in turn got widowed or were deserted. Moreover, intercaste marriages are quite common. Kiranbala had lost her husband and her father-in-law in the same car accident and, 'out of sorrow my mother-in-law also passed away eight months later.' Kiranbala already knew at the time of her husband's death that nobody would give her shelter. Yet, her mother had stayed in a camp and Kiranbala was taken back. Besides, the camp commandant had been very helpful in providing a separate room for her and her children. He had also asked her whether she was interested in remarriage but she had answered negatively since she 'was very serious about the future of [her] two daughters'. Kiranbala herself arranged the marriage of her elder daughter and the younger one had a love marriage with a Bihari rickshaw puller. Mother and daughter had initially been very satisfied with the government and Kiranbala's mother thought that, 'if the government had not provided help we would have been floating on the river.' Yet, when the government withdrew support she had felt as if 'we were alone in the world'. The mother was even denied her pension. Happily enough, mother and daughter stated, 'we have each other.' Besides, Kiranbala added, 'I extremely value the three Bihari families in which I work. They like me as a sister and daughter.' Kiranbala keeps her daughter and son-in-law with her since she fears, 'what will happen to them when I die. I never had to pay any dowry at the time of marriage so I feel I should give my one-room house to them. They will remember me after my death.'

The first marriage of her daughter, which Nityabala Das herself had arranged, ended when the boy left the girl. Yet her daughter remarried with another boy from a refugee family and nowadays lives in Delhi. Though this daughter never sends money and visits her mother only once in two or three years, Nityabala looks after the child born during the first wedlock. Nityabala also arranged the marriage of this granddaughter but she explained:

> Her husband kicked her out because she remained barren. Now she earns money for both of us by making a kind of cigarettes and I add a little by begging. I have tried for her rehabilitation too but the government keeps on telling that since I have no son, they cannot rehabilitate us. Yet, they have promised to take care forever.

Pramoda Sarkar also arranged her daughter's marriage but her husband deserted her, remarried and keeps no relation whatsoever with his first wife. Thereupon, Pramoda invited her daughter to live with her. Though Pramoda had tried to get her daughter remarried, 'we did not succeed since she has a son. I suffer from arthritis. My grandson and I now fully depend on my daughter who makes cigarettes.' After Nirmala Datta and her husband had migrated, communication with relatives had stopped. They arrived in the Mana Camp where both contracted malaria but Nirmala survived. Widowed, Nirmala had felt extremely lonely and helpless. The government sent her to the Hazari Camp where she lived in a small room and received a cash dole. Yet, when Nirmala was offered a maid's job she did not hesitate:

> Nowadays I am a key-member in the family. I never feel I am a refugee, help-less or a barren woman. Once I got engrossed in my work I forgot all the sor-rows of my husband's death, loss of family and the flight from our village. I have rebuilt my destroyed house.

Yet, some relations are not recognised or publicly accepted. His wid-owed aunt had brought up Ashok Kumar Roy. Not having children of her own, Ashok's aunt, being illiterate herself, had looked after his educa-tional needs and had reared him as her own son. Yet the adoption had been informally and Ashok is still fighting, as a refugee, for his rights even after the death of his aunt in 1994.

Late Jamini Dasi's husband had already died before Partition. Kamini Dasi is the only daughter but her lawfulness was contested. Actually, Jamini lost track of her daughter during her passage to India. She was therefore registered as widow without children in the Ranchi camp. Kamini landed up in Dhanbad. Later, Jamini was transferred to the Deoghar camp and Kamini came to know about this. She instantly joined her mother. Kamini received training as a midwife and started working. All grants were therefore stopped. Yet, after her mother's death Kamini remained living in the room with her adopted son. Government officials refused however to transfer 'the house' to Kamini. This implied her son would also have no rights after her death. Meanwhile, other refugees had taken advantage. They claimed the house, stating that Kamini was not Jamini's real daughter and also that the adoption of the son had not been legal. Petitions were filed and even reached the Supreme Court. The case was finally settled in favour of Kamini and her son. The latter is now mar-ried and has three daughters and three sons who all live in the camp as refugees. These cases reveal female agency but also the extreme vulnera-bility of such more uncommon relations.

Living with and Beating the System: Remaining Refugee in a Patriarchal Society

Actually, there are close linguistic, social and cultural similarities between camp inhabitants and the local population outside the camps. Never-

theless, a type of separation is somewhat maintained through the continued identification of the former as refugees (see Mondal 1998: 75).
Interestingly, the life stories of these women illustrate how remaining a
refugee in a patriarchal society made many a woman first of all conscious
of unequal gender relations and also of the need for 'demasculinisation'
of the refugee concept. Besides, though often identifying as refugees this
did not signify victimisation only. It provided them a means to protest
and claim. Pramoda Sarkar maintained it was very difficult for women
like her to run the family 'in a proper way'. 'Male-headed families are
much happier than ours are. They get many more facilities and their position is much higher.' At times this awareness of inequalities stimulated
agency. Though Manju Das' case is extremely tragic it shows that agency
in turn could provide a sense of self-confidence. Manju, her parents and
two brothers had been rehabilitated in another state after a seven years'
stay in a camp. More children were born, yet problems remained and two
sons died. Manju's mother broke down mentally. Upon request, the government resettled them in Bihar but Manju's mother kept suffering from
depression. On top of this, Manju's father died. The depleted family was
again transferred, this time to the Khanjarpur camp. With sadness yet
mixed with great self-esteem Manju narrated:

All responsibility had fallen on my shoulders. Even now my mother does not
receive old age pension or the red ration card nor do we get certificates as
Scheduled Castes. Nevertheless, I got my siblings educated, married them off
and we have applied for rehabilitation.

Pramoda lost several family members during riots. Subsequently, she,
her husband, two sons and two daughters left for West Bengal but the
government sent them to Bihar where her two sons died. Shortly after, her
husband was diagnosed as a tuberculosis patient and was therefore not
rehabilitated. He never recovered and finally died after ten years of free
treatment. Says Pramoda:

No sons were left and the government promised to take care until my death.
Yet, since ten years ago they stopped all facilities, I started working as a maid.
I even arranged my daughters' marriages. I managed everything myself.

Many women perceive their lives as widows in the camps as better
than life outside. Widowhood in India generally involves restrictions on
residence, ownership, remarriage and employment and put widows in a
situation of acute dependence on support from others (Chen 1998). Yet
widows in the camps neither face social constraints nor many ritual and
customary sanctions such as food, dress and employment restrictions or
control over physical mobility. Though some men allege that these widows actually also provide sexual services to the families in which they

work, taboos regarding the sexuality of single women have generally not been reinforced. Initially, the government had recommended a grant of Rs 200 to be paid to each girl or widow for her marriage (Ministry of Rehabilitation 1956–57: 5). Rather than categorising this as a 'liberatory' or 'progressive' policy as Menon and Bhasin (1998a: 162) did, this policy was a means to get them out of the camps and thus to alleviate the government's 'burden'. Now re-marriage by camp residents is neither prohibited nor encouraged. Sons remain dependent on their mother's property and husbands on their wives' (i.e. the daughters of widows) and conditions in the camps will therefore not change easily.

Entering camps, as Menon and Bhasin (1998a: 257) described, generally implied that other identities such as those based on age, gender, class, caste and (sub)regions were subordinated to an exclusive and confining religious and ethnic community. It is important however, to recognise that all aspects of refugee identity are matters of debate and revision in different settings and among different age and gender groups of the community. They are historical images that invoke and stress particular relationships with the contemporary state and society rather than simply being narrations of the past and culture. Women in the permanent liability camps do not use their agency on behalf of the religious, caste or male community but rather on their own behalf as widows. Besides remaining in the camp in order to claim dues, there is another reason for women's continued self-labelling as a refugee. These women obviously remain refugees in order to live with and at times beat the patriarchal system.

Conclusion

Partition plays roles in people's lives even today, not least because some are still identified and identifying themselves as 'refugees'. Actually, labelling of this sort, as well as the type of descriptive characterisation, was central to the formulation and administration of aid by the Indian government. Moreover, the label worked as a structuring mechanism, which established 'spheres of competence and areas of responsibility' and reflected 'patterns of authority and the acceptance of it in the context of particular events and conjunctures' (Wood 1985: 349). In the context of the permanent liability camps in Bihar, however, it is shown that people label back. The latter were not only labelled refugees, but also identified as such. Besides, when the government stopped aid and refused to consider them refugees any longer, people protested. It can be argued therefore that the choice to remain refugees was contingent on the desire to contradict the exertion of state power (see Asif 2000: 2005). These refugees therefore conceive their identity in fundamentally different terms from those who bestowed the label (see Zetter 1991: 40). Rather than seeing themselves as burdens, they keep on reminding the government of its burden. Yet, the impact of the struggle of women against the state will remain limited, as it does not replace the refugee identity. On the contrary, the latter is used as capital within this gender struggle. This blurs the fact that these refugees are part of a wider community of widowed, separated and other single females in Indian society facing common problems. Only when the government reconsiders its schemes and rehabilitates single women on similar lines to men, will these women be able to abandon the refugee label. They then can join hands with other (single) women and proceed with their struggle for equal rights and control over their own lives.

Notes

1. This chapter is one of the outcomes of a research project carried out by the author between July 1997 and July 2000. The research is part of a bigger project supported by the Indo-Dutch Programme on Alternatives in Development (IDPAD) on 'Displaced Populations and Development in the South Asian Context'.

7

New Opportunities: Angry Young Men in a Tanzanian Refugee Camp

Simon Turner

Introduction

This chapter sets out to explore how life in a refugee camp has affected gender and age relations among Burundian refugees in Tanzania, and how refugees interpret camp life in terms of gender, age and class. How do young men manoeuvre in this new space, finding a place for themselves and making sense of their new setting?[1]

The chapter is based on a year's fieldwork in Lukole Refugee Camp in northwest Tanzania. At the time of fieldwork, 1997–98, around 100,000 Burundian Hutu refugees lived in the camp. In conversations and group interviews the refugees gave the impression of living in a world of social and moral decay. This was often expressed in terms of deteriorating gender relations. Responding to a question on the general changes in the camp, one of the men related his hardships directly to problems between husbands and wives.

> Life is much worse in the camp. We have no blankets or other materials. We have to beg. In Burundi we had *shambas* (fields). We have no money to buy things for our wives. Our wives say: You are not feeding me. I'm fed by *wazungu* (white men). (Twa man, August 1997)

When the men can no longer provide for their wives, these women consider UNHCR or the white man to be 'a better husband' and no longer respect the men as they used to and ought to do. Rather than taking these statements at face value or estimating to what degree social structures are actually deteriorating in the camp, I will explore how such perceptions have emerged and what are the consequences for the strategies of refugees in general and of young men in particular.

Equality and Hierarchy

In the refugee camp the relief agencies do their best to treat everyone equally. Every man, woman and child – whether former minister or former peasant – is given the same amount of food and provided with the same basic cooking utensils, blankets and plastic sheeting. In fact, in order to ensure social equality, special relief programmes target 'vulnerable groups' such as the elderly, unaccompanied minors and the disabled.

Furthermore, the agencies are very keen on introducing refugee participation and community development. The refugees still cannot decide what food rations they receive or where to build their huts. They are still not allowed to move beyond four kilometres around the camp. However, by organising elections for street and village leaders, promoting community development projects and introducing women's committees, UNHCR and NGOs attempt to give the refugees a feeling of empowerment. They are in other words directing their programmes towards shaping the subjectivities of the refugees rather than changing structural relations of power. In line with the liberal arts of governing, UNHCR is trying to produce self-governing subjects (see also Foucault 1991; Cruikshank 1999; Dean 1999 for a discussion on the liberal art of governing; also known as *governmentality*).

In these approaches UNHCR is particularly interested in promoting women's participation. UNHCR and its implementing partners have various programmes to promote women's livelihood possibilities (e.g. vocational training) and their influence on decision making (e.g. women's committees). This marks a significant shift from Patricia Daley's findings in the 1980s where UNHCR allegedly supported patriarchy (Daley 1991). As I have argued elsewhere (Turner 2002), a consequence of this mode of governing the camp is that women are perceived by relief agencies to embody a true community spirit while men only cause 'trouble'. Women are constructed as 'helpless victims' that need encouragement to participate, and when they do participate it is seen to be innocent and self-sacrificing. Men, on the other hand, get involved in politics, which is not only illegal in the camp; in UNHCR discourse it is also connected with selfishness and greed. Hence this kind of empowerment and participation is not encouraged. These practices of promoting equality and these gender constructions have implications for gender relations in the camp – although the consequences are quite different to what was intended, as I will show.

The 'problem' in the camp is that the refugees do not interpret UNHCR's governmentality in terms of equal rights. Instead, they interpret their new surroundings in terms of hierarchy, and they see UNHCR's programmes as threatening this, causing social and moral dissolution as women and men no longer know their 'natural' place in the social order. As one street leader explains:

> In the Bible men and women are equal and also with UNHCR laws. But it is not good. A man has to give some orders in his house – and when woman is equal to the man that means woman also has to give orders in the house; some orders to the man. But in Burundi it is forbidden for a woman to give orders to the man. (Village leader, 2 February 1998)

An ideal Hutu wife is quiet and shy and obeys her husband.[2] Loud-mouthed young women are considered prostitutes and will find it diffi-cult to find a husband, I was told. A good husband, on the other hand, is expected to provide for his family and give nice clothes to his wife. At par-ties and ceremonies men would flaunt their wives' *kangas,* and the audi-ence would know exactly how much each item of clothing had cost. Finally, men's failure to be real men providing for their wives leads to women failing to act as women ought to, and they stop obeying their hus-bands. They only obey 'UNHCR laws'.

When confronted with allegations that they no longer respected their husbands, women often retorted that this was not always so. However, rather than denying the tale, they would qualify it. A group of women's representatives that I interviewed reiterated the tale by claiming that '*A man cannot give to his wife. Therefore she begins to behave badly*' (women's representatives, 25.08.97). Another group of women modify this opinion by saying that if a man does not buy clothes for his wife because he has no money, then she will be understanding and there will be no problem (women's sewing group, 12.08.97). In other words, if he genuinely cannot provide for her and is not drinking up the money, then she will show him respect.

A special case is when women work for one of the NGOs in the camp as teachers, medical assistants, community workers or the like and their husbands do not work. I discussed this in a group interview where two young women working in Oxfam's Sanitation Information Team joined the conversation. A man explained what problems could occur when a woman is employed with an NGO and the husband has no income.

> When she comes with her money, the wife becomes a husband. She has to decide everything. She has to buy clothes for her husband. That's why the wife will never respect the husband. (Man, Village E, 25 June 1997)

In other words, the breadwinner – in this case the wife – makes the decisions. In response, the one who is being kept – in this case the hus-band – has to pay respect to the breadwinner. One of the young women working for OXFAM, replies that it need not be so in all cases, as it depends on the woman:

Maybe that may happen. But it depends on the behaviour of the wife. The woman who does that, she is the one who doesn't know the power of the husband – who doesn't know how to treat a husband. The wife who knows how to treat her husband can take half of her money and give it to her husband. (Woman, Village E, 25 June 1997)

In this way she agrees that it can cause problems. But if the woman is 'sensible' she tries not to antagonise him, by giving him half her wages. It is not an inevitable problem but a question of the individual woman's choices, according to this young woman.

Although women may dispute the men's sweeping statements about lack of respect, they only actually dispute the prevalence of the phenomenon. They may contend that not all women act that way, keeping their own path clean while not disputing the phenomenon as such. Secondly, they do not dispute the fact that women ought to respect their husbands, thus accepting and reproducing the dominant gender ideology. In other words, men and women agree that a Burundian (Hutu) woman should respect her husband. And they agree – to varying degrees – that this ideal relationship is under threat in the camp.

There is no doubt that the structural conditions for the family unit have changed drastically since leaving Burundi. With these changes, the family – as it (ideally) was – is threatened, and particularly the male refugees feel this threat very strongly, as these and other testimonies reveal. In other words, there is a feeling that things are not as they used to be, and there is uncertainty about what the future has to bring. The general feeling of loss; loss of certainty, of absolutes, of taken for granted structures of authority, reminds us of the general ambiguous feeling associated with the 'juggernaut of modernity' (Giddens 1991). Moving from a village in Burundi to a refugee camp is similar in some respects to instant urbanisation with all the pros and cons that go with it. When asked about life in the camp, many refugees would simply say 'it is like a city.'

The experienced breakdown in gender relations[3] does not necessarily imply that only gender relations are being challenged. Rather, gender appears to be the perspective through which most refugees attempt to understand social change. The threat to authority is, however, also perceived in other fields of social life, although not so often mentioned.

I would, for instance, hear complaints that the children no longer respect the adults or that parents no longer bring up their children properly.

And in Burundi you can't see a boy wearing a hat and standing up with the hat when he's in front of elders.

That means he doesn't respect?
Yes impoliteness. But here they do so. Everything has changed. (Village leader,
2 February 1998)

Along a similar vein, refugees – poor as well as rich – would complain
that ordinary 'small people' did not show 'big men' enough respect because
'we are all fed by Food Distribution'. A young man who bakes bread rolls
to sell at the market explains that in the camp the poor become rich and the
rich become poor (Mandazi Baker, February 1998). A young teacher
explains how difficult it is for 'big men' to maintain their authority:

> But in Burundi teachers lived in their home and children seldom came to visit
> that area. Here we live together, and maybe children are my neighbours and
> then they don't respect me well. I can give an example. When we go to get
> food, I go there, and I meet my pupils, and they say this is my teacher. (Young
> teacher, 18 June 1997)

The children can see into his *blindé* (hut) and discover that he is eating
the same food as they do. Again, we see that equality is perceived as a
threat to social and moral order. And furthermore, the physical structure
of the camp does not permit superiors to maintain the illusion of their
superiority. The teacher can no longer hide the fact that he also eats beans
and maize like everyone else. The father can no longer allude that he is
the main provider by controlling cash incomes and occasionally buying a
nice *kanga* for his wife.

Although in general the disruptions that I witnessed in the camp
resemble processes of urbanisation and modernity elsewhere, refugees in
Lukole have been experiencing these changes over an extremely short
period of time. In addition, the process is to a large degree controlled by
external actors, or rather: there is a detectable actor, UNHCR, who can be
blamed for the 'evils of social decay'. This is most obvious in the fact that
refugees in Lukole depict UNHCR as the father or husband; the organisation takes the place of the patriarch and it deprives people of control
over their own lives, reducing them to the status of 'infants' and 'women'.

> There is a change. People are not taking care of their own life. They are just liv-
> ing like babies in UNHCR's arms. (Man, 27 years, April 1998)

In sum, the vague feeling of loss and uncertainty that refugees
encounter in the camp is expressed in tales of decay where lack of respect
for men, adults and 'big men' is seen as the 'symptom', while UNHCR's
policy of equality is perceived as the 'cause'. In this manner, gender equality is not only perceived as a threat to patriarchy. It is also seen as a threat
to a Burundian 'way of life' and to morality as such. It is this perceived
threat that the young men are trying to deal with.

Young Men as Liminal Experts

Old values and norms are being challenged, old authorities are losing their grip and a new authority – represented most strongly by UNHCR – is in control of resources, livelihoods and ideological formations (e.g. the ideology of equality between men and women).

Young men are in many ways affected by these changes. They are at a junction in life where they are supposed to be creating a family that they can protect and provide for. They are also expected to find a place in the hierarchy among the other men in their community. However, this process of identity creation has been disrupted at a vital stage by flight and life in the refugee camp.[4]

The feeling of 'in-betweenness', that refugees experience, resembles Victor Turner's liminal phase in *rites de passage* (Turner 1967). The *neophytes in rites de passage* are 'betwixt and between', in an 'interstructural situation' (Turner 1967: 93) where they are neither here nor there, neither this nor that.

Liminality is the suspension of taken-for-granted social structures and norms, thus making 'room for alternative interpretations and potentially dangerous freedom from the convention of society' (Stepputat 1992: 35). In this manner, the refugee camp opens up certain possibilities for transgressing the taken for granted norms and customs and for new social values to emerge. This is exactly where I found the roles of some young men intriguing.

This is not to say that life in a refugee camp is more or less disruptive for young men than for older generations or for women. But women seem to try to carry on things as they were in Burundi, i.e. cooking, taking care of the children, fetching firewood, etc., avoiding the destructuring powers of liminality.[5] And whereas elderly men appear to be paralysed by being in *limbo*, (some) young men make use of this suspension of social structures and try to change things to their own advantage – they are '*liminal* experts'.

A large group of young men, however – probably the majority – does not become 'liminal experts'. They merely pass their time playing cards or urubugu (a game played with stones or seeds and holes in the ground) or just hanging around the *blindés*. The reason for focusing on the successful refugees is thus not due to their numbers but rather due to their possibility of changing existing power structures and perhaps even dominant – ideologies.

Mobility Strategies

There were three main areas where the young men were able to establish influential positions in the camp: as street/village leaders; working for relief agencies; and as businessmen. Often these strategies would coalesce in the informal networks of the new elite in the camp. These networks were structured around the two rival parties in the camp.

When I first arrived in the camp, I was surprised to see young men down to the age of 21 as street and village leaders. These formal leaders constitute the main link between refugees and other actors in the camp such as UNHCR, NGOs and Tanzanian authorities, making sure information flows both ways. Their other main task is to solve disputes involving people in their constituency.

In a survey of sixty two (out of a total of ca. one hundred) street and village leaders I found that seventeen were between twenty-four and twenty-nine years old, while only two were above fifty, the rest being in their thirties (twenty-six) and forties (seventeen).

The refugees give their own explanations to this phenomenon. They say that it is necessary to be mobile in order to reach the offices of the relief agencies or the police post within short notice. They may also have to transfer a message from UNHCR to the whole community. Old men cannot manage that, they argue. Similarly, they claim that women cannot manage such tasks while carrying a small child, taking care of the household or being pregnant.[6] Furthermore, leaders have to be literate to some degree to be able to take notes during meetings. Mastering foreign languages is also mentioned as an asset. In contrast to Burundi, where Kirundi and French are the official languages, knowledge of English or Swahili is a great advantage in the camp in order to communicate better with Tanzanians and expatriates working for NGOs, the UN and the Tanzanian authorities.

These abilities of the male youth – mobility and flexibility – are supplemented with the value of not being 'shy'. They are no longer shy to approach a *muzungu* or to say their opinion in a meeting, in front of elders, officials and foreigners. Just as women are supposed to be shy and timid towards men, so are young men expected to be shy towards their elders. There is also an ethnic twist to this, as shyness is stereotypically a Burundian Hutu trait.[7] The refugees clearly have an ambivalent relation to these Hutu 'virtues' as they realise that they are constantly losing out and being cheated due to their naive timidity. Thus, to be shy is seen as a Hutu virtue but also as a vice, and to learn 'not to be shy' is perceived as an asset in the camp where old values no longer are of much use.

Another strategy for young men is to find a job in one of the relief agencies in the camp. With limited education these young men (and a few young women) get the opportunity to hold quite influential posts. To obtain these positions much of the same abilities are needed as for street leaders: i.e. mobility, adaptability, 'not being shy', languages, and literacy. It is also useful to have good relations with the right people in the right places. It is said that a person who can get another person a job with an

NGO sometimes gets to keep half of that person's salary as payment for the favour.

NGO employees receive meagre salaries (called 'incentives') of between 14,000 and 22,000 shillings per month (US$ 23–36). In addition, there are various windfalls. Apart from direct embezzlement, usually on a minor scale, the jobs have more important indirect benefits. As the employees occupy strategic positions as intermediaries between relief agencies and beneficiaries, the camp population's access to essential resources like medical help, education, and security, goes through these intermediaries. It is important to be on good terms with an NGO employee who can ask favours in return, in this way establishing a patron-client relationship. However, these strategies are not merely avenues to self-enrichment, as the following example illustrates.

Patrick (fictive name) is twenty-one years old and works as a 'community mobiliser' for AEF (African Education Foundation). By investing his salaries in bicycle taxis he had been able to save enough money to go to Nairobi where he wanted to continue his studies. His trip to Nairobi was a failure, however, and at the time of the interview he was trying to save up again, and to find a way of getting a Burundian or a Tanzanian passport. When asked whether other refugees would think that he was running away from the problems, he gave the following reply:

> There are some who can understand that, as you say, I am running away from problems. But there are others who see that it's better to try because *later I can be someone who can help to solve the problems.* (Patrick, September 1997, my emphasis)

His strategy is legitimised through its relevance to 'the struggle'. In other words, Patrick's choices are subject to peer group evaluation, and he feels a certain belonging to the group and its broader objectives of supporting the 'Hutu cause'.

Along a slightly different line we find the 'businessmen'. Some buy extra rations of oil and maize and resell it to Tanzanians. Others brew *mugorigori* (beer made from maize). Some invest in a bicycle and transport goods and people from the junction at the main road to the refugee camp. There are hairdressers, maize mills, brothels, bars, cigarette vendors, butchers and tailors. Young and old, men and women are active in business, but here again young men tend to dominate.

In the camp, where old authorities, expectations, and norms are no longer taken for granted, young men are relatively free to try out new ways of making a living. In other words, the interstructural space of the camp liberates them from their prestructured place in society and permits them to make alternative interpretations of society. To be a successful businessman one needs to be assertive and have a bit of nerve, they explain. The Rwandan refugees who lived in the camps from 1994 to 1996 were generally believed to be good businessmen, and although the Burundian refugees generally disliked the Rwandans' aggressive attitude and rude behaviour, they also envied and admired their success. Many businessmen were proud to say that the Burundian refugees were behaving increasingly like Rwandans. Again we see how the new elite discards Hutu timidity as anachronistic.

The educated elite, working for NGOs or as street/village leaders, tended to perceive the businessmen's strategies as short-sighted and selfish because they were not struggling for the common good and the future of the country. This conception of struggling for the future is most obviously observed in the omnipresence of the two rival political parties in the camp: Palipehutu (*Parti pour la Libération du Peuple Hutu*) and CNDD (*Conseil National pour la Défense de la Démocratie*).[8] Although political activity is banned in the camp, every adult male is forced to take sides in the bitter and often violent struggle between the two parties. The leaders of these parties obviously hold powerful positions in the camp.

Although recent literature on African politics (from Hydén to Bayart) tends to overemphasise the 'politics of the belly', as if ideology in itself is irrelevant in Africa, there is no doubt that politics in the camp – like politics anywhere in the world – is a mixture of ideological conflict *and* local struggles over access to power and resources. It is in this light that we should see young men's involvement in clandestine politics.

The political leadership constitutes a tight network with the elite that works for NGOs and to some degree with the street leaders. It is in this way that the political leadership has such an influence among the population. Especially the CNDD leadership has managed to find many jobs with NGOs causing resentment among Palipehutu cadres who find that they are given unfair treatment due to their political convictions. Palipehutu sympathisers would complain that CNDD members would give other CNDD members the jobs with NGOs and that CNDD members working in the hospitals, for instance, would not treat patients whom they believed to be Palipehutu sympathisers. CNDD members on the other hand claimed that in certain parts of the camp they were being threatened to pay taxes to Palipehutu by 'men in long coats' (hiding long knives). This had resulted in many people moving from one part of the camp to another, creating politically 'cleansed' spaces.

Membership of a party gives access to jobs and other resources in the camp but it is also a way in which young men gain a sense of purpose and combat boredom and laziness. As the earlier quote 'they are just living like babies in the arms of UNHCR' in this chapter shows, there is a feeling that refugees are not controlling their lives. This sense of not being able to act is equally caused by being unable to influence the course of events in Burundi, so vital for their eventual return. By joining a political party and perhaps even doing some kind of military training, these young men show that they are not just being fed by the UNHCR or, worse, 'like someone buried' (Mandazi Baker, February 1998). They are taking their future in their own hands, they are acting, and they are showing strength. Politicians are treated with respect and even fear in the camp. They dare defy the laws of the Tanzanian government and the UNHCR and play by their own rules; the moral rules of the rightful struggle. In other words, they are recouping the masculinity that they believe was taken away from them by UNHCR.

New Opportunities – New Ideologies?

So far we have seen how UNHCR's ideology and practice of equality, coupled with the nature of living in a refugee camp as such has seriously challenged notions of authority. We saw how this feeling of upheaval, similar in many ways to the experience of modernity elsewhere, was often interpreted by the refugees in terms of gender and, to a lesser degree, in terms of age and class. The common perception in the camp was that UNHCR had taken the place of the father, thus turning refugees into 'helpless women' or children having to obey the UNHCR and without control over their own lives – in spite of UNHCR's efforts to promote democracy and participation for all refugees. In other words, the refugees interpreted the governmentality of UNHCR, based on liberal notions of equality and rights, in terms of sovereignty. Finally, we have seen how some young men have managed to take advantage of this liminal situation and create a new space for themselves. We have also seen how these strategies were partially aimed at material gains and partially at creating a new identity as men.

The question is whether these 'liminal experts' will be able to retain their positions in the future; i.e. when and if they return to Burundi. Although the refugees tend to emphasise the negative effects of life in the camp, some would also mention the advantages of having this experience. Businessmen would explain how they were sure to have an advantage when returning while those who stayed in Burundi lack the entrepreneurial spirit of the camp. NGO workers hoped to work for an international agency in Burundi. After all, they speak a bit of English, they know the developmentalist jargon and are not shy to approach a *muzungu*. Stepputat found that Guatemalan returnees would act as 'development catalysts', bringing modern rationalities and techniques of government to the areas where they returned, due to the language and techniques that they had incorporated in the refugee settlements (Stepputat 1999). So there is a great chance that the changes that have occurred in the camp will actually be perpetuated into the future. Apart from the practical skills of leadership, languages and doing business, they believe that the camp has taught them more general social skills. They feel that they have matured and have become less shy and naive and more aware. There is a general ambiguity around these changes. On the one hand the tales of social and moral decay bear witness to a longing for the 'good old days' when every man, woman and child knew his or her place and hierarchic harmony reigned. On the other hand there is a sense that some of these stereotypical Hutu customs are preventing them from being emancipated, keeping them in naive darkness. It is impossible to estimate how this will affect their future in Burundi and the future of Burundi. But there appears to be an attitude of no longer wanting to 'take any rubbish' from the Tutsi.

The question of gender relations is also complex and deserves more attention. It appears that men still dominate decision-making institutions, in spite of UNHCR and NGOs encouraging the 'empowerment' of women and in spite of refugees complaining that women no longer obey their husbands. Street leaders are still men, influential NGO employees are men, politicians are men, etcetera. Furthermore, and more important- ly, the construction of gender roles does not appear to have changed much. It is still considered shameful for a man not to be able to provide for his family. Women are still expected to obey their men. In fact, the breakdown of the authority of the patriarchy (consisting of old men and 'big men') in the camp, and the resulting sense of social decay, has given young men the incentive to fight back. They have broken the monopoly of 'old men' and 'big men' to some degree, while maintaining a male identity on the other. The goal of these young men's strategies is to regain control of their lives and to take back their place as providers.

In this way we see that the relief agencies' ideologies and practices have had quite unintended consequences. They have been based on the implicit assumption that 'our' rational mode of governing will slowly but surely supersede 'their' backward ideas. However, the refugees interpret the structural shift towards gender equality (equal food rations etcetera) in a completely different manner to what was intended by the agencies themselves. The unintended consequence is that existing gender ideolo- gies are strengthened through the male refugees' attempts to combat what they perceive as social and moral decay. And such gender ideologies are crucial: they have very concrete effects for the lives of men and women in the camp. It is due to such ideologies that men still make the decisions while women are carrying the brunt of the workload in the camp.

At a more general level, this paper has shown how important it is to take male gender into consideration. The aim of such a study in my view should not be to do a 'gender analysis' for its own sake, nor to measure how much women or men are oppressed or emancipated; i.e. to deter- mine who gets the greatest slice of the cake. Rather, the fact that the refugees themselves use gender as a major interpretative scheme – gender being central to their identity – is crucial to understanding the broader dynamics within refugee society.

Notes

1. I would like to thank Jeff Crisp, Steffen Jensen, Thomas Hansen, Joke Schrijvers and Finn Stepputat for comments on earlier versions of this paper.
2. Similar constructions of ideal women and men are to be found in ethnographic data from Burundi. See Trouwborst (1962: 129).
3. Joke Schrijvers (1999) notes how breakdown of moral values is a picture assigned to internal refugees by the surrounding Sri Lankan society. This image also pictures refugee women as especially promiscuous, something that Schrijvers could find no evidence of in the camps.
4. Focussing on male gender is not an issue of claiming that we should feel sorry for men (White 1997: 21). Nor is it a question of denying the fact that women in the camps are up against immense problems as has been demonstrated by Judith Benjamin (1998) and Patricia Daley (1991). Rather, by focussing on changing masculinities (Connell 1998), we can understand broader dynamics in the camp.
5. Similar observations were made among internal refugees by Schrijvers (1999).
6. The idea of the father taking care of the baby or cooking while she attends meetings does not occur to them.
7. For a brilliant analysis of this 'salt of the earth' construction of the Hutu self see Malkki (1995).
8. I analyse these two parties and their role in the camp in more detail in Turner (1998).

8

Identities and the Sense of Belonging: Iranian Women Activists in Exile[1]

Halleh Ghorashi

The Iranian revolution of 1979 forced many people to leave their country. Among them were the Iranian women of this study, who as political activists within leftist organisations had to leave Iran when the Islamists assumed absolute power in 1981 and suppressed all opposition. These women became exiles throughout the world, including the Netherlands and the United States, where I conducted my research. My fieldwork, which took eight months in each country, was concentrated in Amsterdam in 1996 and Los Angeles in 1997. During that time, for some months I participated in and observed the Iranian communities in both countries to grasp the dynamics in each context. The majority of women interviewed in both cities have a higher education and jobs related to their fields of study.

In this chapter, I present part of the findings of this research, particularly in relation to the process of identity formation. Identity is here perceived as a process of becoming and as a narrative of life (Giddens 1991). Thus, it is neither fixed nor given, but rather, a dynamic process, a changing view of the self and the other, constantly acquiring new meanings and forms through interactions with social contexts and within historical moments. To understand the process, in which identities are constructed, the life stories of women are essential. These self-narratives are expressions of their experiences of certain events and their identifications with certain groups. When people tell their stories they identify themselves with one or another group or reject some external identification. In this sense, the process of identity formation is not an isolated phenomenon but a relational process that includes both the approval and the rejection of different levels of identification. In what follows, I explain how the process of constructing an identity is influenced by differences between the new contexts.

The Impact of the Revolution

The involvement of women in the Iranian revolution of 1979 took place at many different levels. Their most intense participation was during the two years after the overthrow of the Pahlavi regime (1926–1979). During 1979–1981, which was called 'the spring of freedom', a number of political groups came into existence that at that time were permitted by law. These groups advanced a wide range of ideologies, including forms of Marxism, Islamism, liberalism, and women's rights. Both the extent of the freedom enjoyed during these years and the opportunity for political involvement gave Iranian women the chance to become part of political change in their country on an extensive level for the first time. Nahid, thirty-eight and living in the United States, mentions the following:

> I can say that those years were the better years of my life. I think that I never in my life enjoyed life like that. I gained a lot of personal freedom at that time and socially all those restrictions were not there anymore. You could go wherever you wanted to go, you could do whatever you wanted to do. It was really a safe environment and a democratic one. It was friendly and everything was good. It was as if it was paradise – it was my paradise anyway. Those were the best years of my life.

I listened to the stories of women between the ages of thirty and fifty, those who had lived in the Netherlands and the United States for more than ten years. Age was important in the ways that the memories of the past were narrated. For the younger women like Nahid who were between fifteen and twenty years old during the revolution, the impact of those years was much more pronounced than it was for the older women (for an extensive analysis on this issue see Ghorashi 2002). Nevertheless, the experiences of those years changed the lives of women who talked to me.

These women were involved with various Marxist organisations. Although they came from different social, religious, and economic backgrounds, what all had in common was that their political involvement in a leftist organisation made it possible for them to some extent to transgress the limitation of their background. As Nahid mentions, those years opened the door for them to 'feel free to do whatever they wanted to do'. This meant that being politically active, even for a short time, changed the life of these women drastically.

The 'spring of freedom' did not last. Confrontations had been growing between secular/leftist political groups and the Islamists in power from the first days after the revolution. Those confrontations took a turn for the worse on 18 June 1981. From that date on, the streets of Teheran and other Iranian cities bore witness to terrible violence. Islamists began institution-alising their absolute power. All other political groups were declared illegal, and the majority of their followers arrested, tortured, or killed. Laleh, forty-eight and a resident of the Netherlands, describes those years of suppression.

> In those days you could see only darkness and decay. Everything deteriorated. I could not see anything positive in that time. I could not see any light. There was no place for hope. Not only were all our hopes buried, but also we could see nothing but negativity and darkness, which became worse day by day. ... I always wonder whether people who hear or read about our experiences during that period can ever really understand the depth and painfulness of those events. When you try to explain the situation, it seems as if the words cannot properly describe what you want to say.

Revolution changed the life of these activists and then attempted to take it back from them. Their souls were filled with dreams and ideals, and they were suddenly punished because of those ideals. They suffered during those years of suppression, either being arrested themselves or living in fear of being arrested day by day, or seeing their loved ones arrested, tortured, or killed. Those were the memories that made the women of this research and many others feel like exiles in their own country. Those who had a chance left the country and found themselves in exile outside Iran. A new start in a new country went together with the memories of a lost home and an insecure future.

Continuous Strangers: Iranians in the Netherlands

For many of the women of this study, a new country meant the chance to build a new life. During the first four or five years of their stay all of the younger women were able to learn the language and finish a course of study within higher education. Women from the older generation above the age of thirty for whom the possibilities of study were more limited had to restrict themselves to job-oriented courses. Only one of the women did not choose to study and went directly to work after learning the language. The initial encounter of these women with Dutch society was rather positive. However, this positive feeling was later replaced by a new kind of frustration. Despite their success in mastering the language and in becoming a part of this society, they felt a kind of uprootedness in the later phase of their stay. The disappointment began when they realised that they were treated as strangers by the Dutch despite their desire to be part of the new society. This experience of being 'the other' has to do with a process in which women feel excluded based on their background. This process in the Netherlands has to do with the ways that the negative images of 'the other' are constructed and acted on (see for example Dijk 1987, 1993; Essed 1991; Lutz 1991; and Verkuyten et al. 1993, 1995). In order to understand this process of othering, I explore the link between the approaches toward migration and the feelings of otherness. Then I distinguish different components in the process, such as gender and ethnicity.

The process of othering can be understood in relation to the history of migration in the Netherlands. Despite the fact that a considerable number of migrants in the Netherlands are the product of colonialism, the image of migration has been strongly shaped by the arrival of 'guest labourers' in the 1950s. When economic growth and the need for cheap labour brought the Dutch to look beyond their borders, labour contracts materialised, first with Italy and Spain and later with Turkey and Morocco. Migration was seen as temporary and guest workers as having left their country with the aim to return later. As is the case with exiles who wish to return to their 'homeland' after the hostile political situation changes, the host country assumes that migrant workers will return home upon the completion of their work. In other words, for the guest worker, as for the exile, the notion of 'home' is directly associated with one's native land. Nevertheless, for activists in exile, two factors are of great importance. Firstly, the political ideals of activists play an essential part in their lives, even in exile. Secondly, for years the hope for change in their country keeps a strong link with the past. In this kind of migration, we are dealing with a strong desire for return, which is not the case in other kinds of migration where the choice is to stay (Rushdie 1988; Eastmond 1993; Naficy 1993; Clifford 1994).

This close link between migration and return dominates how the host society approaches migration. The 'myth of return' creates the expectation in the host society of seeing migration as temporary and not as a permanent settlement. When the process of migration becomes a more permanent phenomenon, it goes against the expectations of the host country. The idea that migrants should return creates an understanding in which migrants are always considered guests and not permanent residents or citizens. Considering migrants as guests has to do with the idea that they do not belong in this society. In this way, the construction of otherness is embedded in the ideology and practice of 'who belongs' and 'who does not belong'. This has to do with the construction of certain images of nation that exclude migrants. The migrant as 'other' is 'constructed as not belonging to the nation and yet living inside it' (Räthzel 1995: 165). The effect of this process of othering and the idea of migration as temporary vision is enormous for political refugees with the primary wish to return. When Iranians, for example, start to feel closer to the new society and distanced from old ideals and hope, they face the fact that they are not particularly wanted or welcome in the new society. Even when they are included legally, they are excluded socially. When Iranians are made to feel that they do not belong to the new country, nostalgic feelings toward their 'homeland' grow. The context of the host society strengthens this nostalgic feeling by treating these immigrants as temporary residents.

Exemplifying the social exclusion are the number and frequency of the questions these women have been asked, such as, 'Where do you come from?' and 'When do you hope to return?' These questions may seem harmless in the beginning, but repetition year after year reminds the women of not being part of the new society and contributes to their sense of exclusion from it. Leila, who is forty-five and has lived in the Netherlands for about nine years, talks about her frustration:

> In the beginning when I went to a party or a gathering, if somebody asked, 'Where are you from?' and I replied, 'Iran' I had a feeling that the word 'Iran' sounded very heavy. The reaction was 'Oh, Iran'. Some people are interested and ask questions. You have to explain constantly, about Iran, about yourself, and about your private life. In the beginning I liked that, I felt as if I was giving information to Dutch people, and that this might change their views of Iran. I hoped that after some time they would understand more about Iran and that they would understand where I came from. I hoped that people could see to which category I belong. But after a while, this whole situation became really tiresome. Because all the questions were the same and because my answers were also the same, I became really fed up. In the beginning I thought that I must explain who I am, but after some time I became tired. I repeated it so many times that it now has psychological effects on me. I have to tell my life story over and over again, and then come to political issues. I will give you an example: I go to a cafe to drink some coffee, and somebody comes over to ask me for a match. This person then asks immediately, 'Oh, you are foreigner! What is your mother tongue?' I reply, 'Persian', and then it goes on and on. I go to a cafe to relax, and I end up having to tell my life story. This becomes very boring and difficult after a while.

In addition to the perception of the immigrant as a temporary resident, issues of gender and ethnicity play crucial roles in the construction of the immigrant as an 'other'. On the one hand, dominant images of femininity in Dutch society shape the perception of the immigrant women as 'other'. According to these images, Dutch women are modern and emancipated, while Iranian women are seen as oppressed and traditional. Such stereotypical perceptions disregard the very fact that in every society some women are 'modern' or 'progressive' while others are 'traditional' and 'conservative'. Such ideas also disregard the struggle of these Iranian women activists against the traditional ideas of Iranian women. The revolution changed the life of many women who became politically involved. The new context in the Netherlands did not drastically change these women's ideas about gender, but it gave them a more open space for self-fashioning. However, despite the possibility in the Netherlands for these women to improve themselves, a new burden appeared, namely, the dominant stereotypes of Middle Eastern women, especially Iranian women (Moors 1989; Lutz and Spijkerboer 1994a; Baalen 1997).

Ironically, this means that Iranian women activists who have fought almost all of their lives to improve their situation are considered backward and suppressed people. Women are seen as dependent and passive victims. 'Institutions involved with refugee care tend to patronise refugee women, whom they consider pitiful, traditional and backward' (Essed 1995: 49). These negative images of Iranian women have their ideological underpinnings in what Edward Said has described as Orientalism: a western perception of the Middle East that reduces its people to types (Lutz 1991; Jansen 1996; Behdad 1999). This view confirms that gender as a concept cannot be analysed on its own, but must be intricately linked to other concepts, like ethnicity (Wekker 1998).

Dutch society provides Iranian women with a productive space for self-fashioning, and yet its refusal to acknowledge them as equal beings undermines their ability to feel part of the new society. It is easy to imagine how bitter they become by these kinds of stereotypes. This calls for reactions, especially from the activists who consider themselves emancipated.

Soraya, who is forty-nine and has lived in the Netherlands for sixteen years, says:

> They think of us as backward women, being continually beaten by men. They think that they have to emancipate us. I tell them that the way I was dressed before the time of Khomeini was much better than the way I am dressed now. We had beautiful clothes and in Iran we were very well dressed, here people do not care much about their appearance and I dress worse now than I used to in Iran.

Laleh, forty-eight and single, has worked and lived in the Netherlands for eleven years. She says:

> It is like this, you have to explain constantly. They think that we always had to wear scarves and veils in Iran. They ask: 'Do you like it here now, are you more comfortable here?' My God, the obligation to wear a scarf only began a few years ago, before that we didn't have to. They ask: 'Did your parents arrange your marriage?' For God's sake, we didn't have that. Maybe it happened in villages and among some sections of society, but not with all Iranians. You see? These are the false impressions of our society.

Moreover, the manifestation of ethnicity in physical appearance shapes the perception of immigrants as 'others'. There is a clear-cut division in

Dutch society between the white self and the black other. This division goes further than just the physical appearance, and has strong normative connotations. Despite the fact that the majority of the Dutch population is still white, the process of change and migration has made Dutch society less white than it realises itself. Yet, it is not so much the physical whiteness but the association with a normative concept of whiteness that is important here. I agree with Wekker (1998) when she suggests that definitions of whiteness are invisible while the ones blackness are not (for more on this issue see Frankenberg 1993; Dyer 1997). Wekker pleads for breaking through this invisibility by questioning the neutrality of whiteness. 'Whiteness is a powerful, normative and ethnic category' (1998: 59). When whiteness is a norm, a dark-looking person becomes a deviance from the norm.

The Dutch word *allochtoon*, which refers to ethnic minorities in the Netherlands, is a good example for this division based on colour.

> The notion of *allochtoon* is not used for just any 'non-native', such as U.S., British, or German immigrants, but explicitly for 'non-natives' of colour and for immigrants with real or attributed Muslim identity. The term *allochtoon* is functional in setting apart people from the South, both the newly arrived refugees and the established black and ethnic minority groups, from a constructed image in which 'genuine' Dutch or European identity is a white identity. (Essed 1995: 53)

The racial aspect of otherness is strongly experienced by the women I interviewed in the use of the term *kale-siyah* (blackheads), which is used to express the way Europeans perceive Iranians. Iranians also use this word in some other European countries:

> We are always blackheads (*svartskallar*) in the eyes of Swedes. We can never make a career and are isolated all the time. (from an interview quoted in Graham and Khosravi 1997: 120)

This labelling consists of negative connotations like being stupid, uncivilized, and dangerous. The use of this labelling shows how Iranians feel within Dutch society. They feel strongly perceived as 'the other': an unwelcome other with negative connotations.

Such negative images of Middle Eastern women combined with the perception of migration as a temporary phenomenon make the Iranian women of this study feel like strangers in Dutch society (for more on creation of otherness see Essed 1991; Lutz et al. 1995; Räthzel 1995; Wekker 1995). Moreover, in the Netherlands, the few Iranian group activities and the Iranian network cannot serve as an alternative social resource for women. The absence of a strong ethnic community – well in place in the United States, for example – intensifies their sense of otherness.

Once Iranians become part of the process of othering, they contribute to it by perceiving the Dutch as 'others' in four ways. They first create an image of 'the other' in a static way. The general Iranian image of the Dutch, presented either during the interviews or in gatherings, is that the Dutch are cold, distanced, stingy, and sober. Recognising differences among the Dutch becomes marginalised in order to keep an intact image of 'the other'. Second, Iranians manifest othering by translating questions and remarks by the Dutch in a normative way. Any example of impolite, cold, or insensitive behaviour is interpreted as being 'typically Dutch', while it is often the person and not his or her nationality that determines such behaviour. Third, when Iranians sense not being welcome within a society, they distance themselves from it and call it undesirable. By emphasising certain stereotypical characteristics, such as being aloof or stingy, Iranians construct their identity through the Dutch identity. In short, they stress their differences with the Dutch, differences that marginalise their similarities. The more that Iranians feel that they are being othered, the more this stereotyping of the Dutch increases. Thus, Iranians are not just passive participants in the process of othering in the Netherlands, but in some ways they are actively contributing to it. This dialectical process influences the construction of identity in such a manner that different cultures become exclusive enclaves toward each other. The differential structure of identification thus engenders an exclusive and monolithic notion of cultural identity in which one culture is emphasised at the cost of another's marginalisation.

Defining Iranianness and Dutchness in an exclusive way sets up a situation in which people can only belong to their place of origin. For the women of this study, physical home ('there') is constructed as different and privileged over the place where one lives ('here'). Such an exclusive form of identification creates an imagined place of belonging outside of where people presently live. As Leila mentions:

> Even if I feel that I have adapted myself to the new situation here, I often feel that I do not belong. How can I say it … I feel that my roots are there. I think then that some day I will go back, because I prefer to live in my place [Iran], everybody likes to live in their own country.

The sense of uprootedness in the Netherlands brings women like Leila to search for their roots somewhere else. This makes the possibilities of settlement and feeling comfortable in a new context very difficult, if not impossible. As a result, what prevails in the stories of Iranian women in the Netherlands is that they are not able to articulate the actual relation between their past and their present in order to create a coherent story of their lives. In short, a disrupted sense of time and place prevails. A disrupted sense of life vacillating between the past and the present creates emptiness and insecurity, feelings that displace their sense of belonging.

The stories of the Iranian women interviewed in the United States were quite different from those told by women interviewed in the Netherlands. Despite their relatively similar past, the women positioned themselves differently within the context of each country.

Irangeles: a Better Home Abroad?

Los Angeles is one of the most multicultural areas in the United States. Probably one-third of today's Los Angeles population is foreign-born (Kelly and Friedlander 1993). Los Angeles in particular and Southern California in general are immigrant-oriented communities. Ironically enough, where the racial discrimination linked to the construction of whiteness in the United States seems to be strongly present (Frankenberg 1993; Goldberg 1994; McLaren 1994; Grant et al. 1996), the attitude toward immigration is differentiated. People often immigrate to the United States with the aim to stay, a fact that is commonly accepted by immigrants and citizens alike. But exiles are the exception to this rule; and even more so are political refugees with a political bond to their homeland, who put 'returning home' at the top of their priorities for a long time. Results of my research show, however, that exiles could well experience another reaction toward return after living in Los Angeles for years and becoming both professionally and culturally part of the society: the waning of their myth of return.

In the area of Los Angeles that Iranians refer to as *Irangeles*, the existence of the largest number of Iranians living outside of Iran contributes in different ways to a large Iranian network, activities, and a sense of belonging. Estimates as to the number of Iranians in Los Angeles vary from 200,000–300,000, the number released by the media in the mid 1980s to the U.S. Census Bureau's count of 100,000 (Bozorgmehr et al. 1996: 376, n. 15). Iranians in Los Angeles belong to a group of immigrants who generally arrived with the money, education, and skills to obtain good jobs. They did not 'enter the U.S. economy as an ethnic underclass but as a sort of transnational elite, requiring minor adjustments but not massive retraining' (Naficy 1993: 6). It is also relevant to mention that Iranians in the United States are considered Caucasians, which of course positions them differently than African Americans or Mexican immigrants who are considered nonwhite ethnic minorities.

The Iranian activities in Los Angeles are generally a re-creation of the years before the revolution, an imagined Iran outside of the actual Iran. For many Iranians brought up during the time of the Shah, *Irangeles* feels more like Iran than the Islamic Iran after the revolution. In the diversity present in the reconstructed Iran outside of Iran, many Iranians have found the basis for a sense of belonging. The women that I interviewed, however, had different reasons for this sense of belonging. For these women, it was not so much their participation in various Iranian cultural activities as their affiliation with specific intellectual and women's organisations that made them feel at home in Los Angeles. In fact, based on their political background the women of this study kept their distance from cultural activities with connections to the previous regime in Iran. For these women the variety of choices in Los Angeles seemed to be more essential than the known environment of prerevolutionary Iran. Nevertheless, this same environment given implicit and indirect approval helps them to feel a sense of belonging on a latent level. The whole setting of Iran outside of Iran, or *Irangeles*, can serve as a familiar environment similar to the place where they grew up, and can stimulate their sense of belonging in the new context.

In eighteen interviews, life in Los Angeles is mentioned in a positive sense. Many consider Iran outside of Iran even more positively than Iran itself. When the women talk about Iran the emotions are still there, but the rational choice is explicitly for the life in Los Angeles. When the interviews reveal a conflict between past and present, between the rational and emotional choices for 'there' and 'here', the final choice is often Los Angeles.

When I asked, 'Do you consider yourself a stranger in this society?' Shadi, an artist of forty-five who has lived for more than ten years in the United States, answered, 'Not now'.

Then I asked, 'Has this become your home in a way?' She said,

Yes, I don't like to think of going back to Iran. ... It is possible that I would go back later, and would stay there, but not now in my present situation. I like the kind of life that I have here. A life in Iran has nothing for me. I have expectations from life that I can fulfil here. At least I think this now. Another point is that I have better possibilities on my own here in comparison to Iran. My wishes can be fulfilled here.

When I asked, 'Could you give me some examples?' she replied,

Take for example my work in music. By making music I can give my past a place. You do it through anthropology, I do it through music. There are also my social activities on women's questions. ... Sometimes when I think of Iran, I become emotional. I feel like crying, despite the fact that my whole family is here. However, there is something from my past, which is there, ... I miss my friends. I miss the cities and the people, the streets, all those things. When I am melancholy, I become emotional and feel like crying. Even now, when I say that I do not want to live in Iran, I still become emotional.

When I asked in what ways she misses Iran, Sadaf, an artist of thirty-five who came to the United States about fifteen years ago, responded,

The memories. I know that when I go back to Iran many things will shock me. ... Before, I missed Iran more, but not now.

This has become your home, in some way?

Yes, I feel that.

You told me that you don't feel a stranger here.

I don't feel like a stranger in my daily life, but there are incidents at my work and my school when I feel like a stranger, but in general I am very happy and do not feel like a foreigner. I spoke to a friend who lived in Germany and she told me that there you feel like a foreigner all the time and you have no feeling of belonging. They look at you as a foreigner. This feeling is very weak in me, it is possible that this is somewhere inside me but it is not something I think of very often. ... It is not like that at all here. When I came here, I thought that I had entered paradise. I wrote to my aunt that it is paradise here.

When I asked forty-year-old Jaleh, who has lived for more than ten years in the United States, the question: 'Do you feel at home here?' she answered:

Yes, I do.

Do you feel like a stranger here?

No, I feel that I have become part of this society, in some ways. Maybe I feel like this because my husband is American. However, this feeling is not always present. Even in Iran, I felt that I did not belong to anywhere, but to everywhere.

The majority of the women in this study, eighteen out of twenty, felt as if they were part of the new society. For these women being Iranian and living in the United States are not mutually exclusive forms of identification. They do not feel being othered in the new context and are able to combine their Iranian identity with their present life in the United States. Some of them call themselves Iranian-American, which means that the two cultural identities are not defined in an exclusive way. Iranian women feel a strong sense of belonging in the new context and are able to position themselves multiply in a diversity of cultural practices. This sense of belonging, however, is not a product of their positive interactions with Americans. Iranian women in Los Angeles socialise less with Americans than do their counterparts in the Netherlands with the Dutch. Nevertheless, what distinguishes Iranian women in Los Angeles from their counterparts in Amsterdam is their ability to fashion a more inclusive form of identification. Whereas Iranian women in the Netherlands experience a deep sense of otherness by the exclusive form of identification, Iranian women in Los Angeles tend to ignore expressions of exclusivity, thus feeling more at home in exile.

Many factors contribute to this difference. Firstly, the Iranian ethnic community in Los Angeles is one among others. Differences in physical appearance and language are not seen as strange but normal in daily life. During the interviews, I realised that for Iranian women appearance itself is not an issue in Los Angeles. Although none of them mentioned that they were treated as 'other' because of their dark appearance or their accent, they said that the problems begin when their nationality becomes known. In the Netherlands, by contrast, problems that begin with the appearance and the accent cause them to feel alienated in the new society on a daily basis (Essed 1991).

Secondly, because of the diversity of their interactions in Los Angeles, the attitude of Americans toward the women I interviewed is one of the many they face daily. Therefore, it helps them not to consider it a major factor in their daily lives. In addition, the existence of an Iranian network in Los Angeles is a resource to rely on when the women feel marginalised by Americans. In Los Angeles, women who have many contacts with Iranians are able to see their American contacts in a marginal way. But their interaction with Americans also enables them to distance themselves from the Iranian network when they feel pressured by it. Having two social resources with which to interact enables these women to have more alternatives. One of the women who was less positive about her life in Los Angeles was one who maintained exclusive contact with Iranians, which limited her resources. Unlike other women in Los Angeles, she did not have the opportunity to interact with Iranian and American resources interchangeably. Her situation is similar to that of the single social resource available to the women I interviewed in the Netherlands. The women in the Netherlands are more in contact with the Dutch and become more dependent on the ways the Dutch treat them and interact with them than do the women in the United States. But despite having contact with different kinds of Dutch people, these women seem to generalise their feeling of being 'othered' by the Dutch and do not mention the differences within Dutch society. This is because this feeling of 'otherness' overwhelms Iranian women in Dutch society, a feeling that blinds them to the differences that they encounter in their everyday practices. In Los Angeles, by contrast, women differentiate between intellectuals and other Americans, or between friends, colleagues, and other Americans. In this way, they try to distinguish degrees of difference among Americans. This does not happen with Iranian women in the Netherlands, because they have no sense of such nuances. Their feeling of marginalisation is too strong to admit to the differences even if they face them in their daily life.

Conclusion

The process of othering and the feeling of social exclusion in the Netherlands contribute to an exclusive form of Iranian identity that make achieving a sense of belonging in the new country almost impossible. As a result, the women of this study construct an imaginary notion of an Iranian identity that is nostalgically linked to Iran. This imagined sense of belonging to Iran ironically brings back the painful memories of the past. The need to create a past to belong to, and the uprooted feelings in the present, make the painful memories of the past actually present. The narrative life of the women in the Netherlands is somehow split between the past ('there'), where they imagine their 'root', and the present ('here'), where they are forced to live as exiles. The new achievements and the positive aspects of Dutch society are forgotten when the Netherlands is constructed as an alien land where they feel marginalised.

The context of California, by contrast, gives many women the chance to fashion for themselves a sense of belonging in this new place. Because they feel socially included in American society, they are able to create a coherent story of their lives where the past and the present are linked in a productive way: they shape a nonexclusive form of identity. Their sense of belonging, in short, is not exclusively linked to their past. The actual re-creation of the past in California and the sense of being included in the society enable these women to reconstruct their identities in an inclusive manner. The sense of belonging includes elements of both the past, the cultural and social gatherings and Iranian contacts; and the present, the new achievements in life and sense of freedom in the new context. Such a productive sense of belonging has obviously positive outcomes. First, painful memories of the past are undermined in light of the present and future expectations. Second, the women are free to live where they feel they belong. There is no disruption in their lives by living in one place and feeling they belong somewhere else. The predicament of being between 'there' and 'here' seems to have been solved by living mostly 'here' with the elements of 'there'.

In sum, the construction of a hybrid identity in which the past and the present are productively linked depends on a sense of social inclusion. The process of social inclusion in California gives the women the chance not to be captured between two different places and times, but to be able to bring 'the past' and 'there' closer to 'the present', 'here'. For the Iranian women in the Netherlands, on the other hand, their state of being temporally and spatially split disrupts the construction of a hybrid identity.

Notes

1. I would like to thank Professors Joke Schrijvers, Philomena Essed, and Ali Behdad for their important suggestions and insightful comments on this paper.

Part III
Discouraging Policies; Empowering Agency

9

A Community Empowered? The Bosnia Project in the U.K.

Lynnette Kelly

Introduction

This chapter is about a British programme launched in the early 1990s for the resettlement of refugees from Bosnia Herzegovina. The problem addressed is how refugees have experienced the particular policy interventions implemented in the name of humanitarian aid. The purpose is to offer a critical view based on the presupposition that intentions meant to increase refugee empowerment are one thing, to operationalise these intentions effectively is quite another step.

The outbreak of war in Bosnia Herzegovina in April 1992 produced the largest flow of refugees and displaced persons in Europe since the Second World War. Thousands of people fled outwards and sought safety in other European countries, and the term 'ethnic cleansing' entered the world's vocabulary. The discovery by journalists of the existence of concentration camps in Bosnia eventually led to the closure of those camps, and UNHCR appealed for countries to offer a place of safety for those who had been detained. Britain offered to take one thousand persons, plus their dependants, and eventually around 2,500 persons in total arrived as part of this quota. The Home Office approached the Refugee Council and the British Red Cross to organise reception and resettlement facilities, and at a later date the Scottish Refugee Council and Refugee Action also became part of the programme. Together these organisations formed 'The Bosnia Project', the British programme for the resettlement of ex-detainees and vulnerable persons from Bosnia Herzegovina. In addition, around 6,000 Bosnians came to Britain on their own or as part of humanitarian evacuation convoys (Home Office 1995). These 'nonprogramme' Bosnians were excluded from all areas of Bosnia Project support other than the community development phase. Nonprogramme Bosnians applied for asylum and most were given refugee status or exceptional leave to remain. In contrast, those that came as part of the programme did not usually apply for asylum, as on arrival they were given 'temporary protection', which resembled exceptional leave in many respects but was for a limited period of time (HWIG 1994).

Though a few of those that came as part of the programme have returned to Bosnia, the majority remains in Britain, despite the temporary status they were originally given (UNHCR 2001). This chapter examines aspects of the refugees' experiences in Britain, based on information collected as part of a Ph.D. thesis.[1] This research suggests that their present situation will inevitably have been influenced by the policies of arrival, reception, and settlement. These can be divided into three main areas: the programme and its implementation; the use of temporary protected status and the emphasis on return; and finally the focus on 'the community' as the mode of incorporation into British society. In order to assess the impact of the programme the concept of 'empowerment' seems relevant. Adams' (1996) theory of 'empowerment' is a useful tool for examining these policies, since it allows for the incorporation of the refugees' perspective. This is important, since generally in Britain there is (and has been) a failure to incorporate the opinions of the recipients of services, the refugees themselves, sufficiently, if at all, into any assessment that takes place (Majka 1991). Towards the end of the main project research was commissioned into its operation, and as part of this the views of clients were sought (Graessle and Gawlinski 1996). This exercise led to some changes in the operation of the final stages of the project, but it was the first serious attempt to incorporate the views of those on the receiving end. For most of the time that the project operated, and for the vast majority of its clients, the opinions of the clients were not actively sought

Empowerment

'Empowerment' is a term that is at once theoretical and practical. Its use in recent years has been widespread, so much so that it has been described as, like apple pie and motherhood, a concept beyond reproach (Stevenson and Parsloe 1993). Empowerment has appeared in a range of views, from both the left and right of the political spectrum (Baistow 1994), and appears at times to have lost its meaning (Stewart and Taylor 1995). However, empowerment is still used as a guiding principle in social and community work, and so it can be used as a tool for assessing and evaluating such work if it is clearly defined (Ward and Mullender 1991).

Empowerment has been defined as 'the process whereby individuals, groups, and/or communities become able to take control of their circumstances and achieve their own goals, thereby being able to work towards helping themselves and others to maximise the quality of their lives' (Adams 1996: 5). They must have the power to make decisions about themselves, but also they must have sufficient knowledge so that these are informed decisions. This implies a specific understanding of the nature of power in society, and the view that the distribution of power can be changed. It is also intrinsically connected to the understanding of the effects of policies and their implementation. Power and knowledge, though different, are inseparable, and one cannot exist without the other (Foucault 1985). Empowered individuals and groups have the power to make decisions and choices, and the necessary knowledge and resources in order to be able to make those decisions. Ultimately the aim of empowerment is to encourage self-help and autonomy, and to increase choice (Zippay 1995).

Refugees could potentially benefit the country in which they live, and a government minister has stated that '… refugees bring with them enormous benefits to society' (Barbara Roche MP, Foreword, Home Office 2000). In order to realise their potential, refugees need to be properly incorporated into society, and this cannot happen if refugees are seen as either a burden on society, or as objects of pity. Both views objectify refugees, and impose someone else's perceptions onto their reality. It is only if refugees are truly empowered that they can contribute to society in a meaningful way, both economically and socially.

In British social policy a community approach is often used as a method of attempting to empower the disadvantaged (Favell 1998). Minority ethnic groups are among those considered to be disadvantaged in British society, and community development policies are used as a means of addressing this disadvantage and empowering minority ethnic communities (Barr et al. 1996). Many local authorities also contribute to the community orientation of work with or for minority ethnic groups. Political representation at a local level can often be obtained via local forums such as community relations councils and religious councils, but this route is only open to formally constituted groups. Local authorities often make grants of funds or services to established community groups, and so play an important role in the creation and maintenance of formal associations.

In the absence of any formal policy on the integration of refugees, refugee groups are treated in much the same way as immigrant and minority ethnic groups (Joly 1996a). The integration of refugees has been considered to be an issue for nongovernmental bodies, in line with the prevailing ethos in British society that places emphasis on the role which can and should be played in society by charities, volunteering and active citizenship (ECRE 1998). The Voluntary Services Unit at the Home Office is the only Government body with a specific remit to fund work with or for refugees, and funds agencies such as the Refugee Council and Refugee Action. Its community-oriented approach can therefore be considered to be transmitted to those agencies via its funding relationship.

But the assumption that refugee communities will emerge and play a supportive role in the lives of their members is predicated on the assumption that refugee groups will act in the same manner as immigrant groups made up of labour migrants, and this may not always be the case. With labour migrants, there is the possibility of chain migration that can then lead to the reconstruction and reconstitution of community based on village ties. This is not possible for refugees, whose pattern of migration is determined by the search for safety, and may not be linked to family, and who often lose kinship networks when they go into exile. To have an ethnic minority community, it is necessary to have some form of bond between members, and it is not automatic that people from the same area will create themselves into an ethnic group. The mode of definition for refugees may be different, and be related more to the conflict than to ethnicity.

The empowerment of its clients was one of the principles of the Bosnia Project (Morrison 1994). This was partly due to a consideration of the work of previous programmes for refugees in Britain, and an understanding of their strengths and weaknesses.

The Bosnia Project

The Bosnia Project should be seen against the background of previous government programmes. In most instances, refugees make their own way to Britain and make an individual application for asylum. In particular cases however the government has arranged programmes for the reception and settlement of groups of refugees, for example in the cases of Ugandan, Asian, Chilean and Vietnamese refugees. In each of these programmes a group approach was taken and special measures were introduced to assist the refugees' integration and settlement. The nature of these programmes differed, but the common involvement of some agencies and individuals has meant that to some extent each programme has been influenced by the one before. As with other refugees, an emphasis was placed on the role of the voluntary sector in implementing the programmes.

The Bosnia Project can be seen as having three distinct parts: the reception centres; mid-term support; and community development.

Reception Centre Phase

Though each reception centre had the same broad aims, there were differences between them in staffing levels, policies and standards of service.

The exact level of support received by residents varied between centres, and was also dependent on the level of occupancy of the centre. Some centre staff in the early days had time to accompany residents on driving lessons, though as the centres became busier this practice was rapidly dropped. There were few formal rules on the exact role of reception centre staff (Compass 1997; Robinson and Coleman 2000).

The length of stay in a reception centre was intended to be around three months and the residents were then to be housed in one of the cluster areas, usually in local authority or housing association rented properties. Each reception centre sent residents to specific cluster areas, for example Rugby sent residents mainly to Coventry, Solihull and Birmingham, whilst Dewsbury sent residents to Batley and Newcastle. As initial offers of housing were accepted, the choice for later arrivals became more limited, as cluster areas became 'full'. Housing choice was further limited by the unavailability of larger properties. Many residents wished to be housed in extended family units, but most housing authorities and housing associations had very few properties available with more than three bedrooms. Some families were allowed to remain in the reception centre until suitable accommodation could be found, but in other cases families had to be persuaded to accept two smaller properties instead of one large one.

Offers of housing were made without entering the normal waiting list procedures, and the families were usually not given an option to refuse. They were told that they could apply for a transfer after one year if they were unhappy, but refusal at the offer stage could result in homelessness.

Those that did not arrive as part of the Bosnia Project were not given access to this system. If they arrived as part of a humanitarian convoy, then the people who brought them into Britain arranged crisis accommodation for them, sometimes staying with British families, and then helped them to find rented accommodation. This could be in the public or private sector, depending on what was available in the local area.

Mid-term Support Phase

Once housed in one of the cluster areas, the refugee became the responsibility of the local mid term support team, a team of workers established in each region to provide support and advice. Theoretically this support was to be provided for six months, though in practice the demand-led nature of the service meant that it was difficult for individual workers to define their roles and duties.

The rationale for mid-term support work arose from a consideration of the experiences of those involved in the Vietnamese programme, and of the differences between the two programmes. It was felt that the lack of clarity about the status and length of stay of Bosnians would not encourage local agencies and local authorities to offer the same kind of support they had offered to Vietnamese refugees. It was also felt that settlement would be most successful where there was either an existing community from which support could be drawn, or some form of specialised support. Since there were no established Bosnian communities from which support could be drawn, some form of specialised support would therefore be necessary to avoid problems of isolation and to hopefully avoid the high levels of secondary migration noted amongst Vietnamese (Morrison 1994).

The mid-term support workers carried out a problem-solving and advocacy service on a casework basis, that is they worked mainly on solving individual problems rather than using a group approach. Workers were office-based, but would accompany clients to act as interpreters and advocates in certain situations. These situations were not clearly stated, which meant that the exact nature of the support provided, as with that provided by reception centre staff, was dependent to some extent on the number of clients the support worker had. The mid-term support system was a success in some ways, but the lack of a clear definition of mid-term support led to some confusion on the part of both clients and workers as to the level of service which could be expected.

There was no equivalent service for nonprogramme Bosnians, and instead they were reliant on whatever local support was available. In some cases, this meant that they received very little practical support, but in most cases they were able to use existing advice agencies such as Law Centres and Citizens Advice Bureaux, and Social Services Departments. Although these offered a much more restricted service compared with the Bosnia Project, the advice workers were trained and usually had greater experience of many of the problems that refugees experience, such as in the areas of housing and welfare benefits.

Community Development Phase

The community development phase was based on the model established in the later stage of the Vietnamese programme, whereby community development meant facilitating links between the refugee population, the host community, and local service providers; as well as assisting the members of the community to organise a formal community association. The Bosnia Project agencies actively supported the establishment of community associations in the cluster areas, with assistance from sympathetic individuals and groups in those areas. Initially it was hoped that these would take over much of the support work carried out by the Bosnia Project's mid-term support workers, but thus far they appear to be functioning more as social groups. The Refugee Council's evaluation of the project noted that the community groups existing at the time of its research performed a useful social function, but that 'most practical mutual support takes place outside the community group structure amongst neighbours and relatives' (Compass 1997). The individual community associations vary widely in their activities, degree of organisation, number of members, and level of funding. Of the five community associations examined in detail as part of my research, one existed in name only, and was in the process of trying to reinvent itself. A second was functioning thanks to the hard work of a few individuals, but was rife with internal disputes. A third, where there were no nonprogramme Bosnians, was active and carried out a range of activities, but was dependant on the leadership of one man with a strong desire to further the multicultural aims of the Bosnian government. The final two were in areas where there was a mixture of programme and nonprogramme Bosnians, and were led by Bosnians who had not come from the Bosnia Project.

Return

There is no organised programme of return for Bosnian refugees, unlike in some other European countries. Those who wish are allowed to travel to Bosnia for an exploratory visit of up to one month, without jeopardising their status, in order to satisfy themselves about the conditions should they wish to return. This applies to all those from Bosnia, not just those on the programme.

As the situation in Bosnia became calmer, some refugees returned. The Refugee Council estimates that of the 2,500 who came under the auspices of the programme, up to 250 have returned to Bosnia thus far. This figure includes some medical evacuees who returned as soon as they were well enough to do so.

Stages of Disempowerment

Concentration Camps and Disempowerment

Most of those that came to Britain as part of the programme had either been held in concentration camps in Bosnia, or were their dependants. These camps were the scenes of horrific treatment, and many of the inmates were killed. As such, they were the scene of major disempowerment for the inmates. All future developments for those inmates must therefore be seen as taking place with people who are totally disempowered, with all control over their lives taken away by their captors. The question to be asked about actions once released from the camps is therefore the extent to which the individuals were able to regain control over their own lives.

Those that arrived outside of the programme had mostly not been in the concentration camps, and instead they had fled to refugee camps in neighbouring countries. They were disempowered as well, since once in the refugee camps they were largely dependent on refugee agencies and voluntary groups for support, and for transport to Britain, but they were not starting from the same low point of total disempowerment.

The Programme and its Implementation

Many of those on the programme did not make a deliberate choice to come to Britain. Though theoretically the refugees themselves chose which country they wished to go to, in practice many were placed on the British programme despite preferring other countries, such as Germany or Austria, because at the time it offered the only places (McAfee 1998). In interviews, refugees stated that they either had asked to travel to another country but were told the only country that would accept them was Britain, or they were not allowed to express any preference and were told they had to go to Britain. The decision to come to Britain was therefore a negative decision, one made in the absence of other options, rather than a positive choice. Many families have been divided, and often Bosnians coming to Britain were deprived of support and companionship from family and friends. Research has found that many refugees experience feelings of loneliness and distress caused by this separation (Wilson 1998), and this can be considered as having a disempowering effect. This does not apply to those that were not part of the programme to the same extent. Those that became nonprogramme refugees left their homes and travelled to refugee centres in neighbouring countries when they felt that it was too dangerous to stay where they were, or to get away from the escalating conflict. When in these centres, they had a degree of choice as to whether they should remain where they were or join on of the vehicles offering evacuation. Although they had a very limited range of options, they did have some control over their destiny. However, those on the programme were refugees who had been held in concentration camps or who had been forcibly removed from their homes, and they could not be considered as having exercised any choices in the matter.

The way the policies of reception and mid-term support were implemented, despite the intention to empower clients (Morrison 1994), may have had the opposite effect. Job descriptions and the roles and responsibilities of staff, especially during the early stages of the programme, were not clearly defined either to the staff or clients (Compass 1997). Staff was at times accused of favouritism due to their giving more assistance to one family than another, but this accusation itself reflects the dependent relationship between the residents and the staff. A lack of time and in some cases training meant that workers would sometimes carry out tasks for their clients, rather than assisting the client to complete a task themselves, thus creating dependence.

The cluster-areas housing policy has been considered far more successful than previous dispersal policies (Compass 1997). Whilst refugees from Uganda largely ignored settlement guidelines and went to areas they were told were full, and Vietnamese moved to conurbations and away from areas where there were only one or two families, Bosnians who took part in the programme have on the whole remained in the area where they were first placed (see also Robinson and Coleman 2000). One of the main reasons for this seems to have been that the presence of others from the same area, combined with the availability of assistance from the mid-term support team, made the option of moving away less attractive. It should be noted, though, that the location of cluster areas was decided by the willingness of housing providers to make a quota of properties available, and this emphasis on housing has been to the detriment of employment. This is not the case in some other countries, for example France and Australia, where settlement policies emphasise the role of employment as well as housing. Britain has often concentrated on housing for refugees and ignored employment, which has had a detrimental effect on the ability of refugees to enter the labour market (Joly 1997). If economic independence is important for feelings of self-worth as well as for the economic wellbeing that employment usually brings (UNHCR 1997), then an empowering settlement project must also include employment as one of its objectives. However, in the case of this programme employment was not a priority. Whilst there was no discouragement of employment as such, the emphasis on accessing welfare benefits meant that there was little time available for employment advice.

Although many of the programme Bosnians have remained in the area that they were first housed in, the same pattern is not evident amongst those that were not part of the programme. In one town, I found that all the nonprogramme Bosnians had moved away, and in another around half had moved to another area. Those that had been in contact with people who had moved away said that the reasons for moving included a desire to move to areas were they were more likely to find employment, or they were moving to be close to friends and relatives, or they were searching for better quality housing. Since they had often been actively involved in the initial search for housing and applications for benefits, nonprogramme Bosnians were better equipped with the skills needed in moving from one area to another.

Temporary Protection and the Expectation of Return

The status of temporary protection given to Bosnian refugees who came as part of the programme gave them an additional level of insecurity.

Though it gave many of the same rights as full refugee status, it gave no guarantees as to the future. This was a special status, not given to other refugees or asylum seekers, stating explicitly on the visa document that the holder had temporary protection from the conflict in former Yugoslavia and would be expected to return when the British Government considered it safe to do so. This meant that the question of duration of exile and the issue of return were in the forefront of refugees' minds, regardless of their own view of eventual return. One effect of this found during research was that some of the refugees seemed to be continually waiting for something to happen. They were unable to influence their future by making a positive choice to remain or return, and were waiting for the decision to be made for them. This sense of insecurity about the future affected their interest in language classes and employment. Refugees not only faced many difficulties in learning English and obtaining employment (Hudson and Martenson 1998), but in addition for Bosnians there was little point in learning English if one expected to return shortly. Moreover, there was a strong belief that employers would not be interested in employing people who might be about to leave the country. Those that were not part of the programme often faced the same problems when seeking employment, but since they had refugee status or exceptional leave to remain, they had a degree of security about their status in Britain that those on the programme did not have. They did not have the same fears that the government might deem it safe for them to return to Bosnia and force them to return at short notice, and therefore were able to make more long-term plans.

For those that remain outside Bosnia, the question of return is not a matter of a simple choice between remaining or returning. The Dayton Agreement was the foundation for peace in Bosnia, and allowed for the return of displaced people to their homes or the area where they used to live. Though officially allowed to return, in practice there are many barriers, especially for those who would be returning to an area where they would form part of a minority community. The Dayton Agreement allowed for the creation of a single country, but within that country there are a series of cantons under the responsibility of either the Muslim-Croat Federation or the Serb Republic (Glenny 1999). Return of displaced people to areas controlled by the 'other side' is therefore not a simple issue, as it would affect the balance of power in the area. There is often opposition to the arrival of minorities from nationalist leaders, and there is often a fear on the part of those wishing to return that living under the authority of another ethnic group would be a major threat to their security and livelihood. The Dayton agreement does not alleviate these fears, and the implementation of the agreement has in many cases enhanced rather than dampened the nationalist standpoint (Cox 1998).

Expectations of 'the Community'

The premise which the agencies promoting community development adopted was firstly that the refugees, once housed in an area, would form a community; and secondly that the best way for the needs of this community to be met was through the creation of a formal community association which would empower the community members. This fails to take into account the idea that rather than being a 'natural' process, it may be a reflection more of British society than of immigrant inclinations. It has been suggested that the basis for group formation may lie in the way British institutions create spaces for the recognition of groups rather than individuals (Joly 1996b). Individuals need to form themselves into an association in order to enter into dialogue with the state (Favell 1998). However, the formation of an association can be very difficult for those who arrive en masse as opposed to groups who arrive through chain migration (Gold 1992). This is an important difference between refugee groups and other minority groups, as chain migration is far more common among labour migrants than refugees.

Among refugee groups there is often little group-wide organisation, and a typical feature is factionalism and segmentation (Gold 1992). There are often divisions within refugee groups based upon differences in class, politics, religion, and so forth (Salinas et al. 1987). This factionalism can inhibit attempts to create a formal association, or where an association is formed it may be unrepresentative. Among those who came on the programme, the majority are Muslim but there is a minority who are Catholic or Orthodox, and the question of who should be considered to be part of a Bosnian community can be a source of conflict. The Bosnian government on the whole articulates a notion of being Bosnian as secular, but with a majority Muslim component accepting of Serb, Croat, and other identities. For the refugees themselves, there is sometimes a difficulty in accepting this notion. Whilst many profess to bear no grudges against whole communities, there are some who feel distrust and resentment against all Serbs or Croats. This in itself is problematic, since Bosnia was almost like Orwell's 1984: the war had three protagonists, and allegiances changed during the course of the war. Muslims in the North of the country were imprisoned by Serbs, and many Croats in the region were treated as badly as Muslims. In the South and Herzegovina, Muslims were persecuted by Croats, and some owe their lives to Serb neighbours.

Generally, when refugee organisations are formed, they are organised in order to attempt to meet a specific need of the community (Salinas et al. 1987). The very existence of support services can be a disincentive to the formation of an association, since the provision of services takes away one of the main motives for forming an association (Gold 1992). It may be unrealistic to expect any formal associations formed to have much more than a social role throughout the time that other support mechanisms exist (Wahlbeck 1999). Yet this is precisely what was expected: associations were expected, not to identify the needs of their community and find ways of meeting those needs, but to take over the tasks which outside agencies had decided were important. This is not to suggest that these tasks were not themselves important, but this type of expectation cannot be empowering. To empower, there must be some input on the part of the client, yet in this case there was little client input.

Joly (1996a) suggests that for those refugees who were in a minority group in their country of origin or who had a clear political project, the notion of community association is more likely to be developed. However, if the group was not a minority and had little or no understanding of itself as a group, the process whereby a community is formed and a formal association established will be delayed, and may never happen at all. Refugees from Bosnia mostly did not have a political project in Bosnia, and their involvement in the war is very much portrayed by them as having been forced upon them by circumstances, rather than the result of, say, Muslim Bosnian political ambition. There is little history of formal organisation of Muslim Bosnians within Bosnia outside the area of organised religion. The immediate history of Yugoslavia as being state socialist gave little opportunity for organisation along ethnic lines. Indeed, the conflict in Yugoslavia, though often portrayed in the media as the inevitable result of ethnic or national antagonism, can be seen as having a variety of causes other than the articulation of ethnicity (Janjic 1995). If the ethnicisation of politics in Yugoslavia is recent, then the notion of a distinct Muslim Bosnian identity and hence a Muslim Bosnian community may also be relatively recent.

Unlike the majority of refugees from Vietnam, those from Bosnia do not have a definite project in Britain, that is to say they are unclear as to whether their future lies in Britain or in Bosnia, especially if they came as part of the programme. This means that their community associations are likely to be unclear as to their orientation, leading to difficulties in defining a role.

There was a presumption on the part of the refugee support agencies and some local authorities that refugees from Bosnia would be supported individually and as a group by British Muslims, due to their shared religious beliefs, but this support was not always forthcoming. For Bosnian Muslims to be able to identify with British Muslims, they need to have a concept of Islam as a factor that binds them to Muslims throughout the world. Bringa found that this identification with Muslims internationally was present amongst only a small number of Bosnian Muslims, those who were part of a small urban-oriented economic and religious elite (Bringa 1995). This suggests that an assumption that Bosnian Muslim refugees would automatically look to the wider Muslim community for support would be misplaced.

The practise of Islam in Bosnia was qualitatively different to that found in some other parts of the world, particularly South Asia from where the majority of British Muslims originate. Many in Bosnia were Muslim in name only, and did not practise their religion. Even for those who were practising, there were major differences (Bringa 1995) and these at times led British Muslims to accuse Bosnian Muslims of not being 'proper' Muslims, which in the context of the war in Bosnia was hurtful. Since their persecution and the death of their relatives had been predicated on their Muslimness, how could they then be questioned as to whether they were really Muslim? This lack of understanding between the two groups meant that the support of Britain's Muslim community could not always be depended on, and in seeking to create a community and association other resources had to be sought.

Conclusions

The biography of Bosnian refugees reflects a disempowering process by its very nature, whether or not they came as part of the programme. They were caught up in a war not of their making, and their situation as refugees has been forced on them by circumstances. The agencies supporting them in Britain have to some extent recognised their powerlessness, and the intention of programmes of work was to empower Bosnian refugees. In practice this worked out otherwise, however. If empowerment is about choices and positive decisions, then it is difficult to conceive of Bosnians on the programme as empowered. At almost every stage of the process of their construction as refugees in Britain, their choices have been severely limited or totally absent, and a sense of powerlessness has been reinforced. The particular circumstances of the programme of reception had some positive aspects, but the way it was implemented can be seen as disempowering. The emphasis on the role of a formal association ignores the lack of history of organisation as an ethnic group, and can be considered as imposing an identity on the community rather than allowing the group to find or create its own identity.

The notion of community has been seen as the solution to the refugees' disempowerment. The intention was for refugees to acquire skills and knowledge in order to support and assist each other, through the community, and to present a united front to service providers in order to gain greater resources for the group. Despite these intentions, too little attention was paid to empowerment in practice during the course of the Bosnia Project. Whether this was due to lack of experience or lack of time, the end result was the creation and maintenance of a dependent relationship between refugees and support staff. The high expectations placed on the formal community may eventually be met, but first it will be necessary for the group itself to attain a notion of 'community' in the informal sense.

Successful programmes of work with refugees, where there is a positive contribution to the refugee's quality of life, are important not only to the individual refugee, but also for the welfare of future refugees and asylum seekers. The development of an image of the refugee as an asset rather than a liability to the rest of society can contribute to the creation of a climate of opinion whereby the notion of refugee admission is not inextricably linked to discussions on the abuse of the asylum process (Majka 1991).

Bosnian refugees' experiences are important in the context of the Immigration and Asylum Act 1999. This ended all welfare benefits for asylum seekers and introduced their dispersal. The Government intends that placements of asylum seekers should take into account the need of asylum seekers to move to areas where there are existing communities from the country of origin and where relevant support from voluntary and community groups is available. An assumption appears to be being made on the role of 'community' in the settlement of refugees, an assumption that will not always prove to be correct. In addition, the provision of benefits in kind and the limitation on choice of location of residence could lead to the creation of additional dependence and have an adverse effect on the eventual settlement of successful asylum seekers.

If refugees are to be empowered, then it is not enough that the intention is to empower. It is important that the effects of all the policies surrounding their settlement are critically and carefully considered.

Notes

1. Kelly, L. 2001. 'Programme Policies, People: the Interaction between Bosnian Refugees and British Society', Centre for Research in Ethnic Relations, Coventry: University of Warwick.

10

Refugee-generated Return: The Case of Guatemala[1]

Anita Rapone and Charles Simpson

Introduction

Refugee populations constitute a set of unresolved problems. Given the desire of most refugees to return to their country of origin, the strain which refugees represent for less-developed countries of first asylum, and the increasing reluctance of the industrial world to accept refugees, the best available solution to the refugee crisis is repatriation (Coles 1989). But often the problems which generated a particular refugee flow – civil war, the destruction of infrastructure and the collapse of marketing systems, landlessness and deepening poverty, and government sponsored repression – are chronic and systemic, not episodic. Yet in the view of many refugees as well as host countries and the international community, return cannot await structural reform in their countries of origin. Although the United Nations High Commission for Refugees (UNHCR) has represented refugees in negotiations with host countries and countries of origin in an effort to assure safe reintegration, successful repatriation under hostile conditions has remained elusive (Goodwin-Gil 1989; Stein and Cuny 1991).

For more than a decade, refugee-policy analysts have discussed the relationship between development and successful repatriation. What has emerged in the literature is the view that (1) refugees must be involved in the development process; (2) successful repatriation depends upon appropriate economic and social development, not only for the refugees but also for the regions to which they return; (3) the development process must be linked to refugee aid and (4) successful repatriation is related to the development of civil society and national reconstruction (Cuénod

1989; Rogers 1992; Fagan 1993; Ruiz 1993). The experience of Guatemalans driven into exile in Mexico in the early 1980s indicates that the control and organisation of camp life by refugees themselves is a prelude to successful return, even when conditions in the country generating flight remain hostile to human rights.

In 1986 after several years in Mexican refugee camps, Guatemalan refugees began to discuss possibilities for their repatriation. Within two years they established the Permanent Commissions of Guatemalan Refugees in Mexico, composed of elected representatives from each of the camps, to plan and prepare for their return home and to negotiate the terms of that return directly with the government of Guatemala.

Their success in negotiating a reentry into a militarily conflictive Guatemala was based on their ability to conceptualise their political and social situation in counterhegemonic and empowering terms. The camps of refuge provided key resources, including escape from the control of a hostile state and the presence of a diversity of indigenous groups among the refugees. The refugees' varied community experiences prior to and during the army's 'scorched earth' campaign which sent them into flight, the presence of supportive nongovernmental agencies (NGOs), including the Catholic church, and Mayan neighbours who offered material aid constituted additional resources. In this camp setting, the refugees were able to reconstruct their lives, giving organisational form to an increasingly sophisticated social consciousness. In Freirean terms (Freire 1973: 3–20), they were able to escape the atomising intent of the Guatemalan government's genocidal violence and become subjects determined to shape their own history. Faced with a choice between risking assimilation in camps-with-no-future or possible death if, as isolated families, they returned to rural areas terrorised by government-sponsored paramilitary groups, these refugees gathered the material and organisational resources to forge a third course: human development in the camps while they negotiated their collective return to rural Guatemala as autonomous communities monitored by international human rights organisations.

These Permanent Commissions offer a viable example of orderly and effective repatriation in which refugees play the leading organising role and in which the necessary regional development begins in the camps of the host country.

Development and Violence

While neoliberal ideology treats the elimination of the subsistence peasantry as an essential step to modernisation (Rostow 1960), Guatemalan development from the expansion of coffee estates in the 1870s to the cotton boom of the 1960s has been built on the availability of this sector.

Driven to marginal areas by the plantation building of the elite, indigenous small farmers were permitted to retain relatively autonomous communal life on lands too poor for self-sufficiency. Endemic poverty and, up to the 1940s, national labour laws required the poor to enlist as plantation labourers. Subsidising themselves by farming their own tiny plots, they comprised a rural seasonal proletariat that could be maintained at less than subsistence wages (Simpson 1994).

Development strategy from the 1970s to the 1990s combined coffee and cotton production with 'nontraditional' agri-export production and garment assembly undertaken by women displaced from the countryside. Discontented peasants were shifted into expanding economic sectors in a way that avoided restructuring land tenure. The oligarchy, with new members drawn from the professional and military officer ranks, expanded their landholdings as opportunities arose and employed permanent rather than migrant labour.

This neoliberal development strategy coincided with greater impoverishment of the majority of the population. Between 1980 and 1987, the portion below the poverty line increased from 79 to 87 percent; those unable to secure a minimum diet increased from 52 percent in 1980 to 72 percent by 1990. Two percent of the farms occupied 65 percent of the country's arable land, while 80 percent were crowded into 10 percent – the worst land distribution pattern in the Americas (Jonas 1992: 177–78). In 1993 the Organisation of American States (OAS) found that 'enjoyment of socio-economic and cultural rights is reserved to a small percentage of the population while the rest endure the worst social conditions in the Americas, with the exception of Haiti' (OAS 1993: 105).

Since 1954, this 'caste arrangement' was held in place by government counterrevolutionary violence. The military became both the agent of and a sector within the national bourgeoisie, with arms factories and a banking system. Generals emerged from the violence of the 1980s as cattle barons on what had been national lands or Indian community property. Peasants and labourers who protested against this system were treated as the popular base of the ongoing armed insurgency and repressed.

Flight and Regrouping in Mexico

Between 1981 and 1984, approximately 150,000 Guatemalans fled into Mexico to escape the military's 'scorched earth' campaign concentrated in the northern provinces. Surviving the initial assaults, hiding in the jungle in hopes the army might leave, and the flight to Mexico required an intensified community unity and the creation of pragmatic leadership.

Some communities, unarmed and distinct from the guerrillas, tried to frustrate the military sweeps. When the army interrupted its campaign in the Ixcán in November 1981 to regroup for a new offensive, people sabotaged the landing strips, burned down the barracks, and turned to collective farming to more effectively watch for the army's return (Falla 1994: 47, 137).

The army did return, rolling inexorably from east to west, killing peasants and guerrillas alike. Yet the response of the peasants remained collective. As some went to remote parcelas to gather survivors, they stressed the needs of the community as a whole. One farmer reported that he asked other survivors about the missing and confronted them with the certainty that those who were absent were in fact dead in order to get them to seek cover in the jungle. Orphans were incorporated into new families (Falla 1994: 100–01).

By 1984, about 46,000 of these refugees had settled into small camps along the border in the Mexican state of Chiapas (Manz 1988: 217–18), aided by the Catholic Church and by Mexican indigenous communities who had begun to colonise this rainforest region twenty years before. As a Mayan area, where some ethnolinguistic groups, Mam for example, span the national boundary, it was conducive to the refugees' efforts to rebuild their communities (Méndez 1994: 72–74).

Difficulties, however, were significant. The Guatemalan army crossed the border in 1981 and 1982, kidnapping or killing those it accused of supporting insurgency. Mexican policy was also disruptive. Between 1981 and 1982, approximately 4,000 refugees were deported to Guatemala, and in 1984 15,000 refugees were forcibly relocated to new camps in the Yucatan states of Quintana Roo and Campeche.

From the beginning, the Catholic Church in Chiapas under Bishop Samuel Ruiz assumed a role of protective intervention. It protested the initial deportations of refugees and generated human rights pressure that halted this practice. Ruiz, an exponent of liberation theology, created the Comité Cristiano de Solidaridad in 1979 to work with refugees, initially providing the only institutional assistance available to them. It secured land, on which the refugees could settle and grow crops, and provided food and building materials. When the refugees perceived the need to train their own teachers and health promoters, a Comité team provided the instruction.

The Centrality of Consciousness

While Guatemalan refugees shared a culture that valued community unity, they varied in their experience with community organisation. One subpopulation from the smaller and more remote hamlets of the Guatemalan Highlands had been less touched by the wave of economic and community development of the 1970s. Consequently, their communities had more intact traditional systems: cofradías (religious brother-hoods) celebrating the saints, a civil-religious hierarchy of authority and prestige, and a functioning system of elders who, together with the elected mayor, settled disputes internal to the community. A second group in the camps were those driven from the large resettle-ment colonies in the Ixcán, a population with a clearly shaped social organisation and consciousness as a result of successfully building co-operative economies and social systems. Settlers first arrived in the Ixcán in 1966 with Maryknoll priest Edward Doheny in a joint project of the Church and the National Institute of Agrarian Transformation (INTA). William Woods, the Maryknoll priest who replaced Doheny in 1969, reduced the role of INTA, invited in more people from the Highlands, and insisted on collective ownership. The group was multiethnic and multi-lingual. These communities, developed initially within the context of a government, which saw colonisation as a safety valve to reduce social pressure for systemic land reform, soon became the object of government suspicion and hostility. In 1976 Woods' plane was shot down, presumably by the Army; in 1978 his replacement, the German priest Karl Stettler, was deported. Over the next three years, about fifty cooperative participants were kidnapped and 'disappeared'. With the new presidential regime of Lucas García in 1979, a full-scale war was launched against guerrillas and peasants alike in the Ixcán region of colonisation.

A similar group of refugees came from the Petén, which after the Ixcán, was the point of origin of the largest number of refugees. They had origi-nally migrated to the Petén as part of a colonisation drive by the govern-ment beginning in the 1960s and had settled in a cluster of cooperatives along the Mexican border. Some were ladinos, people who do not social-ly identify as Indians. Displaced by a combination of war and the consol-idation of land into large estates by military and other landowners during the Lucas García administration, these refugees brought significant expe-rience in cooperative work (COMADEP n.d.a; Falla 1994: 19–31; Yoldi 1996).

Giving up their lands in the face of the Army's murderous advance was difficult for all the cooperative settlers.

> Beginning in 1960, many of us campesinos who are now refugees had begun to colonise new lands in Huehuetenango, El Quiché, El Petén and Alta Verapaz which from then were recognised as our property and that we made produc-tive at the cost of the lives of many of our children who died in the labours of colonisation. We succeeded in developing an economy with hopeful possibili-ties that had already begun to give the first fruits for us and our country. (Permanent Commissions 1989: 5)

The refugees accumulated their own direct experience of the repression during the period of massacre and flight. This became their master narrative. It explained their identity, social location, and relationship to one another and to the state of Guatemala. Individual survival stories were shared among refugees and retold to relief workers. Sympathetic audiences validated these tales of loss and survival as parts of a general description of social reality. In this way the refugees overcame the political paralysis and atomisation which was the goal of the counterinsurgency campaign of the Guatemalan Army (Barry 1986). Convinced of the validity of their own understanding, refugees rejected the army's account of the massacres as the fault of the peasants themselves. They also became inoculated with scepticism towards the patriotic declarations of the Guatemalan government as it encouraged individual repatriation into militarily controlled 'model villages' and 'development poles'.

As camp residents became conversant in the vocabulary of moral and legal rights used by church workers, international humanitarian groups, and the UNHCR, they formulated their understanding of political reality and social development as a struggle to secure those rights. This deepened their belief in the moral right to life located in indigenous culture and articulated by progressive priests (Episcopado 1988; Watanabe 1992).

Self-organisation in Refuge

Several factors created space in which the refugees could organise. Because Mexico was not a signatory to the UN Convention on Refugees of 1951 nor the Protocol of 1967, the UNHCR could not work directly and so channelled its aid through the Mexican government agency, the Comisión Mexicana de Ayuda a Refugiados. Early participation of the Catholic Church opened up other nongovernmental channels of support to the refugees. Most importantly, the Comisión was inconsistent in delivering relief and slow to monitor camp administration, providing the refugees with the need and opportunity to organise for their own survival.

Even where refugees received raw land, survival was an immediate concern. Decisions had to be made about the placement of houses and garden plots, latrines and washing areas. Groups were formed to address a variety of functional needs: foraging for wild food and firewood, erecting shelters from plastic sheeting and roofing supplied by aid agencies, turning over and planting common fields. As family shelter was secured, camp residents erected community facilities, including multipurpose structures for general meetings and religious services. Two principles characterised this work: deliberation to achieve consensus on decisions involving the interests of the camp as a whole and the delegation of tasks to appointed or volunteer teams.

Camp organisation consisted of a general assembly and a committee of representatives of neighbourhoods and sectors, that is areas of designated services. Initially these were health, education, and religion, each undertaken by lay promoters. The general assembly comprising all camp residents was the ultimate authority, meeting annually and intermittently as necessary. The committee of representatives handled the day-to-day administration of the camp.

Refugees drew on their past cooperative experiences. At Quetzal Edzná, for example, after a hurricane damaged the ageing temporary housing and the Mexican refugee agency began plans to relocate residents to another camp, the community formed a cooperative of all 370 households. They assessed themselves at five pesos each to create working capital and began the reconstruction of housing.

> We had positive experiences working in a cooperative. It was the form in Guatemala, in the Ixcán and the Petén, that we had gotten land and through which we were commercialising our products like coffee and cardamom. We saw that in working in this form, all the community was benefited, something that individually we had never achieved. Almost all of us were members of a cooperative and some had experience as directors of these cooperatives. We thought to revive and recover this experience that during the refuge was being lost on account of all the movement and dispersion. We saw the need to create again the same structure embracing all the sectors of our community in order to try to solve general problems ... (La Cooperativa 1991: 6)

Struggle for Control of the Return

The possibility of full-scale repatriation arose in 1986 with the return of civilian government to Guatemala. International pressure was building to end the violence and establish a more secure environment for foreign investment. The new president, Vinicio Cerezo, visited Mexico in July 1986 for talks on several topics, including the refugees. The refugees took advantage of his visit to raise their grievances in a public letter affirming their desire to return, protesting the redistribution of their lands, and demanding that those responsible for the massacres be punished (*La Jornada* 1986). When President Cerezo promised to send a delegation headed by his wife, the refugees prepared for this visit by meeting throughout the camps to develop a unified position on repatriation.

In developing political consensus, the refugees faced problems of communication. One mechanism to keep refugees up-to-date on news from Guatemala and other camps was a broadcast programme circulated on audiocassettes that linked the camps to the activities of the popular movement in Guatemala, brought news of guerrilla engagements with the army, listed recent human rights abuses, and exhorted listeners to action:

We should remember always that though we are refugees we are Guatemalans and we have to continue forward, we must not go backward, we must unite. We must not let ourselves be deceived and we must have much faith and much confidence that with the aid of God and with our struggle and the struggle of our brothers in Guatemala, some day we will be free and our children will grow up in a free country where there are not assassinations, kidnappings, nor displaced people nor refugees anywhere. (Broadcast 1986)

With the signing of the Esquipulas II agreement in 1987 that defined displacement as a Central American problem, the refugees in Mexico moved to the centre of regional deliberations. Given participatory self-government within the camps, they were able to respond to this historical opening by creating an organisation to negotiate the conditions of their return directly with the Government of Guatemala. They began intense organising and in December held elections in all camps to choose representatives for this new structure, the Permanent Commissions of Guatemalan Refugees in Mexico. 'The door opened a little for our participation. Each community named a representative, we convoked a general assembly of refugees and 1,000 representatives came' (CONONGAR 1991: 28).

The Permanent Commissions campaigned hard for the right to participate in the Esquipulas process. On 15 February 1988, they sent a letter to the Executive Committee of Esquipulas II, asserting their desire to participate in all discussions of their situation 'since without our participation there will not be a just nor possible solution'. Later that year they sent a letter to Monseñor Rodolfo Quezada Toruño, president of the Committee of National Reconciliation, noting that they were ready to return to Guatemala when 'there are conditions of personal and collective security', and asking for the restitution of their lands. They asked to formally participate in the dialogue 'with voice and vote' (Permanent Commissions 1988a; 1988b).

After a long struggle, the Permanent Commissions were accepted as the legitimate representatives of the refugees in Mexico. In their address at the opening working session in February 1989, they argued their right to self-representation and full participation in negotiations at all levels. The Permanent Commissions presented six demands for their return that formed the core of their negotiations: (1) the right to a voluntary, collective and organised return; (2) the right to return to and take possession of their lands; (3) the right to organise and to free association; (4) the right to personal and community security; (5) the right to national and international accompaniment; (6) the freedom of national and international movement of the Permanent Commissions (Permanent Commissions 1989: 6–9).

These objectives made explicit several points of the refugees' emerging development model. A voluntary and collective return would allow them to build self-regulating communities; obtaining adequate land was a precondition for reestablishing a peasant economy, and the free movement of Permanent Commissions delegations was necessary to identify available land; free association would allow them to interact with the popular movement in Guatemala to rebuild the country; the right to individual and community security, supported by international accompaniment, gave them some assurance that they could begin the process of social reconstruction without army interference.

Community Development for the Return

The consolidation of disparate individuals and groups into self-administering camps required a transformation of consciousness. The experience of the massacres and the flight into Mexico had to be retrieved from the depths of painful subjectivity and made public. As this conceptual framework knit together, it located the camp experience within a broadening historical narrative. On one side, this tale expanded backwards to make meaningful the thirty-year civil war and ultimately the last five hundred years of colonial subjugation. On the forward edge of consciousness, camp life was transformed from an historical end point of displacement and cultural ruin into a new beginning, a preparation for a return to reconstruct Guatemala.

In this process of consciousness building, the approach to education was key. Camp residents understood schooling as having both skills and cultural-political components, able to communicate Guatemalan indigenous values to students and prepare them for the return home. Said one refugee:

> The possibility of our children attending Mexican primary schools was discussed a lot and rejected. We though that if they entered the Mexican schools, our community would break up. (Tidwell 1994: 83)

The solution was to collectively construct school buildings within each camp. Committees of parents selected individuals with a few years of schooling to be educational promoters and closely supervised their work. When the promoters were sent from the camps for further education, they were expected to remain responsible to the community rather than become individuated professionals (Tidwell 1994: 90).

The Comité Cristiano played a supervising role in the organisation of the schools and helped obtain educational material about Guatemala that reflected the perspective of the refugees. The social history book used in El Porvenir, for example, began by celebrating the achievements of the ancient Maya and included passages from the Popol Wuh, a central Mayan cultural text dating from before the Spanish conquest. This refugee-generated text discussed racism and Indian resistance during the colonial period and celebrated the social reforms of the 'democratic spring' from 1944 to the coup of 1954. The text concluded with a discussion of the violence, which sent the community into refuge. One promoter said:

> This is a struggle through education of a people who want to return to their lands without returning to the same kinds of suffering that touched our lives there before. This is a struggle for a more just society. (Tidwell 1994: 100)

Organising schools taught the refugees the necessity of a sophisticated defence of their autonomy. By 1989, the Mexican refugee agency began to believe that refugees should be adjusted to longer-term residence in Mexico. Citing the unconstitutionality of the Church's involvement with state functions, it moved to take control of refugee education and to replace the promoters with Mexican-certified teachers. The refugees interpreted this as an attempt to force them to either Mexicanise or immediately begin repatriation to Guatemala, and they resisted for a year through a committee of promoters and community representatives. While defending their rights as refugees to retain their culture and negotiate their return in an orderly way, the refugees also began to see that Mexican teaching certificates could be valuable resources in Guatemala, allowing them to staff their future schools with their own teachers. So they compromised. The Mexican educational system took over all courses with the exception of social history, which the Comité Cristiano continued to supervise. Using refugee labour, the Comité then constructed a secondary school in Nuevo Huixtán in 1989 to educate refugees and other local indigenous. This school used a Mexican curriculum to prepare students to pass the Mexican teacher certification exams. It also educated health promoters and agricultural technicians 'so youth will acquire the training to better serve their communities' (Comité 1990; Tidwell 1994: 118–23).

In each sector, promoters selected by the community kept it informed about their work. Once trained, they provided leadership for decisions in their respective areas. As they taught others, their knowledge was disseminated horizontally and hierarchy minimised. Like Gramsci's 'organic intellectuals' (Gramsci 1971: 6–20), leaders/promoters remained embedded in their communities, approaching their functions in a broadly political manner.

With human rights abuses still common in Guatemala, the anticipated return required that refugees educate themselves in this new area. The Permanent Commissions, therefore, initiated a set of workshops, with staff provided by NGOs. The participants were drawn from several camps and returned to their communities to teach others. These human rights promoters were then incorporated into the camp organisational structure.

Ecological responsibility was also taught. Just as communities were to derive strength from their cultures and identities, economic growth was seen as having to respect the natural surroundings.

Ecologically sensitive development promotes the satisfaction of community needs through appropriate cultivation which does not degrade the environment, requiring both conservation policies and practical and theoretical environmental education. (COMADEP n.d.b.: 28)

As women began to build their own organisations, they comprised a new community sector. The first inter-camp initiative by women, an assembly in 1990, resulted in the formation of Mamá Maquín. A few months later, with assistance from UNHCR, members conducted a survey of women in the Chiapas camps. Identifying illiteracy as a major problem, they launched a promoter programme for women. Supported by international human rights groups, Mamá Maquín rented a house in Comitán as a training centre to educate refugee women in community participation as well as literacy. Said one promoter:

> In the camps women were never counted on to organise anything. The idea of women as an organised sector was never put forward. Some women were organised with the men around some immediate necessity, like a [corn] mill project. But women never publicly discussed the future or general rights. We knew it would be difficult to organise because of what men would say, but we travelled to all the camps in July of 1990. It was the first time we had travelled like this. Half of the refugees are women. We felt we needed a voice to bring something to the discussion of the return. And we got a good response from men as well as women. Five hundred women attended our initial assembly. (Mamá Maquín 1991)

After the first return of refugees in 1993, the Permanent Commissions created three branches to organise subsequent returns to distinct areas of Guatemala. Mamá Maquín became the women's group for the Northwest Branch; women headed for the Petén organised as Ixmucané, while women returning to the South Coast founded Madre Tierra.

The Struggle of Return

From the beginning of the National Dialogue, it took nearly two years for the negotiations between the Permanent Commissions and the Government of Guatemala to reach a firm footing and another two years to finalise an agreement. During that time, the Permanent Commissions implemented a multilevel strategy of building national and international support and solidarity. In the first ten months of 1991, for example, they enlisted the support of the ambassadors to Guatemala from Canada and

Sweden, sent delegations to the bishops in Guatemala, forged links with both rural and urban popular groups, and hosted a visit of the Guatemalan bishops. By the end of 1991, they had amplified their working concept of return to include the logistics of the move and took the significant steps of involving the governments of Canada, Sweden, France and Mexico in the creation of the International Group of Accompaniers to the Return and establishing mechanisms for addressing land problems. Finally, on 8 October 1992, the Permanent Commissions and the Government of Guatemala signed an agreement that embodied all of the conditions which the refugees had articulated in 1989.

In 1993, the Permanent Commissions began the programme of organised, collective return. While many refugee groups wished to resettle on the land from which they had been driven in 1981 and 1982, such resettlement was complicated. Declaring much of this land to be abandoned, the government had redistributed it to commercial farms and to groups of the internally displaced or otherwise landless. Army influence over these recent settlers through civil patrols and the uncertainty of their tenure caused many to oppose the return of the refugees. The patrols were paramilitary squads organised ostensibly to guard against guerrilla incursions. Working through the patrols, the army was able to gather information about dissenters, conscript peasants into military service, and paralyse independent peasant organisation with the fear of being denounced as guerrillas (Jay 1993).

In addition, the government controlled technical aspects of the return, principally loans for land purchase and permits for settlement in areas defined as ecologically sensitive. Any one of several ministries, reflecting various interest groups among the oligarchy and the army, could bring the approval process to a halt. Delays were common, and the refugees resorted to the intercession of the International Group of Accompaniers and others for mediation. They also resorted to direct action, including at times occupying a Guatemalan consulate in Mexico and crossing the border without approval.

The returns involved protracted struggles, beginning with the first, initially set for July 1992. Anticipating this date, the participants sold belongings and did not plant a crop. Encountering resistance from the Government of Guatemala, the Permanent Commissions postponed the departure to November, and then to 13 January 1993. The issue in contention was political and symbolic: the refugees wanted the first return to include a procession into Guatemala City for a ceremonial welcome; the Guatemalan government insisted on a low-profile journey directly to the remote resettlement area in the Ixcán. With the Permanent Commissions unwilling to give the signal to start the return and the UNHCR and the Mexican refugee agency opposed to any move lacking the support of the Guatemalan government, refugee families moved out of the camps and assembled near the border at Comitán as 13 January neared. The government then caved in and agreed to a route through the capital rather than oppose the refugees with force at the border. The families crossed into Guatemala on 20 January in seventy-seven buses, and continued to Guatemala City and a national welcome (COMADEP 1993). But it was eleven months before the next return and it was not until April 1995 that the first return to the South Coast was accomplished (Activa y Objectiva 1995: 8).

Community Development and the Return

In October 1994, 270 families, comprising La Cooperativa La Unión Maya, arrived on the former commercial farm of Xamán, approximately 5,575 acres of open pasture and wooded hills. They were joined by an additional fifty internally displaced families who were already living there despite the efforts of the former estate owners to evict them. Before their flight to Mexico in 1982, some of the returnees were settlers in this region, but they were unable to occupy their original communities due to hostility from more recent occupants placed there by the army (Yoldi 1996: 173-77). This community, now called Aurora 8 de Octubre, which we visited in June 1996, illustrates the features of refugee-initiated community development in Guatemala.

A year after its establishment, Aurora's social organisation was emphasising unity and cooperation, with a general assembly deliberating strategic decisions and a directive council handling day-to-day administration. The latter integrated representatives of the sectors, representatives to the Permanent Commissions, and delegates from the neighbourhoods of distinct linguistic groups – Mam, Kanjobal, and Ke'kchi. The cooperative, involving all households, organised the common productive life of the community. Sectors extended their reach outside the immediate community. Mamá Maquín held meetings with women's organisations in other communities, while education and health promoters met regionally for training. Aurora's social structure mirrored that which had evolved in the camps of refuge.

Household plots of about 3.5 acres were laid out on graded, unpaved streets leading to the urban centre. These allowed each family to produce food sufficient for its own consumption. Banana trees, corn and vegetables, and foraging goats, chickens, and turkeys were evident on each plot. Houses were also the centre of weaving and hammock making, skills learned or enhanced in the training classes in Mexico. As already mentioned, respect for the ecological limits to development had been part of the planning in Mexico. In Aurora, the results of ecological sensitivity including a potable water system piped to centralised taps at various locations, preservation of the river which runs through the community from silting and pollution, and a project to switch house construction from boards to cement blocks. Residents were selectively harvesting and milling local wood into school desks, window frames, and doors for community use.

The second tier of the economy was cooperative commercial production. Residents quickly learned rubber tapping and planned to expand an existing grove of rubber trees. A planting of cardamom had yet to produce a profitable crop, however. The cooperative was also diversifying into cattle. From an original herd of thirty cows, they planned to increase the number to six hundred. The cooperative obtained a loan from the government development agency to purchase the property. On repayment the money will revert to the community as a fund for further investment, to purchase additional land as the population increases, and for community improvements.

Residents provided community services. Education promoters, trained and certified in Mexico, were recognised by the government that now paid their salaries. The construction of a permanent elementary school was underway at the time of our visit. Six health promoters, who collectively spoke each of the three community languages plus Spanish, staffed a clinic. Mamá Maquín initiated a project to build two diesel-powered corn mills with funding from NGOs and opened a small restaurant, with additional NGO support, in order to raise money for various women's activities.

Solidarity with outside groups was evident. Regionally displaced families were brought into the community as members and the clinic and school serviced the wider area. International NGOs provided essential funding and training at this early stage of community formation. The UN human rights representative had installed a solar-powered radio and internationals acting as human rights monitors were a resident presence in the community.

But Aurora also exemplified the political constraints on development in Guatemala. In October 1995, a few days before the community's first anniversary, a platoon from the regional Army base entered. After a confrontation with residents, who challenged their right to be there under specific provisions of the Accord, the soldiers opened fire, killing eleven and seriously wounding at least thirty. The community subsequently fought the repression on several fronts, including a solidarity tour of the United States and a lawsuit.

Conclusion

The repatriation process of the Guatemalan refugees demonstrates the inseparability of the political process of return from the economic dimensions of rebuilding communities in the country of origin. In the literature on repatriation, four elements have been identified as necessary for a successful return. The experience not only includes these elements; it demonstrates the usefulness of extending them in a direction which takes as its central assumption the autonomy, agency, and community nature of refugee populations.

The first element is involvement of the refugees themselves in the development process. By taking charge of the negotiations for their repatriation, the Guatemalans went far beyond simple involvement. They selected their return sites, contacted surrounding communities to make themselves known, and insisted on an assembly/promoter model for decision making and the provision of education, healthcare, and religious activities.

The second element is appropriate economic and social development both for refugees and the regions into which they are reinserted. In the present case, great care was taken to see that development initiatives fit the human capital of the refugees as a land-based population and their cultural needs as Mayans. The refugees obtained guarantees of their right to land in the Accords negotiated with the Government of Guatemala. This base gave them the flexibility to address their subsistence needs as families and communities as well as engage in market economic enterprises. The assignment of land to community cooperatives and through them to families provided the framework within which the institutions of collective life and mutual aid could be constructed. Community-based social services were consciously made available to surrounding rural populations, specifically, healthcare, schools and access to retail goods.

The third element is the availability of aid linked to development. The Guatemalans received aid from a variety of sources: The United Nations, Mexico, the Catholic Church, and various Guatemalan and international NGOs. Projects reinforced Mayan identity, community control, and the human capital of the refugees themselves as skilled workers and organisational participants. The refugees also sought and obtained what might be called political or solidarity aid. That is, they invited an international presence into their communities from the earliest days of exile and guaranteed in the signed Accords their right to national and international observers during and after their return to Guatemala.

The last element is the development of civil society and national reconstruction. The Accords negotiated by the Permanent Commissions included the right to freely associate with other groups in Guatemala upon their return, providing the freedom to forge ties with national peasant groups, Mayan cultural associations, and worker organisations. In these Accords, the refugees declared their intent to 'return to reconstruct the country'. Whether such a reconstruction of civil rights, open political participation and the rule of law takes place is still in doubt. However, the refugees recognised from the beginning that the only route to such a reconstruction, and hence their own security, was through linkages with broad sectors of Guatemalan society.

Notes

1. This chapter is based on interviews with refugees and human rights and development workers conducted in Mexico City, Chiapas, and Guatemala in July–August 1991, in Mexico City and Campeche in May 1994, Quintana Roo in July 1994, Chiapas and Guatemala in June 1995, and Mexico City in August 1995 and March 1996. We spoke with representatives of the UNHCR, the Comité Cristiano de Solidaridad, the Permanent Commissions and various NGOs. In June 1996 we visited two returnee communities in the Ixcán. The analysis draws on documents from the archives of the Consultoria Mesoamericana de Assistencia y Desarrollo Popular (COMADEP) and CERIGUA News Service in Mexico City.

11

Between Victim and Agent: Women's Ambivalent Empowerment in Displacement[1]

Darini Rajasingham-Senanayake

Introduction

Highlighting gross violations of women's bodies and space in situations of conflict and displacement has been part of an important intervention by activists and women's groups to promote women's rights as human rights internationally. The various and systematic forms of violence that women experience at the hands of armed combatants, whether state armies or paramilitary personnel, in situations of armed conflict and displacement was extensively documented in the former Yugoslavia, Rwanda, and other parts of Africa and Asia. This process culminated in the UN resolution that established rape as a war crime and saw the appointment of the first UN Special Rapporteur on Violence against Women in 1994. But the focus on women as 'victims' of war and displacement in international human rights and humanitarian discourses may have also resulted in the elision of how long-term social upheaval might have transformed gender roles and provided new spaces for women's agency.

Of course, women's agency, or to use a term more commonly found in development policy discourse, women's 'empowerment', is rarely unambivalent. Likewise, it has been argued that agency is not wholly encompassed by political activism (Jeffery 1999). Academic and development policy studies of women in conflict situations have only recently begun to address the deeper social and economic transformations that armed conflicts engender, though the former have often focused on women's political and nationalist mobilisation, and the latter on women in governance, as a point of analytic departure (Schalk 1990; Adele 1993).

This chapter explores women's agency by studying the new roles that women, displaced and affected by the war, perform in their everyday activities in the north and east of Sri Lanka. It traces socioeconomic and cultural transformations in gendered practice by exploring emergent spaces and cultural discourses for women's agency and leadership within changing family and community structures generated by conflict and displacement. I argue that the tendency to view women as 'victims' in popular and humanitarian policy discourse has largely obscured the fact that many civilian women have taken on unaccustomed roles, such as head of household and principal income generator due to loss of male family members and displacement. While many have suffered the trauma of bombing, shelling, loss of family members, (extended) family fragmentation, and displacement, they also increasingly deal with the authorities, from the Government Agent, to the military, to the humanitarian aid agencies in the war zones and refugee camps. They file documents, plead their cases and implement decisions in public and private in the presence or absence of their men folk. The latter are increasingly disempowered or have disappeared, even as they formally take on the role of principal income generator and head of household.

Historically, women who took on various nontraditional gender roles in situations of social stress, conflict, war and revolution, have been 'pushed back into the kitchen after the revolution' as part of a return to everyday life (Enloe 1983; Jayawardena 1986). Arguably, one of the primary reasons that the return to peace often meant a return to the gender status quo was the lack of social recognition and a culturally appropriate idiom to articulate, legitimate and support women's transformed roles and agency in the midst of conflict, trauma, and social disruption. For social transformation to be sustained there needs to be recognition and the acceptance of the legitimacy of women performing new nontraditional gender roles, such as head of household.

For, after all, gender hierarchy is one of the old-established institutions of society, and as Partha Chatterjee (1989) noted women are frequently constructed as the central purveyors of a community's 'culture' and 'tradition', ironically precisely at a time that their lives and social roles might be undergoing great transformations. Likewise, as numerous feminist analyses have pointed out, in periods of violent nationalist conflict women often are constructed as the bearers of a threatened national culture, values and tradition. Hence, often a return to peace is indexed in the return to the gender status quo, a situation that denies women's agency and catalytic roles in conflict and displacement.

Analysing women's new roles and the cultural frameworks that enable or disable women's agency in conflict situations could provide us with an understanding of how to enhance women's agency in postconflict situations. Likewise, unless the cultural frameworks that denigrate women's new roles are challenged and transformed women and men who are coping and trying to recover from the wounds of war will carry a double burden – rather than be empowered in the new roles thrust upon them. In charting the shifting terrain of women's ambivalent agency I start from the premise that conflict affects women and men differently, depending on religion, caste, class, ethnicity, location, political affiliation, etcetera. But conflict also reveals a certain commonality in women's experience. Women experience particularly gendered forms of violence, such as rape and the fear of rape, body searches and the fear of sexual violence, as well as the social stigmas which dog women who have been raped. Fear of sexual violence limits and inhibits most women's mobility and hence their livelihoods, choices and realities. Despite the commonly experienced threat of gendered violence women react differently to nationalist armed violence: some like the women cadres of the Liberation Tigers of Tamil Eelam (LTTE), or the women cadres of the Sri Lanka Army and Air Force, have been radicalised and taken up guns and weaponry for their respective nationalist struggles. Others have become political and social activists for peace, seeking to build alliances across ethnic, cultural and regional borders (Mothers' Front, Mothers and Daughters of Lanka, Mothers of the Disappeared, Women for Peace, and Women's Coalition for Peace).

The first section of this chapter examines displaced women's new roles in light of a critique of the construct of women as 'victims' only: of war, caste and culture.[2] The second part assesses the implications of women's transformed roles for humanitarian interventions and development work in war and peacetime. I draw from ethnographic field research conducted during several field work stints over a number of years (1996–2000) among communities in the 'border areas' – both cleared and uncleared areas as they have come to be termed in the media and popular culture in Sri Lanka. This border constitutes the shifting 'forward defence line', that demarcated land held by the military and the LTTE fighting for a separate state. Roughly, the border runs from the main eastern town of Batticaloa in the east, to Vavuniya at the centre, to Mannar in the west of the island. It encompasses most of the eastern and north central provinces that have experienced cycles of violent armed conflict, including repeated bombing, shelling and displacement of civilian populations. In particular, my observations are drawn from interviews conducted with displaced women living in so-called 'Welfare centres', i.e. refugee camps, and new settlements in Vavuniya.

Women as 'Victims' of War, Caste, Culture

Between 1983 and 2001, when Sri Lanka's ethnic conflict, transmuted into a dirty war perpetrated by a number of armed forces and groups in the conflict, affected north eastern border areas, civilian men and women lived amidst overlapping regimes of 'security'. Between the major contenders in the conflict – the Sri Lanka government's military regime of passes and checkpoints and the LTTE's parallel security regime – civilian men and women also had to contend with the subregimes of several other armed groups – the Eelam People's Revolutionary Front (EPRLF – East Coast) and Rasik group, People's Liberation Organisation of Tamil Eelam (PLOTE – Vanni), Eelam People's Democratic Party (EPDP – Jaffna). Almost two decades of war had generated a number of armed paramilitary groups, terrorising and taxing civilians. They seemed intent only on retaining the power they wielded at gunpoint. Many of these paramilitary groups, bankrolled by the Sri Lanka government, worked with the Army to combat the LTTE. They maintained regimes of terror and torture in the areas they controlled. All these groups, mainly youth, carried guns. In February 2002 the government of Sri Lanka and the LTTE reached a ceasefire agreement. Peace talks have taken place in Thailand, facilitated by Norway. Though progress has been made due to the ceasefire, many internally displaced persons have refrained from resettlement until a more definite peace is reached and more security can be provided.

Violence against women during the war was the stuff of rape, trauma and disappeared persons, torture, assassination. It included the gendered politics of body searches at checkpoints usually conducted by armed youth trained in the arts of terror, torture, and the degradation of their victims. Several instances of checkpoint rape by the Sri Lankan government's security forces have occurred. But unlike in Bosnia rape has not been practised as a systematic policy for ethnic cleansing by any groups in the conflict. Women suffered particularly from the poor security situation in the border areas. Mothers, often fearful for their daughter's safety and sexual vulnerability, tended to confine them to the home or refugee camp. Simultaneously, a sexual service industry developed in Anuradhapura area where soldiers returned from the conflict areas, with many homeless and displaced women engaging in prostitution.

Conditions were considerably worse for displaced women, forced to live in refugee camps where privacy is minimal if not nonexistent and where levels of generalised violence, alcoholism and domestic violence are high. Additionally, both the romanticisation of home and the women-as-victims discourse in the human rights field obscure the realities and transformations of living in conflict. For instance, the Sinhala term *anathagatha kattiya* literally means the abandoned people, while the Tamil term *Veedu attavargal* means people without a home. Despite and because of conflict and displacement women have taken on new roles, but not without doubts and struggles. I suggest the notion of 'ambivalent agency' in order to capture the space between the humanitarian discourses that position women as victims in conflict and the development discourse that would construct women as 'empowered' individuals after the development process has run its course. Following Jayawardena (1986), it is arguable that women who take on new roles such as head of household, principal income generator and decision maker in conflict situations merely carry a double burden, because they would be pushed back into the kitchen afterwards to perform traditional gender roles. Likewise, it has been observed that women militants such as those who join the LTTE are merely pawns or victims in the discourse of LTTE's brand of Tamil nationalist patriarchy. While there is little doubt that women in a war's interregnum carry a double burden and often mobilise on nationalist scripts, viewing women as instrumentalised and merely reactive in the process of war, culture, or patriarchy elides the complexity of women's agency. Positioning women as instrumentalised by social and cultural processes might also mean that they are subject to secondary victimisation — victimhood also often entails the burden of a social stigma. Women who are widowed and/or raped are particularly vulnerable to the double complex of victim.

But the construct of the Sri Lankan Tamil woman as 'victim' also draws from another genealogy. Anthropological, sociological and literary ethnography has tended to represent Tamil women as living within a highly patriarchal caste-ridden Hindu cultural ethos, particularly in comparison to Sinhala women whose lives are seen to be less circumscribed by caste ideologies and purity/pollution concepts and practices. The figure of the LTTE woman soldier – the armed virgin – is one of the few highly problematic exceptions to the representation of Tamil women as victims. Of course, the representation of Tamil women in relation to caste and family is not entirely monochrome in the anthropological literature, which is split on the subject. For many anthropologists have also emphasised strong matrilineal tendencies in Sri Lankan Tamil society, where women inherit property in the maternal line according to customary *Thesawalamai* law and enjoy claims on natal families. This in contrast to the rigidly patriarchal cultures of North India where patrilineal descent and inheritance is the norm (see Wadley 1991). Feminist ethnography, on the other hand, has emphasised the subordinate status of Tamil women in the Hindu caste structure, while frequently noting the split between the ideology of *Shakti* or female power as the primary generative force of the universe (also associated with the pantheon of powerful Hindu goddesses) and the reality of women's apparent powerlessness in everyday life (Thiruchandran 1997). Both schools however emphasise the generally restrictive nature of the Sri Lankan Tamil Hindu caste system on women and often tend to see caste and gender relations as culturally rather than historically determined. By and large however women have rarely been centred in debates on caste, and when they have been, they are more often than not constructed as victims rather than agents of culture.

More recently anthropologists have argued that colonialism permeated by British Victorian patriarchal culture eroded the status of women in the South Indian societies that follow the matrilineal Dravidian kinship pattern, where property is passed in the women's line, from mother to daughter – a practice which usually indicates the relatively high status of women in society. Rather, they highlight how colonial legal systems might have eroded the rights and freedoms that women had under customary law. Significantly, this postcolonial analysis views family, kinship, caste and gender relations as structurally dynamic and historically changing. In this vein, I continue to explore how seventeen years of armed conflict, displacement and humanitarian-relief-development interventions might have altered the structure of the family, caste, land rights and the gender status quo among communities in the border areas affected by the conflict.

Spaces of Empowerment: Reconstitution of Caste, Family and Women's Land Rights

Since the armed conflict commenced in Sri Lanka, the population of displaced people has fluctuated from half a million to 1.2 million, or between a tenth and a fifth of the country's population at various points in the conflict. Ironically, displacement and camp life had also provided new spaces for women's agency. In this section I outline some of the processes of transformation evident in young single and widowed women's lives at the Siddambarapuram camp and adjacent new settlement scheme.

Siddambarapuram Camp was located a few miles outside Vavuniya, the largest town in the north central Vanni region. It had received a large influx of refugees from the north. In many ways the facilities, location and environmental/climatic conditions at that camp and the adjoining new settlements were exceptionally propitious. The relative prosperity of the locale and its residents was evident in the fact that the market in the camp was a vibrant and happening place that had become a shopping centre for nearby old (*purana*) villagers as well. At Siddambarapuram the sense of independence, empowerment and mobility of many women heads of household was tangible and remarkable in contrast to other women I met in camps in less propitious settings. This is explainable in terms of the camp's location close to the larger town of Vavuniya where women could find employment, particularly in the service sector. This is of course not an option for displaced women in other less conveniently located camps.

The Siddambarapuram Camp was initially constructed as a transit camp by UNHCR for refugees returning to Jaffna from India in 1991, who were subsequently stranded when the conflict started again in what is known as the second Eelam War. Many of the people in the camp had been resident for more than five years. One of the oldest refugee camps in Vavuniya, it was exceptionally well-located and serviced. Several young widows I interviewed in the camp and the adjoining new settlement noted that while they had initially had a hard time adjusting to camp life and the burdens of caring for their young families, they had also gained freedom to work outside the household and increasingly enjoyed the role of being the head of the household and its principal decision maker.

Several women said that they had little desire to remarry, mainly due to anxiety that their children might not be well cared for by a second husband, while a Christian woman said that she was being pressured by family members to remarry. Several women commented that previously their husbands would not permit them to work outside the household, even if they had done so prior to marriage. Of course one of the principal reasons for these women's newly found sense of control was the fact that they were able to and had found employment outside the household and the camp. Women in the service sector or in the NGO sectors had done best.

Arguably, the erosion of caste ideology and practice particularly among the younger generation in the camps had contributed to women's mobility and sense of empowerment. Except for the highly Westernised urban Tamil women professionals, caste has historically provided the mainstay of the Hindu Tamil gender status quo since caste belonging often determines women's patterns of mobility, with restrictions on women's mobility being a sign of high status. In the camps – unlike in their home territory in the Jaffna peninsula where village settlement was caste and region based – it was difficult to maintain social and spatial segregation, caste hierarchies, and purity pollution taboos for a number of reasons, including poverty.

Often members of the younger generation simply refused to adhere to caste inhibitions. As one mother speaking about the disruption of caste hierarchies in displacement observed:

> Because we are poor here as displaced people we only have two glasses to drink from so when a visitor from another caste comes we have to use the same glass. Now my daughter refuses to observe the separate utensils and she is friendly with boys we wouldn't consider at home. Everything is changing with the younger generation because they are growing up all mixed up because we are displaced and living on top of each other in a camp ....

This mother went on to detail how it was difficult to keep girls and boys separate in the camp situation. She thought that the freer mingling of youth meant that there would be more intercaste marriages and hence an erosion of caste. Presumably this also means that girls had more choice over who might be their partners.

Loss of male family members during the conflict and displacement had also resulted in the reconstitution of displaced families around women, a fact that resonates with an older gender status quo: that of the precolonial Dravidian matrilineal family and kinship system where women remain with their natal families after marriage, and were customarily entitled to lay claim on the resources of the matri-clan, and hence enjoyed a relatively higher status, in comparison with strictly matrilineal societies. For as Bina Agarwal has pointed out, the existence of matrilineal systems where matrilineal descent, matrilocal residence, and/or bilateral inheritance are practised is usually an indicator of the relatively higher status of women when compared to the status of women in patrilineal groups (Agarwal 1996). Similar observations concerning the status of women in matrilineal communities have been made by anthropologists who have studied the Nayars of Kerala as well as the Sinhalese, Tamils and Muslims of the east coast of Sri Lanka, where matrilineal inheritance is the norm (Yalman 1967). These are also societies where social indicators have been consistently good, with high levels of female literacy, education and healthcare in South Asia.

During the colonial period in Sri Lanka there was however a general erosion of the matrilineal inheritance and bi-lateral descent practice, despite general provision being made for customary common law for indigenous communities – Thesavallamai, Tamil customary law, Kandyan Sinhala law as well as Muslim Personal law. In the same period the modernising tendency to the nuclear family enshrined in secular European, Dutch and British law also privileged male inheritance, thereby reducing the power of women within their families. The switch from matrilineal, matrilocal, to virilocal forms of inheritance, where women take only movable property to their affinal household, might also be traced through various postcolonial land distribution schemes, wherein title deeds for land were invested in male heads of household, with the injunction against the further division of land due to land fragmentation. This set a precedent for male inheritance of the entirety of the family's land. The result has been the tendency towards male primogeniture – with the eldest son inheriting the land and daughters being disinherited from land ownership. Unfortunately the similar pattern of title deeds being invested in male heads of household is evident in the new settlement and land distribution schemes for landless displaced families in Vavuniya under the rehabilitation and reconstruction project. In these projects it is only where the male head of household is presumed dead that title deeds are invested in women. Women heads of household who were unmarried or whose husbands have left them or whose location cannot be ascertained are not deemed eligible for land grants.

Given that customary practices with regard to women's land rights are more liberal than that of postcolonial development policies, it is imperative that relief-development interventions be cultural-sensitive. Clearly, cultural practices (e.g. traditional inheritance patterns) can be mobilised either to enhance women's agency, or to diminish it, even as women take on new roles and enter new spaces in conflict situations. In the case of Muslim women in the war zones, cultural factors have diminished their mobility and freedom. In any event there is a need for cultural analysis of gender practices and women's transformed roles if women are to be empowered by development and humanitarian assistance.

Rethinking Women in Displacement: the Development Challenge

Currently there is growing recognition among those involved in humanitarian relief and development that women frequently bear the material and psychological brunt of armed conflict, and hence there is a need for gender-sensitive relief and rehabilitation work. Yet few programmes have systematically explored how relief might aid recovery from individual trauma and social suffering, and facilitate women's empowerment outside a narrowly defined political and institutional context. Thus many gender programmes organised by the government's relief and rehabilitation authority and NGOs still remain within conventional development thinking rather than attempting to work out *culturally* appropriate and effective strategies for women's empowerment in the context of the social transformations that have occurred over years of armed conflict and displacement.

Despite the psychosocial traumas that displacement entails, it has provided windows of opportunity for greater personal and group autonomy and experiments with identity and leadership for women. Certainly this has been the case for many displaced Tamil women, many of who have lost husbands and sons in the conflict. It is hence that humanitarian aid and development should aim to legitimise and sustain women's agency within transformed community and family structures. Moreover relief should also assist host populations to assimilate the long-term displaced. In Sri Lanka this is particularly necessary if the ethnic conflict is not to spread to new areas where the displaced have found refuge and are often perceived to be in competition with poor local populations.

The assumption of return is a fundamental premise of state, international and NGO policies vis-à-vis internally displaced people. The fact is that these policies might be contributing to prolong the conflict and a cause of trauma for people who fled their home over five years ago. This is particularly true of women for whom restrictions on mobility are difficult. Many of these women who wish to settle in the place where they have found refuge are being kept dependent on relief handouts rather than being assisted to build new lives and livelihoods. Thus, ironically, relief might be prolonging the trauma of the very people it is supposed to assist. Many internally displaced women who have given up the dream of return are in the paradoxical position of being materially and psychologically displaced by the humanitarian interventions and human rights discourses and practices that define them as victims who need to be returned to their original homelands for their protection and for the restoration of national and international order and peace.

Women taking on new roles in a situation of war and displacement are not unambivalent or free of guilt feelings. This was evident in many young widows' uncertainty about whether they should return home if and when the conflict ended. For them displacement clearly constituted the space of ambivalence: a place of regeneration and the hope for a future unfettered by the past, loss and trauma. They were also concerned that return home would mean a return to the prewar caste and gender status quo. Of course, anxiety about return was also related to qualms about personal security and trauma and was mostly articulated by young women heads of households at Siddambarapuram, who had integrated to the local economy, and among those who had previously been landless.

Languages of Empowerment: Recasting Widowhood and the Return to Matrifocal Families

A generation of young Tamil war widows who have been displaced to and in the border areas for many years seem to be increasingly challenging conventional Hindu constructions of widowhood as a negative and polluting condition which bars their participation from many aspects of community life. Several young widows working in Vavuniya town but resident in the camp displayed their sense of independence by wearing the red *pottu*, the auspicious mark reserved for the married Hindu women, despite being widows or women whose husbands had abandoned them. Likewise in Batticaloa several women who had lost husbands to death, displacement or family fragmentation in the course of armed conflict and flight from bombing and shelling, increasingly refused to erase the signs of *sumankali* (particularly the auspicious red *pottu*) they wore when married. The symbolic gesture indexes the refusal to play the culturally prescribed role of widow.

Clearly, the demographic fact of a large number of young widows who are unwilling to take on the role of the traditional Hindu widow might facilitate the transformation of a negative cultural complex that defines widowhood as a polluting and inauspicious (*amangali*) state of being. Young women's response to their changed circumstances marks the space for redefinition of what it means to be an unmarried or widowed woman in the more orthodox Hindu tradition. Consciously and unconsciously, they appear to be redefining conceptions of the 'good woman' as one who lives within the traditional confines of caste, kin group and village. As they struggle with new gender roles and identities, many of these young widows also struggle to find a language and cultural idiom to speak of their changed roles. They refuse to wear the prescribed garb of widowhood and appear to break with the ideology of Kanaki (*Paththini*), the exemplary faithful wife and widow of Tamil mythology and ideology. Rather, they seem to evoke the sign of the *devadasi* – Kanaki's alter ego – who transcended conventional gender roles; the professional woman married to immortality for her talent and skill, most familiar to South Asian audiences in the name of the famed dancer and courtesan Madhavi of the Tamil Hindu-Buddhist epic, *Sillapaddikaram*.

Insufficient insight into the subtle dynamics and ambivalences of cultural transformation in conflict and peace building might also impede recovery from traumatic experiences. This holds particularly for women (and men) who might suffer secondary victimisation arising from the different gender tasks they perform during conflict and displacement. Very few women seem to have found a culturally appropriate language to articulate the transformations that they have experienced. Many feel ashamed, guilty and/or traumatised by their changed circumstances and gender roles arising from conflict. As one woman in a resettlement said 'It is a relief now that he (her husband) is not with me. He used to drink and beat me up.' Yet she felt guilty and anxious to admit that this was the case. While she worried for her personal safety and that of her children in the absence of her husband, particularly at night, she said that anyway she had to support the children mainly on her own even when her husband was with her.

In the course of fieldwork it became apparent to me that though many women had taken on new roles, tasks and jobs they would not have otherwise taken on (e.g. fishing in lakes), they rarely coded these changes in negative or in positive terms. Rather, the livelihood transformations that women had experienced during the course of displacement and in camp life were coded in terms of comparisons between then and now, like 'in the old days we would not have done these things – it would not have been appropriate.' There was also a great deal of ambivalence in how women viewed their new activities and role changes, partly because the new activities they performed were markers of poverty, lower status, and lack of culturally legitimated male support. They were also aware that their new roles had come at great personal and social cost to the community.

Clearly, developing strategies for women's cultural empowerment is at least as important as women's political empowerment if women's new roles are to be recognised, legitimated and sustained. Otherwise they carry a double burden. The victim ideology often found in relief and rehabilitation as well as social health and trauma interventions for women in conflict situations needs to be problematised, as it may be internalised by some women – with damaging psychological consequences. Non-combatant women who have found spaces of empowerment in the conflict need sustained assistance to maintain their new mobility and independence in the face of sometimes virulently nationalist assertions of patriarchal cultural tradition and practices during the conflict and in the period of postwar reconstruction. The return to peace should not mean a return to the prewar gender status quo determined by patriarchal cultural mores, morality and conventions.

It follows that humanitarian and development interventions must creatively support and sustain positive changes to the status of civilian women living in conflict. Unlike in Afghanistan where the situation of women unambiguously deteriorated due to conflict and during the rule of the Taliban, in Sri Lanka the evidence suggests that, despite many women's experiences of traumatic violence and displacement, some changes to the gender status quo wrought by armed conflict might have empowered women whose freedom and mobility were restricted.

Conclusion: Ambivalent Empowerment

Social scientists, development workers, and activists have hesitated to address the issue of how social transformations due to long-term armed conflicts might also have brought desirable changes to entrenched social hierarchies and inequalities, such as caste and gender, among people exposed to it. We have been wary of analysing the unintended transformations brought by war, of seeing positives in violence, lest we be seen to be sympathetic to violence. Yet, for many women who have lost family members peace can never be a simple return to the past. Rather, peace necessarily constitutes a creative remaking of cultural meanings and agency – a third space between a familiar, often romanticised, past and the traumatic present – an ambivalent empowerment?

Women's agency is not a zero-sum game, achieved at the expense of men. War places different burdens on men – a fact that many of the women I interviewed recognised and were sympathetic to. For it is men and boys who are mainly targeted to fight and defend their nation, community, family, and the honour of their women. Men are conscripted into paramilitaries to fight. Men and boys are more easily perceived as a security threat if they are of the wrong ethnic or religious community. They are also more likely to be killed. On the other hand, men who refuse to fight or who are forced to live off humanitarian aid in refugee camps suffer from feeling emasculated because they often cannot support their families and play the socially prescribed role of protector and breadwinner of the family. The result is low self-esteem and a sense of failure that might lead to suicidal tendencies among men and boys. Reports from those living in camps for the internally displaced indicate that alcoholism is high, as is increased domestic violence (see Schrijvers 1997). Clearly, there is need for systematic study of the impact of war and ensuing social and gender transformation on boys, men and the cultural construction of masculinity.

This chapter has sought to develop a framework to analyse women's agency and ambiguous empowerment in conflict situations. It has also argued for the importance of developing cultural strategies to empower women living in conflict and displacement. This has meant exploring gender relations outside the scripted frames of ethnonationalist cultural mobilisation, as well as gender analyses of women in politics, or humanitarian and human rights constructions of women as 'victims' of war and culture. Clearly, noncombatant women are differently implicated in nationalist discourses, and the return to peacetime (which entails the reassertion of the gender status quo) is as problematic for them as it is for combatant women, but for different reasons (see Rajasingham 1995). I have also attempted to develop the idea that violent conflicts might disrupt social, political and gender hierarchies in unexpected ways and benefit marginal groups and individuals. The lacuna in understanding of conflict and its effects has much to do with how we conceptualise peace – as also a return to a (gender) status quo. Peace we still think constitutes a return to things the way they used to be; the certain certainties of familiar, older, ways of being and doing. But to conceptualise peace thus is another kind of (epistemic) violence. For women, wives and mothers who have lost a head of household or seen him 'disappear' in the violence, there is no return to the old certainties of the nuclear family, headed by the father, the patriarch. For the war's widows, for those who have lived intimately with war, the changes wrought by sixteen years of armed conflict in Sri Lanka are too deep, too complex, structural and fundamental. They force us to challenge our certainties about war and peace. In this context, peace is necessarily a third place, between the old and the existing, the past and the present, the space where conflict remakes culture.

Notes

1. Some of the ethnographic material used in this paper appeared in an essay titled 'Post Victimhood', in *Women, Nation and Narration*, edited by Selvi Thiruchandran (1997) and in *Women, War and Peace*, edited by Rita Manchada (2001). This paper has benefited from comments by participants at the Women in Conflict Zones Network meeting in Colombo in December 1988 and comments and discussions with Joke Schrijvers and Shireen Xavier.
2. The social role of women, of holding the family together, of caring for children, the sick and the elderly makes women the first sufferers during conflict.

Part IV
Challenging Dichotomies: Relief versus Development

12

Refugees between Relief and Development

Georg Frerks

The last decade has seen an intensive debate on linking relief and development. Below the main arguments are reviewed. Which conceptual approach is most appropriate after considering the arguments pro and contra linking? Is that a model based on a continuum between relief and development or one which believes that the concept of discontinuity can better deal with the empirical, political and practical realities regarding refugees?

Introduction

The debate on linking relief and development started in the late 1980s with workshops, academic literature and policy discussions devoted to the subject. The magnitude of funds spent on an ever-increasing amount of complex humanitarian emergencies forced humanitarian and development workers to find ways of mutual coordination and even linking their efforts. The justification for this was stated succinctly by Buchanan-Smith and Maxwell:

> The basic idea is simple and sensible. Emergencies are costly in terms of human life and resources. They are disruptive of development. They demand a long period of rehabilitation. And they have spawned bureaucratic structures, lines of communication and organisational cultures, which duplicate development institutions and sometimes cut across them. By the same token, development policy and administration are often insensitive to the risk of drought and to the importance of protecting vulnerable households against risk. If relief and development can be 'linked', so the theory goes, these deficiencies can be overcome. Better 'development' can reduce the need for emer-

gency relief, better 'relief' can contribute to development; and better 'rehabilitation' can ease any remaining transition between the two. (Buchanan-Smith
and Maxwell 1994: 2)

The linking of relief and development was attempted by presenting
relief, rehabilitation and development as steps of a continuum. Most models distinguish an acute emergency phase during or immediately after a
disaster, in which rescue and relief aid take place, a phase of rehabilitation
and reconstruction, and finally a phase in which 'normal' development is
begun again. In fact, disaster was considered a temporary disruption of a
normal, linear development process ongoing in the affected societies. The
different phases were seen as interrelated and followed one another in
time. They were often presented as a cycle, similar to the orthodox project
or policy cycle in development cooperation. Coordination between the
phases was seen to create synergy and to facilitate a quick return to development. Moreover, this approach would help to provide development aid
in such a way as to prevent disaster from reoccurring, while relief aid
could be given in such a way as to contribute to long-term development.
On the basis of the logic of these models, the arguments in favour of linking relief and development are summarised below.

Arguments in Favour of Linking

A first argument relates to the increasing number of emergency situations.
Emergency aid has virtually become a permanent feature in many countries
and what is then more logical than connecting relief aid with ongoing development efforts? This eases the pressure on funding, especially since relief aid
tends to be financed from corresponding cuts in development budgets.
Further savings could result from improved effectiveness and efficiency.

Second, emergency situations undermine past development achievements and set back the development process, often for decades. They also
complicate future efforts. Reasons lie not only in the economic sphere, but
relate to institutional, social and emotional problems too. In addition, the
unprofessional provision of relief aid may hamper future development.
Aid has had unintended, negative side effects that weakened local coping
mechanisms and capacities, or provided disincentives to restart local economic activity after an emergency. Abuse and diversion of humanitarian
aid have prolonged or sustained emergencies. Aid has been manipulated
to serve the interests of parties in conflict, warlords and profiteers (see
Keen 1994; Waal 1997). Linking relief and development could help to
avoid these dysfunctional side effects.

Third, unprecedented refugee flows and large-scale destruction of
civilian infrastructure have led to a renewed interest in the concept of
rehabilitation as the logical junction between relief and development.

Another argument refers to the arbitrariness of the distinction between these concepts since the Third World's poor live in a nearly chronic situation of insecurity, stress and emergency. Whether expressed in health, economic or nutritional indicators, the borderline between their chronic situation and acute emergency is very thin, if not completely artificial. It would seem that – in order to be effective – also bureaucratic and organisational boundaries between aid forms should disappear. In fact, any structural, definitive and sustainable solution of an emergency can only consist of measures moving beyond the provision of relief aid. The vulnerability to disasters is determined by structural factors such as poverty and the distribution of resources and power; in short, by the political economy of a society. Cuny has indicated the limitations of relief aid under these conditions:

> Recognizing poverty as the primary root of vulnerability and disaster in the Third World is the first step toward developing an understanding of the need for change in current disaster response practices. For if the magnitude of disasters is an outgrowth of underdevelopment and poverty, how can we expect to reduce the impact with food, blankets and tents, the traditional forms of assistance? (Cuny 1983: 15)

One way to link relief and development is reducing the population's vulnerability to shocks by decreasing their frequency, intensity and impact. Measures mentioned by Buchanan-Smith and Maxwell include the focusing of resources on the needs of the poor, drought-proofing agriculture, different types of food-for-work programmes and macroeconomic stabilisation (1994: 4). They further propose to integrate emergency relief authorities in the normal state structures and to empower local authorities. They also suggest working through NGOs and providing infrastructure that serves a purpose after the emergency is over. Apart from the fact that these suggestions are not particularly new, they are not necessarily helpful as NGOs and local authorities are frequently part of the problem. In any case, there are as yet not many results to boast about. As Green and Mavie state: 'Results [of linking relief and development] are distressingly modest' (Quoted in Buchanan-Smith and Maxwell 1994: 8). It needs to be examined why this idea of linking relief and development has been implemented so little and why there are so few salient results so far. Below three sets of problems with regard to linking relief and development are elaborated on.

Problems with Linking Relief and Development

A first set of problems is of a *conceptual* nature. The prevailing paradigm holds that gradual progress is the normal pattern and that disasters and emergencies are an irritating, but temporary disruption of that process. It is, however, very doubtful whether this model still has much empirical and analytical validity in the present situation of nearly permanent crisis and conflict in many parts of the world. The old modernist thinking in terms of stability and gradual, progressive change needs to be replaced by a model which incorporates the current instability, conflict and chaos and sheds the notion of linear progress.

Many countries have experienced long-term or sudden processes of deterioration. Emergencies and protracted conflicts have been sustained by powerful private and group interests. They gain from these chaotic circumstances by illicit activities, including trade in drugs and arms, the exploitation of natural resources, extortion, theft and plunder. In these economies of violence, war itself has become an enterprise. In a number of countries involved the state hardly functions anymore, or has collapsed completely. Under such conditions the linking of relief and development becomes a very imaginary exercise. Duffield states that: 'Complex emergencies have a singular ability to erode or destroy the cultural, civil, political and economic integrity of established societies.' He asserts that [the linking debate] 'is unable to come to terms with the reality of permanent emergency' (Duffield 1994: 38, 40).

Macrae et al. (1995: 673) give three more reasons why developmentalist approaches fail under political emergencies. Firstly, aid itself has become a political resource that needs to be considered in the broader process of conflict resolution. Secondly, complex emergencies reduce the resource base of the population critically, resulting in extreme and long-term vulnerability. Finally, the conflict itself must be understood as arising from the failure of the existing political and economic structures. Development models must be redefined instead of applied again gratuitously. A simple return to the situation ex ante is not viable and would only lead to a reemergence of the problems, as the underlying causes of the conflict lay exactly in the political and economic characteristics of that very situation and period.

Macrae et al. further state that rehabilitation cannot simply be seen as the link between relief and development as is done so often:

> This assumes that the content and strategies of relief and development are sufficiently compatible to enable their linkage. This assumption is problematic. The criteria applied to planning relief operations are primarily concerned with the physical survival of individuals; development activities are planned with respect to sustainability and appropriateness of social and economic systems. These are two different categories of objectives which the concept of rehabilitation cannot easily reconcile. (Macrae et al. 1995: 673)

The whole idea of a continuum and of linking, for that matter, is problematic because relief and development differ so fundamentally. Table 1 provides an ideal-typical comparison between relief and sustainable

Table 1: *Ideal-typical comparison between relief and sustainable development*

Factor	Relief	Sustainable development
Objectives	Alleviation of immediate, basic needs of disaster survivors	Improvement of standard of living
Nature of needs	Physical, psychological	Economic, social, political
Type of intervention	Delivery of material provisions and initial reconstruction	Quantitative and qualitative changes in ongoing socio-economic processes
Aid characteristics	Short-term, temporary (external)	Long-term (embedded)
	Incidental	Structural
	Relief of acute needs	Changes in vulnerability and entitlements
Management characteristics	Donor-driven	Recipient-focused
	Top-down, *dirigiste*	Bottom-up, participatory
Main foci	Delivery, speed, logistics and output	Underlying processes, causalities, long-term impact
Context variables	Chaos, instability, conflict	Stability
	Lack of infrastructure and counterparts (failed states)	Infrastructure and counterparts available
	Lack of knowledge and documentation	Knowledge and documentation available
	Media attention, fund raising	Less attention

development, showing the differences in the nature, complexity and intervention logic of both aid forms. As a consequence, it would be better to divide them than to lump them together into a type of continuum blurring their differences.

A second set of problems is of a *political* nature. In some countries, the institutional weakening or even collapse of the state has made the implementation of any type of structural measures and, therefore, the linking between relief and development, illusory.

At the donors' end, relief and development aid differ as to the type of conditionalities involved. Relief aid is normally provided on the basis of humanitarian criteria without any political conditions on the receiving countries. Many of these countries would, however, not qualify for development aid due to political considerations such as violations of human rights or 'bad' governance. Moreover, for a long time donors were hesitant to provide any development aid during a conflict, and were limiting themselves strictly to emergency aid. It was deemed highly improbable that development could take root and become sustainable under conditions of war. In such situations linking itself becomes difficult, if not impossible.

As observed by Macrae et al., shifting relief to development implies a political judgement on the part of donors. Whereas in relief aid the donor often tries to remain neutral and impartial, development assistance, according to Macrae et al., implies decisions about the legitimacy of partners, and of the institutions of the recipient state. They conclude that especially the differences in the political meaning of relief and development aid need to be recognized (1997: 226, 241).

> Unlike development aid, relief aid does not imply international recognition, or legitimation of the government or other authorities controlling territory. In terms of the mandates of donor agencies, and the definition of aid budget lines, far from a smooth link between relief and development assistance, there is a clear threshold, which distinguishes relief and development assistance. This threshold is marked not by material conditions on the ground, but by the foreign policy position of donor countries in relation to recipient countries. (Macrae et al. 1997: 225–26)

These distinctions are frequently formalised in donors' aid policies. In these circumstances linking between relief and development is often not possible.

A final political consideration concerns the need to give relief efforts their own separate profile in the media and vis-à-vis the public. This is done not only with a view to accountability, but also to facilitate fundraising. It is easier to raise funds for emergencies than for structural development purposes. This, however, prevents an emphasis on long-term needs.

A last set of problems refers to *institutional, technical and implementation* issues. Normally, structures and organisations for development and relief are strictly separated and coordination and cooperation are, as a consequence, difficult. There is a fairly poor record as far as coordination between international relief agencies among themselves is concerned. This has been amply documented in the joint evaluation of the international response to the Rwanda genocide (Eriksson 1996: 57–59). Differences between relief agencies can indeed be formidable. They include differences in mandates, ideological, religious and cultural backgrounds, approaches and timeframes. There may also be differences in political stances and types of intervention logic. Finally, agencies may compete for funding, media attention and local personnel. It is difficult to see how such differences can be overcome in the course of a particular emergency operation. Cooperation between relief and development agencies seems even more difficult to realise, leaving aside other actors such as local authorities, local NGOs and the military. In addition, centralisation of decision making at headquarters combined with a highly protocolised way of working in the field makes it difficult to mutually adjust and adapt field operations.

In many emergency situations the local administration finds itself decapacitated. It is hardly involved in the relief work and overall control rests with outside agencies. The same applies basically to the local population and their organisations. Anderson and Woodrow assert that: '... Relief organizations usurp all control and decision-making power from the victims' (1993: 137). They observe that: 'Although they mean well, outsiders who "impose" relief assistance on "victims" (Harrell-Bond 1986) and who themselves assume all decision-making and organizing power for meeting the crisis, may increase the vulnerabilities of those who suffer, leaving them further victimized by the aid itself' (1993: 136). This is compounded by the usual emphasis on physical needs, logistics and speed in relief aid. This aptly illustrates that linking relief and development requires a change of attitudes and established routines. More fundamentally, it is difficult to understand how a proper transition from relief to development can be performed as long as local capacities and responsibilities are not fully recognised.

A final issue relates to the cost of relief and development. Relief is typically a high-cost activity while development is much cheaper. Conflating the different phases in a continuum tends to increase total cost. An extensive and expensive relief phase may actually be blocking a return to more cost-effective development (Frerks et al. 1995: 362–66).

These conceptual, political and practical problems show that linking relief and development has not only benefits as identified earlier, but also implies a number of difficulties. However, the original ideas have been rethought and several qualifications and nuances have been added to the debate on the subject recently. Below these developments are summarised.

Recent Developments in the Linking Debate

It has been recognised by now, that there is no continuum between relief, rehabilitation and development or a necessary temporal and logical sequence between these phases. In fact, there may be differences in sequencing per sector or region leading to a type of 'multitrack' approach. The OECD writes:

> For the purpose of analysis, the transition from emergency crisis to long-term development has often been described as a 'continuum'. This does not, however, conform to actual situations, which follow no set pattern, chronology or order. Emergency relief, rehabilitation work and development assistance all co-exist in times of conflict and crisis, and they interact in innumerable ways. (OECD 1998: 48)

A recent high-level roundtable on the gap between humanitarian assistance and long-term development was premised on the recognition that 'there were "gaps" and that these needed to be addressed systematically' (Brookings Institution 1999: 2). More specifically the roundtable agreed that:

> A response to the needs of post-conflict societies organized on two artificially compartmentalized lines, namely the 'emergency/humanitarian' and 'long-term developmental', did not do justice to the fluidity, uncertainty and complexity that characterised war-torn societies. … and the very fragility of many peace agreements, and the accompanying persistence of violence in most war-torn societies, made it difficult to draw a definitive line between 'conflict' and 'post-conflict situations'. Peace and conflict often occurred simultaneously. Invariably, there was a need for simultaneous relief, rehabilitation, and development interventions. One was not looking at a linear process. The 'continuum' concept was considered obsolete. (Brookings Institution 1998: 4)

Also the UNDP has discarded the idea of the continuum and considers models in which relief organizations hand over responsibilities to long-term development agencies as deeply flawed. In a paper of the UNDP-Rwanda (1998: 16) it is concluded that:

> Relief and development should go hand in hand in order to address relief needs with simultaneous attention to issues such as restoring social services, governance, food security and production, economic revival and job creation. These efforts cannot wait for appropriate conditions for long term development. They must be undertaken during and just after crisis. (UNDP-Rwanda 1998: 16)

Likewise, the Dutch Minister for Development Cooperation has introduced the notion of 'development for peace' in which reconciliation programmes should already start during conflict to create the basis for political reconstruction. Such programmes should be carried out by civil society organizations that function as 'a voice for peace and reconciliation' (Pronk 1996). These quotations illustrate the fact that the concept of a continuum has been done away with in policy circles, and more sophisticated modes of linking are being suggested. These modes are based on the idea that relief, rehabilitation and development could or need to be carried out jointly. The obscure situation on the ground, somewhere between conflict and peace, generally makes it not possible to wait for a full peace agreement before starting rehabilitative and development activity. The UNDP administrator states:

> Surely one way to avoid gaps between relief and development is never to stop development during the crisis, whenever possible. Surely another way to avoid the gap is to build development and post-crisis thinking into humanitarian activities, and to build humanitarian partnerships into reconstruction

and development. ... The walls between peacebuilding, political affairs, humanitarian efforts and development must be breached as often and as thoroughly as necessary to do our jobs. (Speth 1999: 2)

One could not agree more with the critical approach that many agencies are exhibiting towards the continuum model. It is, however, a different thing to imagine sophisticated approaches that do not face the same type of problems as the earlier continuum model. Some agencies have been looking into the institutional, organisational and financial obstacles to carrying out their work properly. The lack of involvement of national (local) actors was mentioned as well as the many disparate projects; the lack of an integrated political strategy, institutional framework and aid programme; and the existence of compartmentalised and uncoordinated relief and development structures and actions on behalf of the international donor community. Also the prevailing funding mechanisms were seen as a serious 'self-inflicted' restriction.

On the positive side, there is a clear recognition of the problems and issues involved in improving the linking of relief, rehabilitation and development, and there is an explicit preparedness to learn from failures and shortcomings. The OECD has formulated lessons learned, best practices and 'key orientations for donors'. The UN has appointed humanitarian coordinators in conflict countries, and the UNDP has established a special unit and put in place quick-action procedures and programming arrangements. There are constructive lessons and examples from pioneering UN efforts in Cambodia, Afghanistan and Burundi. The UNDP-Rwanda paper gives a comprehensive overview of the inadequacy and constraints of the current response and presents ten initiatives for institutional reform and to improve current practices.

At the sectoral level there are increasingly efforts to incorporate long-term perspectives in relief aid. These sectors include, among others, water and sanitation, food aid and food security, agriculture, health and education. Provision of aid is more and more focused on strengthening local coping and organisational capacities, and tries to introduce measures that improve the preventive and mitigating capacity and preparedness for future emergencies.

The Question of the Refugees

In disaster situations the vulnerabilities, capacities and needs of the several involved categories of beneficiaries and target groups are highly specific and may differ considerably from one another. The so-called 'Vulnerability and Capacity Assessments' take the prevailing differentiation into account, not only by gender and class, but also over time. Positions may also change between regions or along the administrative levels in a particular state (see Anderson and Woodrow 1989: 15–20 and IFRC 1993: 1–11). In consequence, the different types of emergency assistance need to be attuned to these realities.

In this connection, the question of linking relief and development must be discussed with reference to the specific position of refugees as well. They are – by definition – cut off from their own environment: physically, economically, socially, culturally, and in many other ways. This has large consequences, not only with regard to their immediate well being and survival, but also with respect to longer-term perspectives and the material, cognitive, social and other prerequisites for future recovery.

It also depends on whether refugees will have to resettle in the host country, or whether they have to stay in refugee camps, often in a completely dependent position, until eventually there may be an opportunity to repatriate. In the latter case, but also partly in the former, the idea of a continuum and other forms of linking relief and development, are problematic. In contrast, these refugees' positions are characterised by a whole series of discontinuities.

Efforts to link relief and future development are not taking place in abstracto or in a vacuum: they are, of course, related to a geographic, economic and sociocultural space, defined by rather unique characteristics. One can definitely try to avoid refugees residing in camps becoming passive and dependent and one can also try to raise levels of generalised knowledge and skills. In the refugee camp itself, structures and activities may be designed in such a way that they may contribute to the development of the area in which the camp is located. This is certainly a positive contribution in view of the imbalance that sometimes exists in the levels of provision to refugees and the host population respectively. It does not, however, provide a link between the provision of relief to the refugees here and now, and their future development needs once repatriated. It is difficult to imagine what type of useful development initiatives can be designed related to their future environment, still far away in time and space and anyhow insecure.

Moreover, the conceptual, institutional, organisational and political constraints of linking relief, rehabilitation and development as mentioned in the earlier section of this paper, may have been recognised and plans formulated to address some of them, but real-life experience has taught that institutional reform is a hard and long-term job. Practices are often deeply embedded in organisational cultures and changing them requires endurance, and especially political will which is a scarce entity. Despite numerous attempts over many years to achieve a meaningful level of coordination between donors in development aid, these have not resulted in significant change. This does not augur well for the fairly drastic changes needed in the humanitarian field.

On a more theoretical plane, insights from rural development sociology lead also to a word of caution. Over the last decade, actor-oriented analysis and the study of interface encounters have gained a prominent place in the theoretical debates regarding development. According to Long (1989), interfaces relate to critical junctures of different levels of social order and are found where governmental and other external agencies intervene to carry out a particular development policy or aid programme. Interfaces usually involve social actors with conflicting and divergent interests and values. Long states with respect to the concept of the interface:

> This interest in interface, however, goes beyond the simple wish to document the types of struggles, negotiations and accommodations that take place between intervening agents and local actors. The concept functions as a metaphor for depicting areas of structural discontinuity in social life generally, but especially salient in 'intervention' situations. In other words, it sensitises the researcher to the importance of exploring how discrepancies of social interest, cultural interpretation, knowledge and power are mediated and perpetuated or transformed at critical points of linkage or confrontation. Such discrepancies arise in all kinds of social context. (Long 1989: 221)

Applying the notion of interface and the inherent concept of structural discontinuity to refugees and aid agencies may help to assess the probability of bridging the gaps between relief and development successfully. It seems that it is easy to underrate the difficulties that are involved in this linking exercise. Whereas the agencies limit their discussions mainly to the policy level, the problem merits a more critical theoretical, analytical and empirical approach. This could contribute to a realistic assessment of intentions that are framed by policy makers and programme managers. They may understandably find it difficult, if not impossible, to incorporate the views and interests of other actors such as the programme beneficiaries: the refugees, the stayees, the internally displaced or the hosts. Here a more full-fledged actor approach may inform and improve practical approaches designed at the policy level.

Conclusion

Attempts to link relief, rehabilitation and development in emergency and post-conflict situations have attracted much attention and debate over the last decade. On the one hand, these efforts have been welcomed. On the other hand, the difficulties involved in this exercise have been underlined. This chapter has given an overview of the arguments pro and contra linking. Though the notion of a continuum has been discarded, more complex modes of linking essentially face similar problems of a conceptual, political and institutional nature. Though international agencies have gained relevant insights and experiences, it remains to be seen whether the necessary changes at the level of institutional frameworks, organisational cultures and funding practices can be effected to attain a meaningful integration of relief and development. Linking relief and development takes place in a concrete setting defined in time and place and characterised by specific economic, social, cultural relationships. The specific position of refugees was, however, seen to imply a whole series of discontinuities.

Consequently, it was questioned whether linking relief and development could be realised in a vacuum or in host country situations that for refugees must differ so fundamentally from those to be rehabilitated and redeveloped after repatriation. It was argued that these situations could be profitably analysed from the perspective of an actor-oriented approach and through the related study of development interfaces that typically emphasise structural discontinuities and cultural and cognitive discrepancies in intervention situations.

Concluding, the political, practical and conceptual obstacles to achieving the linkage of relief and development are quite formidable, beside the more epistemological and theoretical concerns with regard to the existence of structural discontinuities and discrepancies in interface situations. This confirms the quote of Buchanan-Smith and Maxwell who say that: 'It would be unwise to minimise the difficulties which surround attempts to link relief and development in complex emergencies' (1994: 14).

13

Rethinking the Relation between Relief and Development: 'Villagisation' in Rwanda[1]

Dorothea Hilhorst and Mathijs van Leeuwen

Introduction

In the aftermath of the 1990–1994 war and genocide, Rwanda had to face the return of an estimated 2.5 million refugees in a four-year period. In order to address the housing need of these people, the Rwanda Government, with the support of international organisations, started a villagisation programme by the name of *Imidugudu*. From early 1997 on, this programme came to target the entire rural population: the government had decided that all scattered households in the countryside had to be regrouped in villages. Within four years, international organisations helped to build about 250 communities with 85,000 houses. Many more were constructed with local means only. What started as an emergency project turned into a far-stretching development programme.

This case sheds some light on the dynamics and difficulties of integrating development in emergency assistance. Until recently, emergency work was organised on the premise that it should simply address immediate needs generated by disaster or conflict, while rehabilitation and development were postponed until the relief phase was over. Since the mid 1990s, this idea has been increasingly challenged and many have argued that development issues should be integrated into emergency assistance.[2] The case of the Rwanda *Imidugudu* programme may be considered as a large-scale pilot of this idea. It worked on long-term development, while addressing an immediate housing need. However, the programme retained the features of an emergency operation. It was a blueprint policy for the whole country, disregarding local diversity, implemented in a top-down fashion and with little space for popular participation. In the Rwanda case it seems that the opposite was achieved of what was intended: development was not integrated into relief, but the pitfalls of relief invaded development.

This chapter first reviews why international organisations supported the programme, despite the controversy it raised and the ambiguities it contained. It has to be said that there were also many organisations that did not support *Imidugudu*. This chapter, however, is particularly concerned with the question why many agencies did support this programme. Their support was remarkable, especially if we take into account the fact that similar programmes in East Africa had generally failed (see e.g. Ergas 1980; Yachan 1997; Scott 1998; Cannon Lorgan 1999). Then, two village case studies give insight into the practices of implementation of villagisation. The studies make clear that despite the large investments that were made in the programme, little has been achieved of the envisaged integrated approach to settlement, land use and livelihoods. Moreover, the authoritative and top-down implementation raises worries about the political implications of the programme. It evokes some pertinent questions about the possibilities and constraints for integrating development into relief.

International Support to the Programme

Immediately after the war and genocide in 1994, the Rwanda government started to plan villagisation sites, at that time foremost concerning the accommodation of Old Case returnees.[3] Those were mainly Tutsi that had fled earlier outbursts of violence in Rwanda (notably in 1959–63 and 1973) and that had been living in exile for many years.[4] With the massive return of the New Case returnees (who had fled the country as a result of the war and immediately after the genocide) from Zaire and Tanzania in the end of 1996 and beginning of 1997 an acute housing problem was born. Many of their houses were destroyed or occupied by Old Case refugees.

This was the impetus for the Cabinet Council to decide on the expansion of the programme. Not only the homeless returnees, but the entire rural population had to be concentrated in villages. This meant that thousands of families had to abandon and destroy their homestead near their fields to move to one of the new settlements. This was done to address a problem of settlement and land use, which had been an ongoing issue since independence. Despite a continuous population growth and Rwanda being one of the most densely populated countries in Africa, nonagricultural activities had always failed to take off (Hentic 1995). As a result, more and more people had to make their living of the same amount of land. Many writers on preconflict Rwanda regard the pressure on agricultural land as a central factor behind the violence (among others Prunier 1995; André and Platteau 1996; Pottier 1997). In contrast to the prewar government of Habyarimana, which had used the scarcity-of-land argument to access donor funds and to prevent repatriation of Old Case returnees during the 1980s (African Rights 1994: 15), the new government came to favour a completely different rationale. Socioeconomic pressure on land was no longer regarded as a given, but could be solved by better land use planning, better settlement patterns and economic growth outside of agriculture. These were presented as the basic tenets of *Imidugudu* (MININTER 1997). Through *Imidugudu*, the message was to be conveyed that the country had enough resources to sustain all Rwandese people, and that every Rwandese living abroad was welcome to return.

As the dispersed settlement pattern prevalent in many of the Rwandese rural areas was considered as inefficient, the programme aimed at the regrouping of the population in villages. The policy further called for the promotion of activities outside the agropastoral field. At the same time, villages would facilitate the provision of services. They would contribute to security, as it would be easier to defend villages than scattered households. The integration of different ethnic groups in the villages was, moreover, expected to lead to informal and eventually relaxed relations between them.

After the policy was announced in the beginning of 1997, it created much commotion and critique. Questions were raised about the feasibility of its implementation. Right from the start, there were doubts about the government estimates of the numbers of homeless families. Besides, it was questioned whether housing was in all cases the primary need, especially for the high number of families that had found temporary shelter by sharing housing with relatives. This became all the more controversial when the programme was extended to the whole rural population, including people already having secured residence. Many houses had to be destroyed, in order to be rebuilt elsewhere. It raised questions in how far regrouping was voluntary.

Another ambiguity concerned the political objectives behind the programme. Although it claimed to contribute to reconciliation, some critics doubted the sincerity of this rationale of the government. It was suggested that the programme meant to favour the Old Case (Tutsi) returnees. Questions were also raised about the security and surveillance aspect. *Imidugudu* could be interpreted as a device to better control the population and it was hard to estimate how the government was going to use the discretion it so created.

Nonetheless, *Imidugudu* was launched with the help of many international organisations. Numerous NGOs implemented settlement programmes, and different UN agencies provided funding and technical support. As part of our research, we interviewed officers of twenty-five international NGOs and UN organisations, as well as a limited number of donor representatives. Discussing their involvement in villagisation programmes, the narratives of officers invariably centred around the theme of 'emergency'. The immense and obvious need for shelter, due to destruction and the massive repatriation of refugees was cited as a central justification why agencies supported the *Imidugudu* policy. They felt that the extension of the programme to the entire rural population was not their concern, as long as there were still people without houses. Despite all doubts and critique they had about the problems and pitfalls, they considered it simply *necessary* to pursue its implementation in view of the emergency situation of the country.

This sense of urgency was magnified by the feeling among the development community that Rwanda was in need of a radical change to prevent future genocides. *Imidugudu*, with its neat and uniform villages promised – literally – to build a new, radically altered and ordered society. Apparently, the 'dire' need for change overruled the 'laws' of development that social change should be slow and sustained from below in order to be successful.

Upholding the emergency rationale, finally, played into considerations regarding the mandates of different organisations. In 1998, four years after the war, a number of *relief* NGOs and agencies were still staying on in Rwanda. They could maintain their presence by continuing to label the situation in the country as one of emergency or rehabilitation. The *Imidugudu* programme fitted well into this representation. Organisations could engage in housing programmes as an extension of their mandate to provide shelter, on the condition that they treated *Imidugudu* as an emergency programme. An illustration of this was found with UNHCR, which in its writings consistently spoke of 'shelter' programmes instead of 'settlement' or 'housing'.

Hence, we may conclude that the emergency rationale played a central role in international organisations' motivations for involvement in the programme. This reliance of organisations on an emergency rationale to organise their involvement in what really was a long-term, compulsory development programme had several consequences. Under the pressure of this emergency thinking, the international community was prepared to accept a blueprint development programme for the whole country. Moreover, as a result of the emergency rationale and the presentation of the programme as a merely technological intervention, the political implications of the programme disappeared from view. These issues will be illustrated by the experiences with implementation of the programme in two cases.

Imidugudu in Practice

Although the national policy is supposed to provide the guidelines, what really matters, is of course the *interpretation* of the national policy by local authorities, and the way they adapt the guidelines to what they consider as the local particularities. At the same time, the local population inter-prets the policy in a particular way. The following two cases make this clear. In the first one, the local authorities focused entirely on the comple-tion of what they perceived as their mission, namely to relocate the entire population in a short timespan. As a result they failed to address the ques-tion of land and livelihoods. In the second case, the programme bred con-siderable resentment among the population, in whose imagery the pro-gramme was a ploy of ethnic discrimination by the local authorities.

The Case of Kanzenze: Rational, Scientific and Planned Land-use?

In Kanzenze *commune*,[5] *Imidugudu* played an important role. NGOs and the local government had constructed a number of villages in the area, mainly for genocide survivors (Kanzenze was heavily inflicted by the genocide) and returning Tutsi exiles that came to the area following the RPF-victory in the 1994 war. The local authorities took the national rheto-ric about complete regrouping of the population seriously. From the start of the programme, new constructions in the *commune* were only allowed on *Imidugudu* sites. NGO programmes rehabilitating war-damaged hous-es were stopped, and individuals who built outside of the designated set-tlements were fined.

We studied two settlement sites in Kanzenze. In the discussions with beneficiaries and authorities about the sites, the availability of services played an important role. The installation of services lagged behind hous-ing construction. In both sites, the lack of drinking water on the site was a major source of complaint for the population. Although these services were also absent in the localities where people came from, they bothered a lot about the same lack in their new community. The problem was, that services had been promised in order to entice people to move to the set-tlements, so people insisted this promise should be realised.

Although services thus figured prominently in discussions about *Imidugudu*, beneath the surface more problematic issues simmered. The population of the settlement sites in Kanzenze were largely dependent on agriculture for their livelihood. Only a few people had income outside agriculture, and there were no NGO income-generating projects in the area. The dependence on cultivation made the issue of land a very crucial one. From the point of view of livelihood, the location of one of the set-tlement sites was extremely ill-chosen. It was constructed on an infertile piece of land, located in the middle of an area that was used intensively for agriculture by people from the neighbouring village at 250 metres distance. No land was distributed to the newcomers to the site. As a result, only seven of the sixty-one families residing there had land of their own. Other families borrowed land from people living in the neighbourhood, some for free, others had to share part of their produce with the 'owners'. The informal arrangements that people on the site had for land were not long-lasting and could not resolve the actual land shortage. The unregulated grazing of cattle further exacerbated the problem.

Livelihood, then, turned out to be the major problem in this area. The local authorities had not yet addressed the issue. They had not started a reallocation of land. Although there was some idle land, this was a sensitive issue. Partly this land belonged to New Case refugees who could still be expected to come home, partly this belonged to those survivors of the genocide who, being the sole survivor, had inherited from their entire extended family. The authorities were afraid to add insult to injury by taking away some of these lands. On the other hand, some people suggested that some of the local authorities were opposed to redistribution, in order to protect their own landholdings that were sized above average.

A central rationale of the *Imidugudu* policy was its possibility to rationally and scientifically plan settlement and land use. In Kanzenze, no start was yet made with the envisaged integrated approach. The authorities seemed to avoid the problems it would imply, because they were too sensitive or complicated to handle. Instead, they put all efforts in the relocation of the population. In October 1998, the authorities stipulated that the relocation progress was not on target. They decided that from then on, the population itself should start constructing its own houses. NGOs were no longer requested to build villages, but instead to provide large quantities of materials. In March 1999, the environment of Kanzenze had been transformed into a landscape of numerous settlements under construction. Housing and relocation became an isolated endeavour. In this way, the authorities compounded the problems for the future.

The Case of Gisenyi: Imidugudu a Politically Neutral Programme?

One of the major policy objectives of *Imidugudu* was that it could contribute to reconciliation and reintegration. It was presented as a programme that would equally benefit every group in society and was therefore politically neutral. The case of Gisenyi gives us some food for thought on this matter. Gisenyi *secteur* is located in the southeastern Prefecture of Kibungo, which was among the areas to receive the largest numbers of returnees. In Kibungo, *Imidugudu* has gone far ahead, with nearly complete resettlement in a large number of communities. Although a lot of NGOs implemented settlement programmes in the area, the larger part of implementation results from the efforts of the municipal authorities and the population itself.

In Gisenyi *secteur*, the complete population had moved into *Imidugudu*. The original population of the area was predominantly Hutu. Immediately after the war, huge numbers of Old Case (Tutsi) returnees had settled in the area. With the influx of the New Case returnees from the camps in Tanzania, Gisenyi saw its original number of inhabitants doubled. This resulted in a large need for houses and land. Moreover, after the return of the New Case refugees, the area remained unsafe for a long time as a result of infiltration by *Interahamwe* militia, crossing the river marking the border with Tanzania. Spring 1998, for example, witnessed an attack on a settlement site implemented by the Lutheran World Federation, in which eight people lost their lives. Some people in the area had been accused of collaboration with the *Interahamwe*, others had simply been forced to collaborate. There were unconfirmed rumours about retaliations by the army.

In view of the large number of returnees as well as the security situation, the local authorities ordered that all inhabitants of the *secteur*, including the onstaying population, had to move to villages. In early 1999, virtually everybody was living in one of the ten settlement sites of about 150 houses each. The abandoned houses were all destroyed or taken apart by their former owners. Unlike in the case of Kanzenze, in Gisenyi the relocation was accompanied by land redistribution. The authorities had asked all original inhabitants of the area to divide their plots in two and give one of the two hectares to a family of Old Case returnees.[6]

The programme enabled Old Case returnees to acquire a house lot and some land. A number of New Case returnees, on the other hand, experienced a sense of loss and felt their situation had deteriorated because of the resettlement. Their major source of complaint was the displacement from the land to the village. People said that when living on the land, more work could be done on it, and more could be harvested. It had become a lot of work to bring the harvest back home and to bring manure to the fields, and the fields could not be watched for theft or harm by wild animals. Although many could understand the population had to be temporarily concentrated when urged by the security situation, they objected to the idea that their move had to be permanent. Quite a few people assured us, that if there were a possibility, they would return to their old houses.

The question remains if and how *Imidugudu* contributed to reconciliation. At first sight, the programme in Gisenyi contained a form of equity. Land was shared between the 'originals' (as they called themselves) and the repatriates. Since houses could not be shared, the decision that everybody had to move represented a kind of 'Judgement of Solomon', in which nobody was favoured with the entitlement of the old houses, and everybody was equally burdened with the hassles of constructing and moving places. However, this was not how the local population perceived the programme. Many New Case returnees displayed a sense of political deprivation. They felt that the *Imidugudu* programme, as it was implemented in Gisenyi, was meant to serve the interests of the 'others', i.e. the Tutsi returnees. The remark that 'power is with the repatriates,' which we heard several times, expressed this feeling very well.

These sentiments seemed to implicitly point to a generalised ethnic tension. This was, among others, apparent in the derogatory labels New Case returnees used for Old Case returnees. However, the issue was more complicated. The resentment of New Case returnees was not primarily directed to those Old Case repatriates with whom they had to share their land. The more problematic relation was concentrated in the interface of cultivators and authorities. The major frustration was evoked by the treatment that ordinary cultivators received from authorities. On their own account, those authorities interpreted how the programme was going to be implemented in their area, including decisions such as which individuals were allowed to stay or had to move elsewhere. Locally, such personal decisions were interpreted as politically motivated. The interface between cultivators and authorities manifested indeed an ethnic dimension, in the sense that Hutu returnees felt deprived by mainly Tutsi authorities. It matters not so much whether the returnees were right or not about the political motivations of the local officials. What matters is their *image* of the programme as ethnically discriminatory. In this case, instead of bringing reconciliation, due to its enforced character, the programme bred resentment that got expressed in ethnic terms, thus leading to increased social tension. This makes the issue of the top-down character of the programme and the lack of consultation or participation a very pertinent one.

The two case studies of Kanzenze and Gisenyi bring out several issues. In the first place, it appears that the outcome of *Imidugudu* and the way it is implemented varies in different areas. It is given different emphasis by local authorities and is interpreted differently by the local population. Secondly, they show a variety of problems with the implementation of the programme, ranging from planning difficulties to issues of livelihood and politics.

Conclusion: *Imidugudu* as a Case of Emergency Development

Imidugudu represents an enormous effort to solve the housing need of the Rwandan population and to contribute to a better land use and reconciliation of the population. Indeed, a large number of homeless people have been settled through the programme. On the other hand, it has also forced many people to vacate their house and diverted away the attention and resources to solve other needs. This programme usurped much of the donor money that the country had received right after the war and genocide, without taking into account possible alternatives.

The prospects that *Imidugudu* will lead to integrated rural development are dim. Although a few communities flourish, with the help of international NGOs, enormous costs will be implied to transform all the sites that have been built into sustainable communities. It is doubtful whether the international community is going to supply the funds needed – although perhaps they should, given the fact that they are co-responsible for the programme as it has evolved. As the case studies show, *Imidugudu* was not implemented in the integrated way it was envisaged. In the localities, the local authorities redefine *Imidugudu*, and actual local implementation depends largely on the efforts and persistence of these authorities. While in some areas they adjust the programme to the local conditions, in others, as in Kanzenze, they relentlessly pursued a regrouping of the population. Eventually, the programme will be shaped by the responses of the inhabitants of the villages. If given a chance, we do not know how many will move out of the villages, either to return to their scattered settlements, or to move to bigger cities.

It is thus clear, that *Imidugudu* worked out well in some communities, but in many others failed to bring improvements or made matters perhaps even worse. At this point, then, we may conclude that the programme should not have been imposed on the whole country, but should have been implemented on a case-by-case basis, where policies for settlement got integrated with approaches for land distribution and land use, services, livelihoods and future habitation needs. Valid as this may be, it leaves certain questions unanswered.

One of the most remarkable aspects of *Imidugudu* is that it was implemented in the 1990s, after decades of experience with and learning about top-down development, and villagisation in particular. One has become well aware of the fact that these kinds of top-down, authoritative and generalised programmes are bound to fail. Numerous authors have shown the limitations of planned development interventions (see Long and van der Ploeg 1989; Long and Long 1992; Scott 1998). Development agencies emphasise the complexity of social change and advocate bottom-up and participatory approaches.

Why then, did so many agencies cooperate with the implementation of *Imidugudu*? An answer, as we suggest, may be found in the fact that they responded to an emergency situation. Roe stipulated that in cases of a lot of ambiguity and pressure to act one tends to resort to broad explanatory narratives and standard approaches (Roe 1991). In the case of the returning refugees in Rwanda, both the ambiguities and the pressure to act were enormous, creating the need for a straightforward narrative from which an equally straightforward line of action followed. The narrative on *Imidugudu* fitted this purpose. However, acceptable as this may be during an acute emergency, it does not explain the continuity of the narrative's acceptance.

Apart from the possible lack of feasibility and effectiveness of the programme, we worry particularly about its political implications. James Ferguson (1994) has likened development to an antipolitics machine. In comparison, *Imidugudu* could be called an antipolitics roller-coaster. By adopting a technocratic bid for sustainable development, the political intentions and implications of the programme remained largely unaddressed and hidden. The programme has been implemented, even though a lot of ambiguity prevailed on the precise political intentions of the Rwandan government with regard to democratisation and reconciliation. For example, although the security situation in the country legitimised certain measures, it has been suggested that *Imidugudu* was a means for the government to have a firmer control on the entire rural population.

Even if the intentions of the programme were indeed to contribute to social reconciliation, this may not have worked out as such in practice. This was exemplified by the case of Gisenyi. Despite a claim of equity and nondiscrimination, ordinary people perceive the programme differently. This is important, because their perception determines their responses. As a result, even if the programme lived up to its apolitical, technological character, it turns into a highly political venture during local implementation. This is exacerbated by the top-down, authoritative style of implementation. Rwanda has a long history with top-down governance, which may even be blamed for contributing to past atrocities, considering the organisation of the genocide and other outbreaks of ethnic cleansing (Prunier 1995; Des Forges 1999). It is an important warning for the dangers in such a style of governance. To make matters worse, the government has stipulated by decree that ethnicity should be abolished, thereby impairing public discussion about ethnicity. If ethnic tension is building up again, it remains hidden.

The case of Rwanda confirms recent findings that when refugees come home this is the start of a long process of reintegration and development, rather than an end-good-all-good closure of a period of exile (Allen 1996). In view of this, Tim Allen as well as numerous other authors have advocated an end to separating emergency relief from development and instead opt for an integrated approach. The idea of such an approach is that relief is organised in such a way as not to jeopardise and possibly to enhance long-term sustainable development. *Imidugudu* meant to be such an integrated programme. It may be labelled as 'emergency development', which was launched under the pressure of an emergency situation and addressed immediate needs, but at the same time had far-stretching consequences for future development. The difficulty is that the emergency situation seems to have lured agencies to accept a blueprint policy, which under 'normal' conditions of development planning they would not have accepted. As a result, the programme lacked participation, and the local knowledge and perceptions of the Rwandan population were not taken into account. This case then, cautions against overenthusiastically embracing the new idea of integrating development into relief. We may end up combining the worst of both worlds.

Notes

1. This chapter has parallels with an earlier article in the *Journal of Refugee Studies* (Hilhorst and van Leeuwen 2000) but questions more in detail the linking of relief and development. It is based on research implemented between May 1998 and March 1999. We are grateful to the Joint Reintegration Programming Unit (JRPU), the International Rescue Committee (IRC) and ZOA Refugee Care, that facilitated the research in Rwanda, and to all those people who commented on earlier drafts. Correspondence regarding this paper can be addressed to: Wageningen Disaster Studies, P.O. Box 8130, 6700 EW Wageningen. E-mail: disaster.studies@alg.asnw.wau.nl
2. For a critical discussion of this issue, see Frerks et al. (1995) and Frerks (1998).
3. In the discourse of emergency operations, in general those are referred to as 'Old Case Load'. However, we shall avoid the term 'Load', and instead refer to Old and New Case refugees and returnees.
4. As a result of the 1993 Arusha Agreement they had lost their rights to reclaim their former entitlements and land (see a.o. Reyntjens 1994).
5. In Rwanda, the term *commune* refers to a municipality, of which there are 155 in total in Rwanda. Each commune is divided in about ten *secteurs*.
6. The area had previously been part of a *paysannat*, which was a resettlement programme in the late 1960s, in which every family had been given two hectares of land.

14

Dilemmas of Humanitarian Aid: Supporting Internal Refugees in Sri Lanka

Joke Schrijvers

Introduction

With the increase of long-lasting intrastate conflicts, the extent and nature of forced migration have changed. Today, 'internally displaced people' by far outnumber refugees. According to conservative estimates, there are altogether 20–25 million internal refugees as against 12 million refugees (Hampton 1998: xv; UNHCR 2001). The 1951 UN convention does not protect internal refugees, but all agencies providing humanitarian aid in crisis situations are confronted with people who are uprooted within their own countries. More often than not these people belong to minority groups. The question of how to provide help to internal refugees in situations where sovereign governments fail to do so urgently needs attention.

Internal conflicts and civil wars tend to last for decades or more, with repeated upsurges of violence in particular regions. These crises hardly ever seem to be really over. People who have fled to other regions in their own countries more often than not are unable or highly reluctant to return home. In such situations, humanitarian relief for 'internally displaced people' is not enough. They need not merely short-term humanitarian relief, but support to build up a sustainable, secure and self-reliant life in their new environments. Precisely because of the nature of internal conflicts and civil wars, with their repeated and sudden outbursts of violence over a long period of time, it has become highly problematic to distinguish separate phases of 'emergency', 'rehabilitation' and 'reconstruction'. Likewise, distinctions between humanitarian and development aid have become increasingly artificial in conflict-ridden and war-torn societies.

In this contribution, drawing on my research experiences between 1993 and 1998 with uprooted people of Tamil origin in Sri Lanka, I will discuss some of the dilemmas of providing support to these internal refugees. My focus is in particular on issues of engagement versus neutrality. What are the implications of trying to provide the necessary help, particularly when dealing with the internally displaced who officially fall under the protection of a sovereign state? Can humanitarian relief and development efforts be linked together, and what are the moral and political dilemmas at stake?

Relief versus Development Aid

Two extreme positions have developed in the debate on the nature of humanitarian aid. One is that humanitarian intervention should be strictly separated from development efforts. According to this view humanitarian aid should be provided as sheer emergency relief from a neutral stand, whereas development should be the responsibility of other, development-oriented, agencies. According to the second view humanitarian aid alone is not enough; donors and agencies should aim at an integration of relief and development aid. Particularly in view of the increasing length of time that refugees cannot return home, and the actual merging of the phases of 'emergency', 'rehabilitation' and 'reconstruction', there is need of 'a more human response to refugee needs' (Zetter 1995: 1665). The idea that refugees, because they cannot and do not return home, should be seen as part of the host society and not as a completely separate category of people, was already put forward in the 1980s (see Harrell-Bond 1986; Cuénod 1989; Kuhlman 1989). In the 1990s it was even seen as 'dehumanising' not to take advantage of the development potential the refugees and their hosts represent (Harrell-Bond 1996: 185; cf. Zetter 1992). A UN report (1997) points to the need 'to couple relief efforts with more comprehensive approaches that include promoting political settlements, rebuilding capacity and restoring economic opportunity'.

The first view, that relief and development should be strictly separated, regained support in the late 1990s. This in spite of the recent experiences of agencies operating during internal conflicts and crises, that have made clear how in practice the politics of humanitarian intervention and more structural aid have become more intertwined than ever before. Even the providers of 'neutral' military UN protection have been drawn into conflicts, like for instance in Rwanda and in Former Yugoslavia. The role of 'Dutchbat' in Srebrenica is one of the well-known examples. Agencies providing relief and rehabilitation in such regions have ended up with dirty hands. In the Netherlands, in the late 1990s, there was sharp criticism of the negotiations about development aid of the then Minister of Development Cooperation with the Taliban in Afghanistan. At about the same time, the Netherlands' Advisory Council on International Affairs (1998) brought out an advice that propagated humanitarian aid in its original mandate. The advice focused on an 'emergency package' for people in crisis situations and distinguished clear-cut stages of emergency and reconstruction with separate forms of aid by separate agencies. It emphatically stressed the need for neutral aid. This advice turned the clock back by at least ten years. But it also brought into the open the dilemmas created by the actual merging of conflict and development, and the linking, in practice, of humanitarian and development-oriented aid.

Would it indeed be wise and just to return to a narrow concept of humanitarian aid, supported by the belief in taking a neutral stand? Theoretically, it is hard to maintain that development and aid can be kept separate from conflict and from the ensuing 'refugee crisis'. Exclusion of large sections of society from the benefits of development and globalisation, together with growing poverty, polarisation, ethnicisation and gender disparities, have gone hand in hand with the increase of violent conflicts the world over (Childers 1991; Schrijvers 1993; 1996; Bradbury and Adams 1996; Goor et al. 1996). And precisely this is reflected at the level of practice in the increasing difficulty and artificiality of distinguishing humanitarian aid and development aid.

Researchers engaged in development-oriented research have been facing similar problems. Development and conflict have become intertwined, and therefore the old issues of engagement versus neutrality need new critical reflection as well. When looking at my own work, for instance, I have always argued for consciously siding with the people in more vulnerable positions. In the late 1970s and 1980s I studied the conditions of life of poor rural women in Sri Lanka (e.g. Schrijvers 1985; 1993). In the 1990s, however, during my research on internal refugees in war-torn Sri Lanka, taking sides proved to be far more problematic. Firstly, internal refugees, whether women, men, or children, were all excluded from society, although in different ways (Schrijvers 1995; 1997; 1999). Secondly, explicit partiality was politically highly dangerous in the ongoing war between the government and the Liberation Tigers of Tamil Eelam (LTTE). At the same time, as practitioners pointed out to me, it had become almost inevitable to get dirty hands in the ongoing crisis, however neutral they presented themselves as being.

What are the implications of this, particularly when dealing with internal refugees who officially fall under the protection of sovereign states? I will first introduce the case of Sri Lanka, and then discuss the moral and political dilemmas at stake.

Internal Refugees and Relief in Sri Lanka

After independence from the U.K. in 1948, Sri Lanka, the former Ceylon, gained international respect for its prosperity and democracy. However, under the successive Sinhalese-dominated governments internal relations rapidly deteriorated between the Sinhalese majority and the two main minorities, the Tamils and the Muslims (who, Muslim by religion and mostly Tamil-speaking, in Sri Lanka are considered a separate ethnic community). Communal tensions escalated into violent riots in 1956, 1958, 1971, and 1981. Tamil youth radicalised, with the LTTE standing out as the most militant and strongly organised group. The particularly gruesome riots against the Tamils in 1983 are generally considered the turning point at which the conflict developed into a violent civil war between the government and the LTTE. This war was going on without a solution in sight, until in February 2002 a serious cease-fire agreement was reached between the government and the LTTE. This led to the cessation of hostilities and stopped the movement of people. Subsequently peace talks have taken place in Thailand, facilitated by Norway. After the ceasefire some internally displaced people have started to resettle, though many prefer to wait until a more definite peace agreement has been concluded and donor-supported resettlement programmes are started. In the following, I will not focus on the causes and consequences of the conflict as such (see Kloos 2000), but on the situation of internal refugees and the dilemmas of providing support during conflict and civil war.

The war has affected the whole population of around eighteen million, of whom some 800,000 fled the country, to India, Australia, Western Europe and North America. A fluctuating number of half a million to 1.2 million people have been internally displaced, during and in between three major upsurges, in the late 1980s, the early 1990s, and from 1995 onwards. Most of these internal refugees are self-settled or stay with relatives or friends. Around 150,000 people are 'temporarily' kept in schools or temples turned into camps – in local terminology 'welfare centres'. Between 1990 and 1992 there was a complete breakdown of communal relations between the Tamils and Muslims in the east, with ten thousand dead, thousands widowed, and at least 80 percent of the population displaced. In October 1990 the LTTE 'ethnically cleansed' the north by forcing all 75,000 Muslims to leave. Most Sinhalese who were still living in the north or east also left, but almost all of them have been able to resettle elsewhere. At present, internal refugees for the majority are staying in the LTTE-ruled north of the Jaffna peninsula and the Vanni, and along the whole northeast war frontier (see Brabant 1998). They are predominantly Tamil-speaking, the majority of them Tamils, a minority Muslims.

In this process, because of ethnic identity politics the different communities in Sri Lanka have been polarised into rigid 'ethnic' groups

(Rajasingham-Senanayake 1999). In fact each of the three groups comprises very different communities. The term 'Tamils', for instance, covers vastly different communities: the 'Sri Lanka' Tamils consisting of the 'Jaffna' and 'Batticaloa' Tamils in the north and east respectively, who have lived in Sri Lanka since times unknown; and the 'Indian' or 'Plantation' Tamils who are the descendants of a plantation workforce imported by the British from Tamil Nadu in South India, in the nineteenth century. These Indian Tamils were disenfranchised immediately after independence, thus losing their citizenship rights. There are important sociocultural differences between Tamils from the north and the east, as well as significant class, caste, and gender differences within all Tamil communities. My research related to both Tamil and Muslim internal refugees, in Colombo, Batticaloa District, and Vavuniya (see Schrijvers 1997; 1998; 1999). In this contribution I will focus on Tamil internal refugees.

During the war, refugees from the north in growing numbers crossed the war frontier to the south in search of security. In 1998, during my last field research, there were 12,500 refugees in camps in Vavuniya alone – once a small provincial town at the Sinhalese side of the frontier. The relief, which looked quite impressive on paper, did not routinely reach the people, and supplies were always poorer in quantity and quality than implied by official rules. Many involved in the aid hierarchy and war-related business could benefit. UN organisations such as UNICEF and UNHCR had to operate under strict government control. They worked mainly through local NGOs that had mushroomed since camps had been established for the refugees, in Colombo and all along the northeastern war frontier. There was an NGO consortium through which efforts were made to coordinate activities. These activities varied from pure food aid to healthcare, preschool activities and training in income-generating skills, especially for girls. After the courses were over, however, no support was offered for selling their products or for entering some form of employment. It struck me that the philosophy according to which these activities were organised was purely philanthropic. It reminded me of the old 'soup-kitchen' mentality of development workers – an attitude that twenty years ago in development circles was already found to be unacceptable.

Governmental and nongovernmental relief was top-down and mostly unconnected with the primary needs of the refugees. For instance, there had been no consultation about the food items to be provided, and people told me they would have preferred money rather than this bad quality food. The refugee self-organisations were bypassed when taking decisions about the relief and support to be given, and there was little encouragement for women to formulate their specific needs, such as private space for bathing.

Packed together in inhuman circumstances, male and female refugees primarily needed support to regain their sense of self, their self-confidence and human dignity. They wanted active involvement in shaping a new life. However, the aid provided encouraged passivity and dependency rather than participation or self-reliance. Having lived in these circumstances for years, most refugees had adopted habits of dependency. The camp enclosure had become a way of life.

'Resettled' in War Zones and Detention Camps

Lacking means to stay with relatives, rent a room, or leave the country, the people who had remained in the camps formed an 'underclass' among the refugees. Many of them had lived in camps for long periods – sometimes for over ten years. People who had first fled from Jaffna or Mannar in the north to camps in Colombo were later 'resettled' in camps in Vavuniya, as the war was still going on in their home areas. Likewise, since 1992 returnees from India had been 'resettled' in camps in this town. In January 1998 I had a chance of visiting Vavuniya. Compared to the situation in the camps in Colombo, the atmosphere here was extremely tense. Refugees were strictly controlled for an indefinite period of time. New refugees arriving daily from the northern war zone, instead of first being thoroughly screened, were sent to a closed prison-like camp where they had to stay for a month. Then they were moved to other camps for an indefinite period. To leave these places a pass was needed, which often was refused when there had been a political 'incident' again, whether in Vavuniya or elsewhere.

After ongoing pressure, a special 'evaluation committee', consisting of military men, government administrators and politicians, was established which had to study their files. But only very few refugees were given permission to leave the camps in order to go to Colombo or elsewhere. Even those who wished to return to Jaffna, which in 1995 had been recaptured by the government forces, were kept waiting endlessly. This not only increased resentment, but also bribery to get things done. Those who remained in the camps were the very lowest in the refugee hierarchy: mostly Plantation Tamils who had no property, no money, no relatives or relations who were better-off, and no relatives in the diaspora who could send money.

One of the camps I visited had been established by the UNHCR in 1992, originally to receive returnees from India. It was open for visitors so that they would get a positive impression of the Vavuniya 'welfare centres'. In contrast to the other camps, where people were packed together behind barbed wire, this one was quite spacious. There were little gardens and trees in between the 'lines' consisting of rooms for each family. It looked rather like a poor, low-caste dry-zone village in the north. The main difference was the lack of freedom to enter or leave this 'village.' Accidentally, I met a group of women there whom I had already met in 1993 when they were staying in a camp in Colombo. When that camp was closed by the government, they had been sent to Vavuniya, to a closed 'transit camp'. 'We got cooked meals, but it was just like a prison, we were not allowed to leave the camp at all.' They ate and slept in the same hall. From there they were taken to another camp, and stayed there for a year. After that, in 1995, they were brought to this camp. First they were given three-month passes so that they could go out for work. But since there had been many incidents, more often than not they were not given permission to leave. So they had to depend on food aid again, but the quality of the food was very bad. 'We want to get a permanent pass, we want to work and earn again,' they told me.

We talked about the camp in Colombo, how was it to live there compared to this place? 'Oh, there was enough food, but no pocket money, no soap.' There were a number of foreign and local NGOs that helped them. They received plastic pots, soap, clothes. There they could go out for work; they did not need a pass. They went out to do casual labour, the men doing masonry, the women working as housemaids, or packing for a firm, or sewing. There was sufficient work and they earned enough. But here in this camp, they had to pick the leaves from the trees to cook additional curries. It was as if they were talking about an idyllic past – but I saw them in my mind, packed together in that big hall in Colombo where in my view they were living an inhuman life. I asked them about medical and educational facilities and was surprised that in this regard the situation in Vavuniya seemed to be far better. It amazed me, therefore, when they insisted that life in the Colombo camp was so much better. 'Because we earned enough money, there were NGOs to help us, and we did not have the pass system'. They agreed with me that the hall in Colombo was too small and too crowded, and that the meals indeed were not regularly delivered and of very poor quality. And just like in Vavuniya they suffered from the men who after drinks started harassing their wives and children. And of course, there, too, they did not want to be refugees, they wanted to work and earn their living. But there they were at least free to move around. If given the choice now, they would leave for India immediately, where there was work, food was cheap, and, most importantly, they did not need passes.

It was unpredictable for how long these refugees would have to remain under control in this camp. It was unlikely that the war would come to an end soon. The government, assisted by UNHCR-funded local NGOs, was now implementing a resettlement programme along the war frontier, but only relatively few refugees could be selected for a plot of land.

Discussion: Relief or Development for Internal Refugees?

The above case suggests that relief and development for internal refugees should be linked together. With civil war and displacement continuing, internal refugees need support to build up a self-reliant life in their new environments. Arguments that, in the case of internal refugees, state sovereignty stands in the way of more structural outside help are not convincing. Structural adjustment programmes for development have undermined the sovereign power of the receiving states far more dramatically. The question is not so much whether relief and development aid should be integrated when working with internal refugees, but to what extent it can be integrated. How to weigh the moral, and political, choices involved?

In the case I described, internal refugees of Plantation Tamil origin found themselves at the wrong end of the rope in all regards. They were not even the Tamils for whom the LTTE has been fighting to create a 'Tamil homeland'. Nonetheless, being labelled as 'Tamils' by the Sinhalese, they had severely suffered during the successive anti-Tamil riots. The government equally treated them as dangerous, terrorist 'Tamils'. All Tamils, whether or not of Plantation origin and whether or not supporting the LTTE, were categorically considered state enemies to be strictly controlled. The camps in Vavuniya served this goal. The majority who had fled from the north ended up in these camps, lacking the means and networks of relations to bribe the officials and find their way to Colombo or abroad. Only a few families got a chance to 'resettle' – close to the dangerous war frontier. These resettlement projects in Vavuniya, meant as support to internal refugees for rebuilding their lives in new areas, were a combination of relief and development. Cynics I spoke to however referred to these projects as 'cannon fodder'. The refugees were resettled precisely in areas where they were most likely to be either killed or forced to flee again. Surely, for the (UNHCR-supported) non-governmental organisations involved this meant dirty hands.

I wondered what I myself would do if I were one of the field officers. Would this be my 'moral bottom-line' (Waal, 1993)? I am not sure because there is little choice in such a situation, and moreover I would depend on the work for my salary. The other choice available would be to participate in pure relief activities for semidetention camps, helping army and government to control the people. Morally speaking, I would find this equally impossible. Yet this is what the humanitarian agencies were actually doing for internal refugees. They helped them survive behind barbed wire, enabling visiting officers from all over the world to have a peep inside – including researchers like me – thereby further undermining their humanity. In April 1998 a group of refugees in one of these camps demanded that no visitors be allowed any longer, to spare them the indignity. Later, hunger strikes were held to speed up decision making, without the desired result either. As nobody did it for them, refugees themselves tried to bring back morality.

Even if humanitarian agencies have succeeded in saving lives, the question arises whether in such conditions this can be called a success (an assumption underlying many evaluation studies, see for instance Apthorpe 1997). My criticism of course does not mean that I am against saving lives, but I am emphasising the importance of the quality of life – a dominant view in development circles since the 1970s. Neither would I know an alternative; government policy does not provide much room to manoeuvre. The Government Agent in Vavuniya for example, a Tamil himself and highly experienced, was doing what he could in his capacity, which was very little. In this frontier zone the military were the ones in actual control.

What, then, are the choices left? When dealing with internal refugees in a country like Sri Lanka, when it was torn apart by civil war, the main space left for making moral choices is, I think, in the approach taken towards the people. This applies to humanitarian agencies and researchers alike. At the very least, humanitarian aid could be organised in a less top-down, more participatory manner, and researchers could create knowledge to support this. Much can be learnt from participatory development theory and practice (see Nelson and Wright 1995). An Oxfam (1996) report on internal refugees in Sri Lanka stresses the need to find out the needs of the people themselves. Women's needs, such as water and sanitation, health and safety are mentioned in particular. Whereas in the development debate this has been propagated for decades, in circles of humanitarian aid this approach is quite new. And of course in the context of war, listening to people is not an innocent approach at all. It is a choice with highly political implications. Particularly when they are negatively affected by war, the views and opinions of people are never neutral. What they have to say always relates to politics, even if only 'innocent' people like 'women' are asked about 'innocent' matters of sanitation or food. With whom, for instance, are people prepared to share the toilets? Why do they detest the food prepared according to Sinhalese taste?

Sooner or later, politics come in explicitly. After the communal slaughters, for instance, the government decided not to put refugees of supposedly different 'ethnic' backgrounds together in camps. This decision, although probably unavoidable in the middle of the violent crisis in the late 1980s and early 90s, further legitimised the ethnicisation process. Indeed, hostile interethnic relations were the main topic of conversation among the male refugees I spoke to (Schrijvers 1997). I found this alarming. When women told me they did not want 'to talk politics like the men', I considered this statement a political cry for peace in a country torn apart by interethnic violence. What could I do as a researcher? As a foreigner I was politically less vulnerable than my colleagues in Sri Lanka (see Kloos 1995). I could more explicitly problematise the status quo with its taken for granted concepts of ethnicity. I tried to combine my research with advocacy work, and I published my findings in Sri Lankan journals as well.

What is the room for manoeuvre for agencies dealing with internal refugees in such countries? Most internal refugees are to be found in the north of Sri Lanka where the war escalated over the years, with increasing numbers of 'casualties' and the majority of the population continuously on the move. This area is predominantly under LTTE control. All NGOs that since the 1980s have remained active in the north have had to collaborate with the LTTE, bound to follow their rules. This implies that they have been supporting a violent, repressive regime that has ignored most international standards of human rights. Agencies active in the south, on the other hand, have had to follow the government's rules and regulations. As I have shown above this does not mean that they have had much space for playing a fair and just role either. The agencies can keep their hands clean on neither side. Moreover, whether active in the north, the east or the south, they have been contributing to the economy of war, knowingly 'helping' people who are merely pawns in the struggle (see Slim 1997).

Does all this support the view that humanitarian aid should be 'cleansed' from development activities? Would it be better to reduce it to pure relief provided from a 'neutral' position, as was the advice of the Advisory Council for International Affairs (1998) in the Netherlands? In my view, this is naive and unrealistic. In the years to come, in the world as a whole an increase rather than decrease of intrastate and 'terrorist' violence can be expected, with the resulting increase of (internal) refugees. Inevitably, both relief and development aid will have to be provided in the context of dirty wars. Efforts to help internal refugees survive and build up their lives cannot be 'clean'. Splitting up agencies into either relief- or development-oriented is no solution when crisis has become the normal state of affairs. The two fields of activities in practice cannot, and should not, be separated, as internal refugees like others are entitled to a human life. Neither can agencies act 'neutrally', involved as they are in the very heat of war and political violence. Slim (1997: 3) speaks of the growing unease among policy makers and field workers who feel confronted by moral dilemmas. 'In such situations, helpers soon find themselves dining with the devil (…).' Morality in this context is almost a synonym of politics. More often than not 'neutrality' supports the more powerful parties, whose interests do not reflect the needs of politically vulnerable people – who have been marginalised, discriminated against, violently repressed, or slaughtered. Providers of humanitarian aid would morally strangle themselves if, for fear of contamination by the dirtiness of war, they let go the ideal of people's basic human right to development – to participation, self-reliance and equity. The argument that it is too difficult to aim at relief-cum-development aid in crisis situations, that we dirty our hands too much, and that we may negatively influence the dynamics of the conflict, does not hold. The same objections have been made with regard to development aid. Development workers at all levels have dirtied their hands, unintentionally contributing to the widening gap between those who have and those who have no access to the benefits of 'development' or, for that matter, globalisation. Repeatedly development workers themselves have indicated to me that they could not reach certain groups of people. They were aware that their work enabled the accumulation of wealth and power of the (slightly) more powerful, and the exclusion of more vulnerable people such as the semi-landless, poor women, or minorities (see Hancock 1991). And precisely this has contributed to further exclusion and the increase of violent conflicts by which people are forced to flee. Politicians, policy makers, practitioners and researchers are all involved in this process. If 'dining with the devil' (Slim 1997) is unavoidable, then it is crucial to have the right people and parties around the table. Internal refugees know very well how to choose from the menu and to negotiate during dinner. Their expertise is badly needed.

Bibliography

Activa y Objectiva (1995) 2: 8.

Adams, R. (1996) *Social Work and Empowerment*. London: Macmillan.

Adele, A. (1993) *Women Fighters of Liberation*. Publication Section LTTE. Jaffna: Thasan Printers.

Advisory Council on International Affairs (AIV) (1998) *Humanitarian Aid: Redefining the Limits*. No. 6, November.

African Rights (1994) *Rwanda: Death, Despair and Defiance*. London: African Rights.

Agarwal, B. (1996) *A Field of One's Own: Gender and Land Rights in South Asia*. Cambridge: Cambridge University Press.

Allen, T. (ed.) (1996) *In Search of Cool Ground: War, Flight and Homecoming in Northeast Africa*. London: James Currey.

Allen, T. and H. Morsink (1994) *When Refugees Go Home: African Experiences*. London: James Currey.

Allen, T. and H. Morsink (1994) 'Introduction: When Refugees Go Home', in T. Allen and H. Morsink (eds.) *When Refugees Go Home*. London: James Currey.

Amnesty International (1991) *Sri Lanka – the Northeast. Human Rights Violations in A Context of Armed Conflict*.

Anderson, M.B. and P.J. Woodrow (1989) *Rising from the Ashes, Development Strategies in Times of Disaster*. Boulder and San Francisco: Westview Press.

Anderson, M.B. and P.J. Woodrow (1993) 'Reducing Vulnerability to Drought and Famine', In J.O. Field (ed.) *The Challenge of Famine. Recent Experience, Lessons Learned*. West Hartford: Kumarian Press.

André, C. and J.P. Platteau (1996) *Land Relations Under Unbearable Stress: Rwanda Caught in the Malthusian Trap*. Working paper, Cahiers de la Faculté des Sciences Economiques et Sociales, No. 164. Namur: FUNDP.

Apthorpe, R. (1997) 'Some Relief from Development: Humanitarian Emergency Aid in the Horn of Africa (including Sudan), Rwanda and Liberia', *The European Journal of Development Research*. 9, (2): 83–106.

Asif, M. (2000) 'Why Displaced Persons Reject Project Resettlement Colonies', *Economic and Political Weekly*. 35, (24): 2005–8.

Baalen, A. van (1997) 'Asiel in wonderland: de partiarchalisering van vluchtelingen', *Tijdschrift voor vrouwenstudies*. 18, (4): 418–32.

Baistow, K. (1994) 'Liberation and Regulation? Some Paradoxes of Empowerment', *Critical Social Policy*. 14, (3): 34–46.

(ed.) *The Psychological Problems of Refugees*. London: The British Refugee Council and European Consultation on Refugees and Exiles.

Bakewell, O. (1999) *Refugees Repatriating or Migrating Villagers? A Study of Movement from North West Zambia to Angola*. Ph.D. Thesis, University of Bath.

Barker, M. (1981) *The New Racism*. London: Junction Books.

Barnett, H.C. (1953) *Innovation: The Basis of Cultural Change*. New York: McGraw-Hill.

Barr, A., S. Hashagen et al. (1996) *Monitoring and Evaluation of Community Development*. A Report for the Voluntary Activity Unit, Department of Health and Social Services, Scottish Community Development Centre.

Barry, T. (1986) *Low Intensity Conflict: The New Battlefield in Central America*. Albuquerque, NM: Inter-Hemispheric Education Resource Center.

Bascom, J.B. (1994) 'The Dynamics of Refugee Repatriation: the Case of Eritreans in Eastern Sudan', in W.T.S. Gould and A.M. Findlay (eds.) *Population Migration and the Changing World Order*. Chichester: John Wiley.

Bauman, Z. (1989) *Modernity and the Holocaust*. Ithaca, NY: Cornell University Press.

Behdad, A. (1999) 'Sevruguin: Orientalist or Orienteur?', in F.N. Bohrer (ed.) *Sevruguin and the Persian Image: Photographs of Iran, 1870–1930*. Seattle, WA: Arthur M. Sackler Gallery / University of Washington Press.

Benjamin, J. (1998) 'Issues of Power and Empowerment in Refugee Studies: Rwandan Women's Adaptive Behaviour in Benaco Refugee Camp', *Refuge, Canada's periodical on refugees*, 17, (4): 27–33.

Black, R. and K. Koser (eds.) (1999) *The End of the Refugee Cycle? Refugee Repatriation and Reconstruction*. Oxford: Berghahn Books.

Boyd, M. (1989) 'Family and Personal Networks in International Migration: Recent Developments and New Agendas', *International Migration Review*. 23, Fall: 638–70.

Bozorgmehr, M., C. Der-Martirosian and G. Sabagh (1996) 'Middle Easterners: A New Kind of Immigrant', in R. Waldinger and M. Bozorgmehr (eds.) *Ethnic Los Angeles*. New York: Russel Sage Foundation.

Brabant, K. van (1998) 'Sri Lanka', in J. Hampton (ed.) *Internally Displaced People: A Global Survey*. London: Earthscan.

Bradbury, M. and M. Adams (1996) 'Editorial: Development and Conflict: Situating the Debate', *Anthropology in Action*. 3, (3): 1–5.

Bringa, T. (1995) *Being Muslim the Bosnian Way*. Princeton, NJ: Princeton University Press.

Broadcast (1986) Transcript.

Brookings Institution (1999) *Report on the Roundtable on the Gap between Humanitarian Assistance and Long-term Development*. 15 January 1999, Washington, DC.

Buchanan-Smith, M. and S. Maxwell (1994) 'Linking Relief and Development: An Introduction and Overview', *IDS Bulletin*. 25, (4): 2–17.

Butalia, U. (1998) *The Other Side of Silence*. New Delhi: Viking.

Cannon Lorgan, C. (1999) *The Experience of Villagisation: Lessons from Ethiopia, Mozambique, and Tanzania*. London: Oxfam Great Britain.

Castles, S. (2001) 'Studying Social Transformation', *International Political Science Review*, 22, (1): 13–32.

Chambers, R. (1986) 'Hidden Losers? The Impact of Rural Refugees and Refugee Programs on Poorer Hosts', *International Migration Review*. 20, (2): 245–63.

Chatterjee, P. (1989) 'The Nationalist Resolution of the Women's Question', in K. Sangari and S. Vaid (eds.) *Recasting Women: Essays in Colonial History*. New Delhi: Kali for Women.

Chen, M. (ed.) (1998) *Widows in India. Social Neglect and Public Action*. New Delhi: Sage.

Childers, E. (1991) *Strengthening International Response to Humanitarian Emergencies* (Opening Address). International Seminar on Forced Migration, sponsored by The Roberts Centre and the Refugee Studies Programme. Oxford: Worcester College.

Clifford, J. (1994) 'Diasporas', *Cultural Anthropology*. 9, (3): 302–38.

Cockburn, C. (1998) *The Space Between Us*. London: Zed Books.

CODHES (1999) *Un Pais que Huye. Desplazamiento y Violencia en Una Nacion Fragmentada*. Consultoría para los Derechos Humanos y el Desplazamiento. Bogotá: CODHES/UNICEF.

Coles, G. (1989) 'Approaching the Refugee Problem Today', in G. Loescher and L. Monahan (eds.) *Refugees and International Relations*. Oxford: Oxford University Press.

Colson, E. (1972) *The Social Consequences of Resettlement: The Impact of the Kariba Resettlement Upon the Gwembe Tonga*. Manchester: Manchester University Press.

COMADEP (1993) *Apoyo al Retorno de los Refugiados Guatemaltecos, (nov. 91–abril 93)*.

COMADEP (n.d.a.) *Política de Refugiados Guatemaltecos*.

COMADEP (n.d.b.) *Desarrollo de la Comunidad* (4).

Comité Cristiano de Solidaridad (1990) *Solidarios*. Mayo.

Compass (1997) *The Bosnia Project: Stage 2 Evaluation, Final Report*. London: Refugee Council.

Connell, R.W. (1998) 'Masculinities and Globalization', *Men and Masculinities*. 1, (1): 3–23.

CONONGAR (1991) *Diagnóstico de la CONONGAR sobre la Situación de los Refugiados Centroamericanos en México*.

CONPES 2804 (1995) *Programa Nacional de Atención Integral a la Población Desplazada por la Violencia*. Documento CONPES 2804 del 13 de septiembre. Departamento Nacional de Planeación and Ministerio del Interior. Bogotá: Departamento Nacional de Planeación.

Cox, M. (1998) *Strategic Approaches to International Intervention in Bosnia and Herzegovina*. Sarajevo and Geneva: Rehabilitation of War-Torn Societies Project, and Centre for Applied Studies in International Negotiations.

Cruikshank, B. (1999) *The Will to Empower: Democratic Citizens and Other Subjects*. Ithaca, NY: Cornell University Press.

Cuénod, J. (1989) 'Refugees: Development or Relief', in G. Loescher and L. Monahan (eds.) *Refugees and International Relations*. Oxford: Oxford University Press.

Cuny, F.C. (1983) *Disasters and Development*. Oxford: Oxford University Press.

Daley, P. (1991) 'Gender, Displacement and Social Reproduction: Settling Burundi Refugees in Western Tanzania', *Journal of Refugee Studies*. 4, (3): 248–66.

Daniel, V. (1989) 'The Semiotics of Suicide in Sri Lanka', in B. Lee and G. Urban (eds.) *Semiotics, Self, and Society*. Berlin: Mouton de Gruyter.

Daniel, V.E. and J.C. Knudsen (eds.) (1995) *Mistrusting Refugees*. Berkeley/Los Angeles, CA: University of California Press.

Daniel, V. and Y. Thangaraj (1995) 'Forms, Formations, and Transformations of the Tamil Refugee', in E.V. Daniel and J.C. Knudsen (eds.) *Mistrusting Refugees*. Berkeley/Los Angeles, CA: University of California Press.

De Munck, V. (1996) 'Love and Marriage in a Sri Lankan Muslim Community: Towards Reevaluation of Dravidian Marriage Practices', *American Anthropologist*. 23, (4): 698–716.

Dean, M. (1999) *Governmentality – Power and Rule in Modern Society*. London, Thousand Oaks, CA, New Delhi: Sage.

Deas, M. and F. Gartán Daza (1995) *Dos Ensayos Especulativos Sobre la Violencia en Colombia*. Bogotá: FONADE and Departamento Nacional de Planeación.

Dekker J. and B. Senstius (1997) *Dit is mijn huis: verhalen over tien jaar opvang van asielzoekers*. Amsterdam: Jan Smets.

Des Forges, A. (1999) *Leave None to Tell the Story: Genocide in Rwanda*. New York, Washington, London, Brussels, Paris: Human Rights Watch, the International Federation of Human Rights.

Dijk, T. van (1987) *Communicating Racism: Ethnic Prejudice in Thought and Talk*. London: Sage.

Dijk, T. van (1993) *Elite Discourse and Racism*. Newbury Park, CA: Sage.

DIRB (Documentation, Information and Research Branch, Immigration and Refugee Board, Ottawa) (1997) 'Sri Lanka: Information from RCMP Cpl. Fred Bowen on Alien Smuggling and Document Forgery'. 9 June 1997, Index: LKA 26917. EX.

Duffield, M. (1994) 'Complex Emergencies and the Crisis of Developmentalism', *IDS Bulletin*. 25, (4): 37–44.

Dyer, R. (1997) *White*. London: Routledge.

Eastmond, M. (1993) 'Reconstructing Life: Chilean Refugee Women and the Dilemmas of Exile', in G. Buijs (ed.) *Migrant Women: Crossing Boundaries and Changing Identities*. Oxford: Berg Publishers.

ECRE (1998) *The State of Refugee Integration in the European Union*. Antwerp: ECRE Task Force on Integration.

Engbersen, G. and J. Burgers (2000) 'De Ongekende stad: illegale immigranten in Nederland', *Migrantenstudies*. 16, (2): 69–80.

Enloe, C. (1983) *Does Khaki Become You? The Militarization of Women's Lives*. London: South End Press.

Episcopado Guatemalteco (1988) *El clamor por la tierra*.

Ergas, Z. (1980) 'Why did the Ujamaa Village Policy Fail? Towards a Global Analysis', *The Journal of Modern African Studies*. 18, (3): 387–410.

Eriksson, J. (1996) *The International Response to Conflict and Genocide: Lessons From the Rwanda Experience*. Synthesis Report. Steering Committee of the Joint Evaluation of Emergency Assistance to Rwanda.

Essed, P. (1991) *Understanding Everyday Racism: An Interdisciplinary Theory*. Newbury Park, CA: Sage.

Essed, P. (1995) 'Gender, Migration and Cross-Ethnic Coalition Building', in H.A. Lutz, A. Phoenix and N. Yuval-Davis (eds.) *Crossfires: Nationalism, Racism and Gender in Europe*. London: Pluto Press.

Essed, P. (1996) *Diversity: Gender, Color and Culture*. Amherst, MA: University of Massachusetts Press.

Evenhuis, W. (1996) *De Zijkant van het asielbeleid*. Utrecht: Greber.

Fagan, P. Weiss (1993) 'Peace in Central America: Transition for the Uprooted, *World Refugee Survey*. 1993: 30–39.

Falla, R. (1994) *Massacres in the Jungle: Ixcán, Guatemala, 1975–1982*. Boulder, CO: Westview Press.

Favell, A. (1998). *Philosophies of Integration: Immigration and the Idea of Citizenship in France and Britain*. Basingstoke: Macmillan.

Ferguson, J. (1994) *The Anti-Political Machine: Development: Depoliticization, and Bureaucratic Power in Lesotho*. Minneapolis, IN, London: University of Minnesota Press.

Fernando S. (1995) 'Social Realities and Mental Health', in *Mental Health in a Multi-Ethnic Society, A Multi-Disciplinary Handbook*. London: Routledge.

Forbes, M.S. (1992) *Refugee Women*. London: Zed Press.
Foucault, M. (1985) *The History of Sexuality*. New York: Vintage Books.
Foucault, M. (1991) 'Governmentality', in G. Burchell, C. Gordon and P. Miller (eds.) *The Foucault Effect: Studies in Governmentality*. London: Harvester Wheatsheaf.
Frankenberg, R. (1993) *White Women, Race Matters: The Social Construction of Whiteness*. Minneapolis, IN: University of Minnesota Press.
Freire, P. (1973) *Education for Critical Consciousness*. New York: Seabury Press.
Frerks, G.E. (1998) *Omgaan met rampen*. Inaugural Lecture. Wageningen: Wageningen Agricultural University.
Frerks, G.E. et al. (1995) 'Correspondence: "a Disaster Continuum?" ', *Disasters*. 19, (4): 362–66.
Freund, P.J. and K. Kalumba (1986) 'Spontaneously Settled Refugees in North-western Province, Zambia', *International Migration Review*. 20, (2): 299–312.
Fuglerud, Ø. (1999) *Life on the Outside: The Tamil Diaspora and Long-Distance Nationalism*. London: Pluto Press.
Gasper, D. and R. Apthorpe (1996) 'Introduction: Discourse Analysis and Policy Discourse', in R. Apthorpe and D. Gasper (eds.) *Arguing Development Policy: Frames and Discourses*. London: Frank Cass/EADI.
Ghai, D. (1993) 'Preface', in D. Turton *Refugees Returning Home*. Report of the Symposium for the Horn of Africa on the Social and Economic Aspects of Mass Voluntary Return Movements of Refugees. Geneva: UNRISD.
Ghidei Biidu, D. (1995) *Door het oog van de naald: een commentaar op de praktijk van de asielprocedure*. Utrecht: Greber/Isis.
Ghorashi, H. (2002) *Ways to Survive, Battles to Win: Iranian Women Exiles in the Netherlands and the US*. New York: Nova Science Publishers.
Giddens, A. (1991) *Modernity and Self-Identity: Self and Society in the Late Modern Age*. Cambridge: Polity Press.
Glenny, M. (1999) *The Balkans 1804–1999: Nationalism, War and the Great Powers*. London: Granta.
Gold, S.J. (1992) *Refugee Communities: a Comparative field study*. London: Sage.
Goldberg, D.T. (1994) *Multiculturalism: A Critical Reader*. Oxford: Blackwell.
Goodwin-Gil, G. (1989) 'Voluntary Repatriation', in G. Loescher and L. Monahan (eds.) *Refugees and International Relations*. Oxford: Oxford University Press.
Goor, L. van de, K. Rupesinghe and P. Sciarone (eds.) (1996) *Between Development and Destruction: an Enquiry into the Causes of Conflict in Post-Colonial States*. Basingstoke: Macmillan.
Graessle, L. and G. Gawlinski (1996). *Responding to a Humanitarian Emergency: an Evaluation of the UK's Bosnia Project to offer 'Temporary Protection' to People from Former Yugoslavia, 1992–1995*. London: Planning Together Associates.
Graham, M. and S. Khosravi (1997) 'Home is Where You Make It: Repatriation and Diaspora Culture among Iranians in Sweden', *Journal of Refugee Studies*. 10, (2): 115–33.
Gramsci, A. (1971) *Selections from the Prison Notebooks*. New York: International Publishers.
Grant, M.D., L.M. Oliver and A.D. James (1996) 'African Americans: Social and Economic Bifurcation', in R. Waldinger and M. Bozorgmehr (eds.) *Ethnic Los Angeles*. New York: Russel/Sage Foundation.
Hägerstrand, T. (1969) 'On the Definition of Migration', *Scandinavian Population Studies*. 1: 63–72.
Hampton, J. (ed.) (1998) *Internally Displaced People: A Global Survey*. London: Earthscan.

Hancock, G. (1991) *Lords of Poverty*. London: Mandarin Paperbacks.

Hansen, A. (1979) 'Once the Running Stops: Assimilation of Angolan Refugees into Zambian Border Villages', *Disasters*. 3, (4): 369–74.

Hansen, A. (1982) 'Refugee Dynamics: Angolans in Zambia 1966 to 1972', *International Migration Review*. 15, (1): 175–94.

Hansen, A. (1990) *Refugee Self Settlement versus Settlement on Government Schemes: the Long Term Consequences for Security, Integration and Economic Development of Angolan Refugees*. UNRISD Discussion Paper 17. Geneva: UNRISD.

Harrell-Bond, B. (1982) *Ugandan Refugees in Sudan: The Quest for Self-sufficiency in Planned Rural Settlement*. UFSI (Universities Field Staff International Inc.), No. 49: 1–12.

Harrell-Bond, B. (1986) *Imposing Aid: Emergency Assistance to Refugees*. Oxford: Oxford University Press.

Harrell-Bond, B. (1996) 'Refugees and the Reformulation of International Aid Policies: What Donor Governments Can Do', in A.P. Schmid (ed.) *Whither Refugee? The Refugee Crisis: Problems and Solutions*. Leiden: PIOOM.

Hathaway, J.C. (ed.) (1997) *Reconceiving International Refugee Law*. The Hague: Martinus Nijhoff Publishers.

Havinga, T. and A. Böcker (1999) 'Country of Asylum by Choice or by Chance: Asylum-seekers in Belgium, the Netherlands and the UK', *Journal of Ethnic and Migration Studies*. 25, (1): 43–61.

Hentic, I. (1995) *La Politique Urbaine au Rwanda 1962–1992: 30 ans d'Antiville*. Symposium International sur la Gestion Urbaine dans les Villes en Développement, UQAMHNRS-Urbanisation.

Hiatt, L. (1973) 'The Pattini Cult of Ceylon: A Tamil Perspective', *Social Compass*. 10: 231–49.

Hilhorst, D. (2000) *Records and Reputations: Everyday Politics of a Philippine Development NGO*. Wageningen: Ponsen and Looyen.

Hilhorst, D. and M. van Leeuwen (2000) 'Emergency and Development: the Case of Imidugudu, Villagization in Rwanda', *Journal of Refugee Studies*. 13, (3): 264–80.

Hollands, M. (1998) *Nieuwe ruimte: integratie als avontuur*. Utrecht: Jan van Arkel.

Home Office (1995) *Asylum Statistics*. London: HMSO.

Home Office (2000) *Full and Equal Citizens: a Strategy for the Integration of Refugees into the United Kingdom*. London: National Asylum Support Service.

Hoole, R. et al. (1988) *The Broken Palmyra: The Tamil Crisis in Sri Lanka – an Inside Account*. Claremont, CA.: The Sri Lanka Studies Institute.

Hudson, D. and H. Martenson (1998) *Refugees and Employment: The European Context, An Analysis of the ECRE Task Force on Integration Survey of Refugee Employment*. London: Refugee Council.

Hughes, J. and F. Liebaut (1999) *Detention of Asylum Seekers: Analysis and Perspectives*. Dordrecht: Martinus Nijhoff Publishers, Kluwer Law International.

HWIG (1994) *Survey on the Implementation of Temporary Protection*. Humanitarian Issues Working Group of the International Conference on Former Yugoslavia. Geneva: UNHCR.

IFRC (1993) *Vulnerability and Capacity Assessment: A Federation Guide*. Geneva: International Federation of Red Cross and Red Crescent Societies (IFRC).

Ismail, Q. (1995) 'Unmooring Identity: The Antinomies of Elite Muslim Self-Representation in Modern Sri Lanka', in P. Jeganathan and Q. Ismail (eds.) *Unmaking the Nation*. Colombo: Social Scientist' Association.

Janjic, D. (1995) 'Resurgence of Ethnic Conflict in Yugoslavia: The Demise of Communism and The Rise of New Nationalism', in P. Akhavan and R. Howse (eds.) *Yugoslavia, the Former and Future.* Washington, D.C.: Brookings Institution.

Jansen, W. (1996) 'Dumb and Dull: The Disregard for the Intellectual Life of Middle Eastern Women', *Thamyris.* 3, (2): 237–60.

Jay, A. (1993) *Persecution by Proxy: The Civil Patrols in Guatemala.* New York: Robert F. Kennedy Memorial Center for Human Rights.

Jayawardena, K. (1986) *Feminism and Nationalism in the Third World.* London: Zed Books.

Jeffery, P. (1999) 'Agency, Activism and Agendas', in P. Jeffery and A. Basu (eds.) *Resisting the Sacred and the Secular.* New Delhi: Kali for Women.

Joly, D. (1996a) *Between Exile and Ethnicity.* Coventry: Centre for Research in Ethnic Relations, University of Warwick.

Joly, D. (1996b) *Haven or Hell? Asylum Policies and Refugees in Europe.* Basingstoke: Macmillan.

Joly, D. (1997) *An Agenda for Reception and Integration: the Western European Experience and Central Europe.* Budapest: UNHCR.

Jonas, S. (1992) *The Battle for Guatemala: Rebels, Death Squads, and U.S. Power.* Boulder, CO: Westview Press.

Jong, J. de (2000) 'Psychiatric Problems Related to Persecution and Refugee Status', in F. Henn, N. Sartorius, H. Helmchen, and H. Lauter (eds.) *Contemporary Psychiatry.* Volume II. Berlin: Springer, 279–99.

Karadawi, A. (1983) 'Constraints on Assistance to Refugees: Some Observations from the Sudan', *World Development.* 11, (6): 537–47.

Kearney, R.N. and B.D. Miller (1987) *Internal Migration in Sri Lanka and its Social Consequences.* International Studies in Migration. Boulder, CO and London: Westview Press.

Keen, D. (1994) *The Benefits of Famine: A Political Economy of Relief in Southwestern Sudan, 1983–1989.* Princeton, NJ: Princeton University Press.

Keller, S.L. (1975) *Uprooting and Social Change: The Role of Refugees in Development.* Delhi: Manohar Book Service.

Kelly, R. and J. Friedlander (1993) 'Introduction', in R. Kelly and J. Friedlander (eds.) *Irangeles: Iranians in Los Angeles.* Berkeley, CA: University of California Press.

Kibreab, G. (1987) *Refugees and Development in Africa: The Case of Eritrea.* Trenton, NJ: The Red Sea Press.

Kibreab, G. (1990) *The Wage-Earning Settlements in Eastern and Central Sudan: From Subsistence to Wage Labour.* Trenton, NJ: The Red Sea Press.

Kibreab, G. (1993) 'The Myth of Dependence: Camp Refugees in Somalia 1978–1989', *Journal of Refugee Studies.* 6 (4): 321–49.

Kibreab, G. (1995) 'The African Refugee Regime with Emphasis on Northeastern Africa: The Emerging Issues', in H. Adelman (ed.) *Legitimate and Illegitimate Discrimination: New Directions in Migration.* York University Press.

Kibreab, G. (1996a) *Ready and Willing … But Still Waiting: The Dilemma of Return of Eritrean Refugees in the Sudan.* Uppsala: Life and Peace Institute.

Kibreab, G. (1996b) *People on the Edge in the Horn: Displacement, Land Use and the Environment in the Gedaref Region, Sudan.* London: James Currey Publishers.

Kibreab, G. (1996c) 'Eritrean and Ethiopian Refugees in Khartoum: What the Eye Refuses to See', *African Studies Review.* 39, (3): 131–78.

Kibreab, G. (1998a) *Returning Refugees in Eritrea: Reconstruction of Livelihoods* (Research Report, Department for International Development, London).

Kibreab, G. (1998b) Computer Printout – preliminary findings of a survey conducted among returnees, stayees and demobilised ex-combatants in Gash Barka and Anseba Regions, Eritrea.

Kibreab, G. (1999) 'The Consequences of Non-Participatory Planning: Lessons from a Livestock Provision Project to Returnees in Eritrea', *Journal of Refugee Studies*. 12, (2): 135–60.

Kibreab, G. (2000) 'Resistance, Displacement and Identity: The Case of Eritrean Refugees in Sudan', *Canadian Journal of African Studies*. 34, (2): 249–96.

Kloos, P. (1995) 'Publish and Perish: Nationalism and Social Research in Sri Lanka', *Social Anthropology*. 3, (2): 115–28.

Kloos, P. (2000) 'Democracy, Civil War and the Demise of the Trias Politica in Sri Lanka', in H. Antlöv and Tak-Wing Ngo (eds.) *The Cultural Construction of Politics in Asia*. Richmond, VA: Curzon Press.

Kommitee Zelfstandig Verblijfsrecht Migrantenvrouwen (1999) *Informatief.* Juli 1999.

Krulfeld, R.M. (1994) 'Buddhism, Maintenance and Change: Reinterpreting Gender in a Lao Refugee Community', in L.A. Camino and R.M. Krulfeld (eds.) *Reconstructing Lives, Recapturing Meaning: Refugee Identity, Gender, and Culture Change*. New York: Gordon and Breach Publishers.

Krulfeld, R.M. and L.A. Camino (1994) 'Introduction', in L.A. Camino and R.M. Krulfeld (eds.) *Reconstructing Lives, Recapturing Meaning: Refugee Identity, Gender, and Culture Change*. New York: Gordon and Breach Publishers.

Kuhlman, T. (1989) *Burden or Boon: A Study of Eritrean Refugees in the Sudan*. Amsterdam: VU Press.

Kunz, E.F. (1973) 'The Refugee In Flight: Kinetic Models And Forms Of Displacement', *International Migration*. 1, (7), 2: 125–46.

Kunz, E.F. (1981) 'Exile and Resettlement: Refugee Theory', *International Migration Review*. 15: 42–51.

La Cooperativa Agrícola y Servicios Varios EL QUETZAL (1991) *Sí! Somos Capaces! La Reconstrucción de Quetzal Edzná. '90–'91.*

La Jornada (1986) 1 July.

Lakeman, P. (1999) *Binnen zonder kloppen. Nederlandse immigratiepolitiek en de economische gevolgen*. Amsterdam: Meulenhoff.

Lammers, E. (1999) *Refugees, Gender and Human Security: A Theoretical Introduction and Annotated Bibliography*. Utrecht: International Books.

Lauren, G.P. (1998) *The Evolution of International Human Rights*. Philadelphia, PA: University of Pennsylvania Press.

Leun, J.v.d., G. Engbersen and P.v.d. Heijden (1998) *Illegaliteit en criminaliteit: schattingen, aanhoudingen en uitzettingen*. Rotterdam: Erasmus Universiteit.

Lipsky, M. (1980) *Street-level Bureaucracy: Dilemmas of the Individual in Public Services*. New York: Russel Sage Foundation.

Long, N. (ed.) (1989) 'Conclusion: Theoretical Reflections on Actor, Structure and Interface.' In *Encounters at the Interface: A Perspective on Social Discountinuities in Rural Development*. Wageningen: Wageningen Agricultural University.

Long, N. and J.D. van der Ploeg (1989) 'Demythologizing Planned Intervention: An Actor Perspective', *Sociologia Ruralis*. 29, (3/4): 226–49.

Long, N. and A. Long (eds.) (1992) *Battlefields of Knowledge: The Interlocking of Theory and Practice in Social Research and Development*. London, New York: Routledge.

Long, N. (2001) *Development Sociology. Actor Perspectives*. London, New York: Routledge.

Lutz, H. and A. Moors (1989) 'De Mythe van de ander: Beeldvorming over Turkse migrantes in Nederland', *Lover*. 16, (1): 4–7.

Lutz, H. (1991) 'Migrant Women of "Islamic Background": Images and Self-Images', *MERA Occasional Paper, No. 11*. Amsterdam: Middle East Research Associates.

Lutz, H., A. Phoenix and N. Yuval-Davis (eds.) (1995) *Crossfires: Nationalism, Racism and Gender in Europe.* London: Pluto Press.

Mabogunje, A.L. (1974–75) 'Migrants and Innovation: Definition of A Research Field', *African Urban Notes.* Ser. B. No. 1, 1974–75.

Macrae, J. with the assistance of Anthony Zwi and Vivienne Forsythe (1995) 'Aid Policy in Transition: A Preliminary Analysis of Post-conflict Rehabilitation of the Health Sector', *The Journal of International Development.* 7, (4): 669–84.

Macrae, J. and Duffield, M. (1997) 'Conflict, the Continuum and Chronic Emergencies: a Critical Analysis of the Scope for Linking Relief, Rehabilitation and Development Planning in Sudan', *Disasters.* 21, (3): 223–43.

Majka, L. (1991) 'Assessing Refugee Assistance Organisations in the United States and United Kingdom', *Journal of Refugee Studies.* 4, (3): 267–83.

Malkki, L. (1992) 'National Geographic: The Rooting of Peoples and the Territorialisation of National Identity among Scholars and Refugees', *Cultural Anthropology.* 7, (1): 24–44.

Malkki, L. (1995) 'Refugees and Exile: From "Refugee Studies" to the National Order of Things', *Annual Review of Anthropology.* 24: 495–523.

Malkki, L. (1995) *Purity and Exile: Violence, Memory, and National Cosmology among Hutu Refugees in Tanzania.* Chicago, IL: University of Chicago Press.

Mamá Maquín (1991) Interview.

Manhanda, R. (ed.) (2001) *Women, War and Peace in South Asia: Beyond Victimhood to Agency.* New Delhi: Sage Publishers.

Manz, B. (1988) *Refugees of a Hidden War.* Albany, NY: State University of New York Press.

McAfee, B. (1998) *Instead of Medicine: Report of the Bosnian Mental Health Pilot Project.* London: Refugee Action.

McGilvray, D.B. (1974) *Tamils and Moors: Caste and Matriclan Structure in Eastern Sri Lanka.* Unpublished Ph.D. thesis, University of Chicago.

McGilvray, D.B. (1989) 'Households in Akkaraipattu: Dowry and Domestic Organisation Among the Matrilineal Tamils and Moors of Sri Lanka', in J.N. Gray and D.J. Mearns (eds.) *Society from the Inside Out: Anthropological Perspectives on the South Asian Household.* New Delhi: Sage Publications.

McLaren, P. (1994) 'White Terror and Oppositional Agency: Towards a Critical Multiculturalism', in D.T. Goldberg (ed.) *Multiculturalism: a Critical Reader.* Oxford: Blackwell.

Meertens, D. and N. Segura-Escobar (1996) 'Uprooted Lives, Gender, Violence and Displacement in Colombia', *Singapore Journal of Tropical Geography.* 17, 'December' 2: 165–78.

Meertens, D. and N. Segura-Escobar (1999) *Exodo, Violencia y Proyectos de Vida.* Informe final de investigación, Bogotá, Universidad Nacional de Colombia y Colciencias.

Meertens, D. (2001a) 'Facing Destruction, Rebuilding Life: Gender and the Internally Displaced in Colombia', *Latin American Perspectives.* 28 (1): 132–48.

Meertens, D. (2001b) 'Victims and Survivors of War in Colombia: Three Views of Gender Relations', in C.R. Bergquist, Peñaranda and G. Sánchez (eds.) *Waging War and Negotiating Peace: The Violence in Colombia 1900–2000.* Wilmington, DE: Scholarly Resources.

Meloen J., K. Wuertz, F. Buijs and H. Tromp (1998) *De Opvang van asielzoekers.* Jan van Arkel.

Méndez, P.E. (1994) *Identidad Etnica de los Refugiados Indígenas en México.* Mexico: Tesis de licenciado, Escuela Nacional de Antropología e Historia.

Menon, R. and K. Bhasin (1998a) *Borders and Boundaries (Women in India's Partition)*. New Delhi: Kali for Women.

Menon, R. and K. Bhasin (1998b) 'Partition Widows: The State as Social Rehabilitator', in M. Chen (ed.) (1998) *Widows in India: Social Neglect and Public Action*. New Delhi: Sage.

Meurs, P. (1997) *Nobele Wilden. Inaugurele Rede.* NVZD: Erasmus Universiteit Rotterdam.

MININTER (1997) *Main Orientations of the Policy of Regrouped Settlement Sites in the Rural Areas of Rwanda.* Kigali: Ministry of the Interior, Communal Development and Reinstallation.

Ministry of Rehabilitation (1950–1966) *Annual Reports.* New Delhi: Government of India.

Mister, R. (1982) *Participation in Refugee Development Programmes: Contrasting Experience from Somalia.* Oxford: Oxfam (typescript).

Mondal, S. (1998) 'Immigration, Adaptation and Ethnicity: A Study of Refugees in Northern Districts of West Bengal', *South Asian Anthropologist.* 19, (2): 71–78.

Monroe, K.R. (1996) *The Heart of Altruism: Perceptions of a Common Humanity.* Princeton, NJ: Princeton University Press.

Morelli, C. and K. Braat (1999) *Kinderen zonder status.* Amsterdam: Defence for Children International.

Morrison, J. (1994) 'Permanent Settlement or Temporary Refuge?', *Projector, Newsletter of the Bosnia Project.* (3).

Mukherjee, S. (2001) 'Rehabilitation of the Bengali Refugees in Eastern and Northeastern India: an Unfinished Struggle', in S.K. Roy (ed.) *Refugees and Human Rights: Social and Political Dynamics of Refugee Problem in Eastern and North-Eastern India.* Jaipur: Rawat.

Naficy, H. (1993) *The Making of Exile Cultures: Iranian Television in Los Angeles.* Minneapolis, MI: University of Minnesota Press.

Nationale Raad voor de Geestelijke Volksgezondheid. Gezondheidszorg voor Illegaal Verblijvende Vreemdelingen (1995) *Advies over de gevolgen van de koppelingswet voor de gezondheidszorg.* Zoetermeer.

Nelson, N. and S. Wright (eds.) (1995) *Power and Participatory Development: Theory and Practice.* London: Intermediate Technology Publications.

OECD (1998) *Conflict, Peace and Development Cooperation on the Threshold of the 21st Century.* Paris: OECD.

Olwig, K.F. (1997) 'Cultural Sites: Sustaining a Home in a Deterritorialized World', in K.F. Olwig and K. Hastrup (eds.) *Siting Culture: the Shifting Anthropological Object.* London and New York: Routledge.

Organisation of American States (OAS) (1993) *Fourth Report on the Situation of Human Rights in Guatemala.*

Oxfam (1996) *Listening to the Displaced: Conversations in the Wanni Region, Northern Sri Lanka.* Oxford: Oxfam.

Pakrasi, B. (1971) *The Uprooted: a Sociological Study of the Refugees of West Bengal, India.* Calcutta: Editions Indian.

Pécaut, D. (1999) 'Las Configuraciones del Espacio, del Tiempo y de la Subjetividad en Un Contexto de Terror', *Revista Colombiana de Antropología.* 35, 'January–December': 8–35.

Permanent Commissions (1988a) CCPP to the Executive Committee of Esquipulas II, 12 February.

Permanent Commissions (1988b) CCPP to Monseñor Rodolfo Quezada Toruño, President of the Committee of National Reconciliation, 11 September.

Permanent Commissions (1989) *El Retorno.*

Pottier, J. (1997) *Social Dynamics of Land and Land Reform in Rwanda: Past, Present and Future.* Paper presented to the conference on 'Understanding the Crisis in Central Africa's Great Lakes Region', Refugee Studies Programme, Oxford.

Pronk, J.P. (1996) *Development in Conflict. Speech for the Conference 'Healing the Wounds: Refugees, Reconstruction and Reconciliation'.* Princeton, NJ: UNHCR.

Prunier, G. (1995) *The Rwanda Crisis: History of a Genocide.* New York: Colombia University Press.

Rajasingham, D. (1995) 'On Mediating Multiple Identities: The Shifting Field of Women's Sexuality in the Community, State and Nation', in M. Schuler (ed.) *From Basic Needs to Basic Rights.* Washington, D.C.: Women, Law and Development International.

Rajasingham-Senanayake, D. (1999) 'Democracy and the Problem of Representation: the Making of Bi-Polar Ethnic Identity in Postcolonial Sri Lanka', in J. Pfaff-Czarnecka, D. Rajasingham-Senanayake and A. Nandy (eds.) *Ethnic Futures: State Building and Identity Politics in Asia.* New Delhi: Sage.

Räthzel, N. (1995) 'Nationalism and Gender in West Europe: the German Case', in H. Lutz et al. (eds.) *Crossfires: Nationalism, Racism and Gender in Europe.* London: Pluto Press.

Reyntjens, F. (1994) *L'Afrique des Grands Lacs en Crise: Rwanda, Burundi (1988–1994).* Paris: Karthala.

Richters, A.J.M. (1991) *De Medisch antropoloog als verteller en vertaler.* Heemstede: Smart.

Richters A.J.M. (1994) *Women, Culture and Violence. A Development, Health and Human Rights Issue.* Women and Autonomy Centre (Vena), Leiden University.

Robinson, V. and C. Coleman (2000) 'Lessons learned? A Critical Review of the Government Program to Resettle Bosnian Quota Refugees in the United Kingdom', *International Migration Review.* 34: 1217–44.

Roe, E. (1991) 'Development Narratives, or Making the Best of Blueprint Development', *World Development.* 19, (4): 287–300.

Rogers, R. (1992) 'The Future of Refugee Flows and Policies', *IMR International Migration Review.* 26, (4): 1112–43.

Rogge, J. (1994) 'Repatriation of Refugees: A Not So Simple "Optimum" Solution', in T. Allen and H. Morsink (eds.) *When Refugees Go Home.* London: James Currey Publishers.

Rostow, W.W. (1960) *The Stages of Economic Growth: A Non-Communist Manifesto.* Cambridge: Cambridge University Press.

Roy Chaudhury, P. (1960) *Bihar District Gazetteers Champaran.*

Ruiz, H.A. (1993) 'Repatriation: Tackling Protection and Assistance Concerns', *World Refugee Survey.* 1993: 20–29.

Rushdie, S. (1988) *The Satanic Verses.* New York: Viking.

Salinas, M., D. Pritchard et al. (1987) 'Refugee Based Organisations: Their Functions and Importance for The Refugee in Britain', *Working Papers on Refugees.* Oxford/London: Refugee Studies Programme and British Refugee Council, 3.

Schalk, P. (1990) 'Birds of Independence: On the Participation of Tamil Women in Armed Struggle in Sri Lanka'. December: Unpublished Essay.

Schans, W.v.d. and J.v. Buuren (1999) *Dossier Europa: Europees asielbeleid in 2000.* Breda: Papieren Tijger.

Schrijvers, J. (1985) *Mothers for Life: Motherhood and Marginalization in the North Central Province of Sri Lanka.* Delft: EBURON.

Schrijvers, J. (1993) *The Violence of Development.* Utrecht: International Books, New Delhi: Kali for Women.

Schrijvers, J. (1995) 'Participation and Power: a Transformative Feminist Research Perspective', in N. Nelson and S. Wright (eds.) *Power and Participatory Development: Theory and Practice*. London: Intermediate Technology Publications.

Schrijvers, J. (1996) 'Violent Conflict and Development', *Anthropology in Action*. 3, (3): 6–10.

Schrijvers, J. (1997) 'Internal Refugees in Sri Lanka: The Interplay of Ethnicity and Gender', *The European Journal of Development Research*. 9, (2): 62–82.

Schrijvers, J. (1998) 'Tamil-Muslim Violence, Gender and Ethnic Relations in Eastern Sri Lanka', *Nethra (Quarterly Journal of the International Centre for Ethnic Studies, Colombo, Sri Lanka)*. 2, (3): 10–39.

Schrijvers, J. (1999) 'Fighters, Victims and Survivors: Constructions of Identity, Gender and Refugeeness among Tamils in Sri Lanka', *Journal of Refugee Studies*. 12, (3): 307–33.

Sciortino, G. (2000) 'A Political Sociology of Entry Policies: Conceptual Problems and Theoretical Proposals', *Journal of Ethnic and Migration Studies*. 26, (2): 213–28.

Scott, J.C. (1976) *The Moral Economy of the Peasant: Rebellion and Subsistence in Southeast Asia*. New Haven, CT: Yale University Press.

Scott, J.C. (1998) *Seeing Like a State: How Certain Schemes to Improve the Human Condition Have Failed*. New Haven, CT, London: Yale University Press.

Sen, A. (1989) 'Development as Capability Expansion', *Journal of Development Planning*. 19: 41–58.

Simpson, C.R. (1994) 'The Collapse of the Developmentalist Model: Guatemalan Rural Modernization Considered as Economic and Community Breakdown', in J. Kleist and B.A. Butterfield (eds.) *Breakdowns: The Destiny of the Twentieth Century*. New York: Peter Lang.

Sinha-Kerkhoff, K. (2000) 'Futurising the Past: Partition Memory, Refugee Identity and Social Struggle in Champaran, Bihar', *Sarwatch*. 2, (2): 74–93.

Slim, H. (1997) *Doing the Right Thing: Relief Agencies, Moral Dilemmas and Moral Responsibility in Political Emergencies and War*. Studies on Emergencies and Disaster Relief No. 6. Uppsala: Nordiska Afrikainstitutet, in cooperation with SIDA.

Sobernigo, J. (1990) *El Proyecto de Vida, en Busca de Mi Identidad*. Madrid: Sociedad de Educadores / Atenas.

Speth, J.G. (1999) *Linking Relief to Development: Lessons and Perspectives*. Washington, D.C.: Brookings Institution, 15 January 1999.

Spijkerboer, T. (1994a) 'Sheherazade en haar zusters', *Nemesis*. 4: 95–106.

Spijkerboer, T. (1994b) *Women and Refugee Status: Beyond the Public/Private Distinction*. Den Haag: Emancipatieraad.

Stein, B.N. (1981) 'The Refugee Experience: Defining the Parameters of a Field of Study', *International Migration Review*. 15, (1): 320–30.

Stein, B.N. and F.C. Cuny (1991) 'Repatriation Under Conflict', *World Refugee Survey 1991*: 20–29.

Stein, B.N., F.C. Cuny and P. Reed (1995) *Refugee Repatriation during Conflict: a New Conventional Wisdom*. Papers from the CSSC Conference in Addis Ababa, Ethiopia, October 1992. Dallas: Centre for the Study of Societies in Crisis.

Stepputat, F. (1992) *Beyond Relief? Life in a Guatemalan Refugee Settlement in Mexico*. Ph.D. dissertation, University of Copenhagen.

Stepputat, F. (1999) 'Repatriation and Everyday Forms of State Formation in Guatemala', in R. Black and K. Koser (eds.) *The End of the Refugee Cycle? Refugee Repatriation and Reconstruction*. New York, Oxford: Berghahn Books.

Stevenson, O. and P. Parsloe (1993) *Community Care and Empowerment*. York: Joseph Rowntree Foundation with Community Care.

Stewart, M. and M. Taylor (1995) *Empowerment and Estate Regeneration*. London: Polity Press.

Swaan, A. de (1996) *Zorg en staat*. Amsterdam: Bert Bakker.

Thiruchandran, S. (1997) *Ideology, Caste, Class, and Gender*. Delhi: Vikas.

Thomeer-Bouwens, M. and M. Smit (1998) *Alleenstaande minderjarige asielzoekers op eigen benen*. Leiden: Rijks Universiteit Leiden.

Tidwell, M. (1994) *Education for a Change: Appropriation and Control Efforts in the Mayan Refugee Schools*. Ph.D. dissertation, University of Pittsburgh.

Trautman, T.S. (1981) *Dravidian Kinship*. Cambridge: Cambridge University Press.

Trouwborst, A. (1962) 'Le Burundi', in M. d'Hertefelt, A. Trouwborst and J. Scherer (eds.) *Les Anciens Royaumes de la Zone Interlacustre Meridionale (Rwanda, Burundi, Buha)*. London: International African Institute.

Turner, S. (1998) 'Representing the Past in Exile: The Politics of National History Among Burundian Refugees', *Refuge, Canada's Periodical on Refugees*. 27, (6): 22–30.

Turner, S. (2002) 'Between the Edge of the World and the Eye of the Storm: Refugees, Relief and the International Community in Tanzania', *Politique Africaine*. (85): 29–45.

Turner, V. (1967) *The Forest of Symbols; Aspects of Ndembu Ritual*. Ithaca, NY: Cornell University Press.

UN (1997) *UN Report (A/52/1) of the Secretary General to the General Assembly*. New York: United Nations.

UNDP-Rwanda (1998) *Linking Relief to Development*. June 1998.

UNHCR (1997) *The State of the World's Refugees: Humanitarian Agenda*. Geneva: UNHCR.

UNHCR (2001) *2000 Global Refugee Trends. Analysis of the 2000 Provisional UNHCR Population Statistics*. Geneva: UNHCR, Population Data Unit/Population and Geographic Data Section.

UNHCR (2001). *Returns Summary to Bosnia and Herzegovina from 01/01/96 to 30/06/01*. Sarajevo: UNHCR.

UNRISD (1993) *Refugees Returning Home*. Report of the Symposium for the Horn of Africa on Social and Economic Aspects of Mass Voluntary Return Movements of Refugees, Addis Ababa, September 1992. Geneva: UNRISD.

UTHR (1990) University Teachers for Human Rights, Report No. 5, Colombo.

Veenman, J. (1996) 'Ontwikkelingen binnen een multi-etnische samenleving: demografie en sociaal economische positie', in E.D. Haveman and Uniken Venema (eds.) *Migranten en gezondheidszorg*. Houten, Diegem: Bohn Stafleu, van Loghum.

Verkuyten, M., W. de Jong and C.N. Masson (1993) 'Gedeelde waarden in racistisch en antiracistisch discours: Nederlandse buurtbewoners over etnische minderheden', *Sociologische Gids*. 40, (5): 386–407.

Verkuyten, M., W. de Jong and C.N. Masson (1995) 'The Construction of Ethnic Categories: Discourses of Ethnicity in the Netherlands', *Ethnic and Racial Studies*. 18, (2): 251–76.

Von Oppen, A. (1995) *Terms of Trade and Terms of Trust: the History and Contexts of Pre-colonial Market Production around the Upper Zambezi and Kasai*. Hamburg: Lit.

Waal, A. de (1993) *Human Rights, Complex Emergencies and NGOs*. London: Mimeo for Save the Children Fund.

Waal, A. de (1997) *Famine Crimes: Politics of the Disaster Relief Industry in Africa*. Bloomington, IN: Indiana University Press.

Wadley, S. (ed.) (1991) *The Powers of Tamil Women*. New Delhi: Manohar.

Wahlbeck, O. (1999) *Kurdish Diasporas: A Comparative Study of Kurdish Refugee Communities*. Basingstoke: Macmillan.

Ward, D. and A. Mullender (1991) 'Empowerment and Oppression: An Indissoluble Pairing for Contemporary Social Work', *Critical Social Policy*. 11, (2): 21–30.

Warner, D. (1994) 'Voluntary Repatriation and the Meaning of Return to Home: a Critique of Liberal Mathematics', *Journal of Refugee Studies*. 7, (2/3), 160–74.

Watanabe, J.M. (1992) *Maya Saints and Souls in a Changing World*. Austin: University of Texas Press.

Wekker, G. (1995) '"After the Last Sky, Where do the Birds Fly?" What Can European Women Learn from Anti-Racist Struggles in the United States?', in H. Lutz et al. (eds.) *Crossfires: Nationalism, Racism and Gender in Europe*. London: Pluto Press.

Wekker, G. (1998) 'Gender, identiteitsvorming en multiculturalisme: notities over de Nederlandse multiculturele samenleving', in K. Geuijen (ed.) *Multiculturalisme*. Utrecht: Lemma.

Wesenbeek, R. (1996) 'Racisme en overdracht', in J. de Jong and M.v.d. Berg (eds.) *Transculturele Psychiatrie and Psychotherapie*. Lisse: Swets and Zeitlinger Publishers.

White, C.M.N. (1960) *An Outline of Luvale Social and Political Organization*. Rhodes-Livingstone Papers No. 30. Manchester: Manchester University Press.

White, S. (1997) 'Men, Masculinities and the Politics of Development', in C. Sweetman (ed.) *Men and Masculinity*. Oxford: Oxfam.

Wieringa, G. (1997) 'Ik vraag me af of mevrouw Schmitz nog wel een oog dichtdoet'. *Opzij*. November.

Wilkinson, R.G. (1973) *Poverty and Progress*. London: Methuen.

Wilson, R. (1998) *Health in Exile: The Experience of Refugees and Evacuees in Leeds*. London: Refugee Action.

Wood, G. (1985) 'The Politics of Development Policy Labelling', *Development and Change*. 16, (3): 347–73.

Yachan, A. (1997) *Notes on Some African Experiences in Rural Development and Resettlement*. Kigali: UNDP-UNHCR, Joint Reintegration Programming Unit.

Yalman, N. (1967) *Under the Bo Tree*. Berkeley, CA: University of California Press.

Yoldi, P. (1996) *Don Juan Coc, Príncipe Q'eqchí' (1945–1995)*. Guatemala: Rigoberta Menchú Tum Foundation.

Zetter, R. (1991) 'Labelling Refugees: Forming and Transforming a Bureaucratic Identity', *Journal of Refugee Studies*. 4, (1): 39–61.

Zetter, R. (1992) 'Refugees and Forced Migrants as Development Resources: The Greek-Cypriot Refugees from 1974', *The Cyprus Review*. 4, (1): 7–39.

Zetter, R. (1994) 'The Greek-Cypriot Refugees: Perceptions of Exile under Conditions of Protracted Exile', *International Migration Review*. 28, (2): 307–22.

Zetter, R. (1995) 'Incorporation and Exclusion: The Life Cycle of Malawi's Refugee Assistance Program', *World Development*. 23, (10): 1653–67.

Zetter, R. (1999) 'Reconceptualising The Myth of Return: Continuity and Transition Amongst The Greek-Cypriot Refugees of 1974', *Journal of Refugee Studies*. 12, (1): 1–22.

Zippay, A. (1995) 'The Politics of Empowerment', *Social Work*. 40, (2): 263–67.

Notes on Contributors

Oliver Bakewell is an independent consultant and researcher based in London. He has worked in relief and development programmes throughout Africa, in the former Yugoslavia and in the former Soviet Union. He is a specialist in the social aspects of refugee migrations, settlement and return and his doctoral research at the University of Bath focused on processes of repatriation of Angolan refugees in Zambia. His current research interests include the use of rights-based approaches in humanitarian assistance programmes for refugees.

Philomena Essed is Senior Researcher at the University of Amsterdam and Visiting Professor at the University of California, Irvine. Her research and teaching cover the areas of gender, race critical theories, social identities, leadership, and research methodologies. Her books include *Understanding Everyday Racism: An Interdisciplinary Theory* (1991), *Diversity: Gender, Color and Culture* (1996), and *Race Critical Theories* (2001, coedited). Forthcoming are *A Companion to Gender Studies* (2003, coedited) and *Humanizing Leadership*.

Georg Frerks is a rural sociologist with a Ph.D. from Wageningen Agricultural University, The Netherlands. Currently he is Professor of Disaster Studies at the Rural Development Sociology Group of Wageningen University and also holds a Special Chair in Conflict Prevention and Conflict Management at Utrecht University. He is Head of the Conflict Research Unit of the Netherlands Institute of International Relations 'Clingendael'. His research interests and publications relate to rural development, policy aspects of conflict and disaster management, local coping mechanisms and the interface between intervening organisations and the local population.

Oivind Fuglerud is a social anthropologist with a Ph.D. from Oslo University (1996). Much of his work has been related to Sri Lanka, and his theoretical interests include nationalism, political violence, and international migration. He has published two books: *Life on the Outside: the Tamil Diaspora and Long-Distance Nationalism* (Pluto Press, 1999) and *Understanding Migration: Movement, Racism, Globalisation* (Oslo University Press, 2001, in Norwegian language only). Oivind Fuglerud works as a Research Director at Norwegian Social Research and as associate professor at the Department of Anthropology, University of Oslo.

Halleh Ghorashi is Assistant Professor of Intercultural Management in the Department of Culture, Organisation, and Management at the Vrije Universiteit in Amsterdam. She came to the Netherlands in 1988. In 1994, she completed her MA degree in Anthropology at the Vrije Universiteit. She received her Ph.D. in 2001 from the University of Nijmegen. She is the author of *Ways to Survive, Battles to Win: Iranian Women Exiles in the Netherlands and the US* (2002, Nova Science Publishers, New York) and of several articles on questions of identity, Diaspora, and the Iranian women's movement.

Dorothea Hilhorst is a development sociologist at Wageningen University, where she lectures on the sociology of conflict, disaster and humanitarian assistance. She specialises in NGOs and organisation studies, and recently published *The Real World of NGOs: Discourses, Diversity and Development* with Zedbooks. She can be contacted at: thea.hilhorst@wur.nl

Lynnette Kelly received her doctorate in 2002 from the Centre for Research in Ethnic Relations at the University of Warwick. Her thesis examined the situation of refugees from Bosnia Herzegovina who were living in Britain. She is currently based at the Centre for Research in Ethnic Relations, coordinating and working on a number of research projects on refugees and asylum seekers in Britain and Europe.

Gaim Kibreab has published widely on population displacement and development. Author of *People on the Edge in the Horn: Land Use Environment and Displacement* (Oxford: James Currey Publishers, 1996), and *Common Property Institutions, State Intervention and the Environment in Sudan, 1898–1998* (Edwin Mellen Press, in press). At present he is affiliated to the South Bank University in London.

Mathijs van Leeuwen is a development sociologist. As part of his studies at Wageningen University he conducted field research in Rwanda. Since his graduation he has been affiliated to the Conflict Research Unit of the

Institute of International Relations 'Clingendael' in the Hague, and has worked for Pax Christi the Netherlands with a women and peace organisation in Kenya and southern Sudan. At the moment, he is a research fellow at Wageningen Disaster Studies.

Donny Meertens, anthropologist, lectures in Gender Studies at the National University of Colombia. She has been a research associate and visiting professor at the University of Amsterdam and CEDLA, the Netherlands. She co-authored a book on Colombian violence (*Bandits, Peasants and Politics*, University of Texas Press, 2001), and is currently preparing a book on Gender and Displacement, based on several years of research in Colombia. E-mail: sanmeer@colnodo.apc.org

Darini Rajasingham-Senanayake is currently a Fellow at the International Centre for Advanced Studies at New York University and at the International Centre for Ethnic Studies in Colombo. She is the co-author of *Ethnic Futures: the State and Identity Politics in South Asia* (Sage, 1999). She has written extensively on the political economy of armed conflict, as well as on multiculturalism and cultural hybridity.

Anita Rapone is Professor of History at the State University of New York at Plattsburgh. Her most recent work includes 'Community Development from the Ground Up: Social-Justice Coffee', *Human Ecology Review*. 7: (2000) 46–57, written with Charles R. Simpson.

Joke Schrijvers, social anthropologist, is emeritus Professor of Development Studies at the University of Amsterdam. Her teaching and research cover the fields of (feminist) anthropology, development, conflict and refugee studies. She is author of many books and articles, including 'Internal Refugees in Sri Lanka. The Interplay of Ethnicity and Gender,' *The European Journal of Development Research*. 9, 2: (1997) 62–82, and 'Fighters, Victims and Survivors: Constructions of Ethnicity, Gender and Refugeeness among Tamils in Sri Lanka', *Journal of Refugee Studies*. 12, 3 (1999): 307–33.

Charles Simpson is Professor of Sociology, State University of New York at Plattsburgh. His research interests include the intersection of community, agriculture, and the state. His most recent article, with Anita Rapone, was 'Community Development from the Ground Up: Social Justice Coffee,' *Human Ecology Review*. 7 (2000): 46–57.

Kathinka Sinha-Kerkhoff received her Ph.D. in 1995 and is now a Senior Fellow in the Asian Development Research Institute (ADRI) in Patna (Bihar) and affiliated to the International Institute of Social History (IISG)

in Amsterdam (the Netherlands). At present, she is among others involved in a project on 'Partition Memories: Minority Identities and Those Who Stayed: a Comparison of Muslims in India and Hindus in Bangladesh'.

Simon Turner is Assistant Professor in International Development Studies at Roskilde University, Denmark. His Ph.D. thesis is on 'The Barriers of Innocence: Humanitarian Intervention and Political Imagination in a Refugee Camp for Burundians in Tanzania'.

Rianne Wesenbeek is a social scientist, specialising in ethnic relations. Her field of expertise is (mental) health care. She is co-founder and co-ordinator of the Intercultural Mental Health Care Foundation and chair of the board of the Amsterdam Patient and Consumer Platform. Her publications include *Ethno-Psychiatry and Intercultural Policy* (1991), *Racism and Transference* (1996), *Suicidal Behaviour Among Young Migrant Women* (2000), and *Intercultural Mental Healthcare in the 21st Century* (2000).

Index

A

access
  to business licences, 21
  to land, 34
  to markets, 34
  to retail goods, 149
Accompaniers to the Return,
  International Group of, 146
accountability, 2, 172
adaptation, innovative, 23
advice, 125
  Citizens Advice Bureau (U.K.), 126
advocacy service, 126
Afghanistan, 50, 162, 175, 192
Africa, 151, 180
African Americans, 114
African Education Foundation (AEF),
  101
age
  assessment through 'bone tests', 58
  characteristics, 12
  configurations, 10
  relations, 94
aggressiveness, 22
agriculture
  collective farming, 138
  extension services, 36
  labourers, 73
  and livestock, 75
  in Meheba refugee settlement, 37–38
  planting common fields, 140
  pressure on land, 181
  production, 26
  technicians, 144

women's participation, 26
agri-export production, 137
agropastoralists, 26, 28
aid budget lines, 172
aid hierarchy, 194
AIDS, 59
Akkaraipattu, 48
alcohol
  prohibition of drinking and selling,
  23
  smuggling, 23
alcoholism, 154, 163
alienation, 25, 117
Ali Gidir, 29
allochtoon, 112
Alta Verapaz, 139
altruism, 60
ambassadors, 145
'ambivalent agency', 154
  and empowerment, 162
Amnesty International, 44
Amparai, 44
  District, 49
Amsterdam, 56, 106, 116
analysis
  actor-oriented, 177
  comparative, 16
  contextualised, 16
  gender-specific, 16
  historical, 16
anathagatha kattiya, 154
Angola, 6, 31–41
  peace process, 37, 39
Anseba region, 28

Anuradhapura, 154
approach(es)
  actor-oriented, 14, 16, 177
  bottom-up, 187
  community-oriented, 124
  'developmentalist', 15
    and public emergencies, 170
  group, 126
  holistic, 16
  integrated, 188
  interdisciplinary, 16
  longer-term historical, 15
  migration, 41
  multitrack, 173
  participatory, 187
  participatory research, 16
  standard, 187
arbitrariness, 57
arbitrary treatment, 76
armed conflict, 69, 71, 78–9
arms trade, 170
Arusha Agreement (1993), 189
Asia, 151
Assam, 82
assimilation, 136
asylum
  abuse of process, 134
  application, 122, 124
  controls, 45
  eligibility, 53
  seekers, 130, 134
atomisation, 140
audiocassettes, 141
Aurora 8 de Octubre, 147–8
Australia, 48, 129, 193
Austria, 128
authority
  hierarchies of, 11
  notions of, 103

B
bad governance, 171
Bangladesh, 85
Barentu, 28, 29
barter, 38
Batley, 125
Batticaloa, 44, 153, 160
  District, 49, 50, 194
  lagoon, 45
  Peace Committee, 44
  Thimilar caste, 50
  Town, 44
beneficiaries, 175

best practices, 175
Bhagalpur District, 83
Bihar (India), 8, 81–93
Birmingham, 125
bishops, 146
blindés (huts), 99
blueprint policy, 189
body searches, 11, 153
  at checkpoints, 154
Bogotá, 71–72, 76
'bone tests', 58
Bosnia, 121–34, 154
  concentration camps, 121
Bosnia project (U.K.), 7, 15, 121–34
  community development phase,
    124, 126–27
  implementation, 128–29
  mid-term support phase, 124–26,
    128
  mid-term support team, 129
  reception centre phase, 124–25, 128
breakdown of communal relations, 193
bribery, 195, 197
British Home Office, 121
British Red Cross, 121
British Refugee Action, 121, 124
British Refugee Council, 121, 124, 126
broadcasting, 141
Bucaramanga, 72
bureaucracy, 40
  criteria, 53
  inefficient, 76
  street-level, 53
burden, 111
  of Government, 92–93
burnout, 64
Burundi, 10, 94–105, 175

C
California, 114, 118
  immigrant-oriented communities,
    114
Cambodia, 175
camouflage uniforms, 72
Campeche, 138, 150
campesinos, 139
camp life, 136
camps
  adjustment to life in, 136, 157
  education, 141
  leadership roles, 11
  'orphan', 85
  participatory self-government, 142

permanent liability, 8, 81–93
permission to leave, 195
political activities, 102
rural, 20
self-administration, 143
social structures, 94
transit, 196
with-no-future, 136
Canada, 46, 145–46
cardamom, 141, 148
cash-crop production, 26
caste, 86, 92, 156, 160–62, 194, 196
certificates, 86, 91
hierarchies, 11, 157
ideology, 11, 155; erosion of, 157
structure, 47
categorisation, 36, 53, 71, 91
Catholic church, 136, 138, 140, 149
cattle, 148, 184
cattle barons, generals as, 137
Caucasians, 114
causalities, 42
Cazombo, 35, 37, 40
cease-fire agreement, 154, 193
Census Bureau (U.S.), 114
Cerezo, Vinicio, 141
certificate of 'displacedness', 77
Ceylon, 193
chain migration, 46, 124, 131
Champaran District, 84
charity, 60, 123
checkpoints, 154
Chenkaladi, 44
Chiapas, 138, 145, 150
children, 37, 44, 58, 64, 139, 142–43, 161, 192, 196
age assessment, 58
conceived through rape, 58
(basic) education, 29, 75, 86–87
hiding from recruitment, 72
illegally residing, 59
looking after, 76
and marriage, 34
prostitution, 64
and respect for adults, 97
traffic in, 64
Chile, 124
chronic diseases, 61
chronic suffering, 31
church, 76, 139
involvement with state functions, 144
workers, 140

circumcision, 34
citizenship, 19, 28, 61, 78
active, 123
rights, 194
civic organisations, 72–73
civil (dis)obedience, 10, 12
and professional ethics, 54
tolerance of, 64
civil patrols, 146
civil rights, 149
civil servants, 76
civil society, 135
organisations, 175
civil war, 43, 47, 143, 190, 193, 198
clan, 21
clandestine politics, 102
clinics, 34–37, 39
cluster areas, 125–26, 129
code of secrecy, 60
coffee, 141
estates, 136
production, 137
cofradías (religious brotherhoods), 139
collapse of the state, 171
collective ownership, 139
collegial loyalty, 64
Colombia, 10, 53–65
Colombo, 44, 48–49, 163, 194–97
colonialism, 109, 156
colonisation, 139. *See also* decolonisation
Comisión Mexicana de Ayuda a Refugiados, 140
Comitán, 145, 147
Comité Cristiano de Solidaridad, 138, 143–44, 150
Committee of National Reconciliation, 142
communal organisations, 73
communal tensions, 193
communication, 90, 141
community-based social services, 149
community development
phase, 122
projects, 95
promotion, 131
refugee-initiated, 147
community identity, 7
community, notion of, 133
community organisation, 138
community relations councils, 123
community spirit, 95
community unity, 138

concentration camps, 121–34
confiscation, 77
Congo, 33
consciousness building, process of, 143
conscription, 146
Conseil National pour la Défense de la Démocratie (CNDD), 102
conservation policies, 145
consultation, 194
Cooperativa La Unión Maya, 147
cooperative community production, 148
Copperbelt, 33, 35
corn-mill project, 145
    diesel-powered, 148
cotton
    boom, 136
    picking, 26
    production, 137
counterinsurgency, 140. *See also* insurgency
Coventry, 125
creativity, 23
crisis accommodation, 125
Croats, 131
cross-border trade, 23
cultivation, 27, 145, 183
cultural practices,
    diversity of, 116
'cultural sites', 47
cultural threat, 56
cultural traditions, 50
cultural values, 47
customary sanctions, 91

D
data, 77
database systems, 54
Dayton Agreement, 130
decolonisation, 4, 56
dehumanisation, 10, 191
Delhi, 86, 89
demobilised soldiers, 27
'democratic spring', 144
democratisation, 188
dependency, 15
depopulation, 35. *See also* population
    Western Zambia, 40
deprivation of power, 10
devadasi, 161
development and relief. *See* relief
development budgets, 168
'development for peace', 174

'development poles', 140
Dewsbury, 125
diaspora, 195
differentiation, 72, 75
dignity, 54
    lack of, 10, 79
    threat to, 19
'dining with the devil', 200
dirty hands, 192, 200
disasters, 168–69, 179
    needs generated by, 179
    as temporary disruption of development process, 169
    vulnerability to, 169
discouragement, policy of, 56–57
discrimination, 4, 35, 61, 81, 199
    collective, 78
    ethnic, 10; by local authorities, 183, 186
    fear of, 78
    in labour market, 26
    protection against, 55
    racial, 114
dispersal policies, 129
displaced person,
    recognition of status as, 77
dispute settlement, 139
distrust,
    political, 78
    social, 78
diversification, 9
    economic activities, 25
divorce, 34, 59. *See also* marriage
Doheny, Edward (Maryknoll priest), 139
domestic labour, 75
domestic servants, 73, 79
domestic violence, 58–59, 154, 163. *See also* violence
donor
    coordination, 176
    key orientations, 175
    representatives, 182
    supported resettlement programmes, 193
dowries, 46–47, 89
    and house, 47–48
    inflation in, 47
    negotiations, 46
    transfer at marriage, 51
    See also marriage
drinking water, lack of, 183
drug-related violence, 70

drugs trade, 170
drug traffickers, 70
confiscation of properties, 77
'Dutchbat', role in Srebrenica, 191

E
European harmonization policies, 57
Eastern Europe, 56
ecological limits to development, 147
ecologically sensitive areas, 146
ecologically sensitive development,
    145, 147
economic bargaining power, 47
economic independence, 129
economic migrants, 39, 40, 78, 80
'economies of violence', 170
education, 9, 29, 54, 72, 144
    in camps, 141
    for children, 75
    in community participation, 145
    and consciousness building, 143
    environmental, 145
    facilities, 196
    of Iranian women in the
        Netherlands, 108
    job opportunities in, 38
    limited, 100
    in Meheba refugee settlement, 37
    permanent elementary school, 148
    promoters, 143, 147–8
    and relief aid, 175
    through NGOs, 101
Eelam People's Democratic Party
    (EDPD), 154
Eelam People's Revolutionary Front
    (EPRLF), 154
Eelam War, Second, 156
Ejército de Liberación Nacional (ELN),
    70
Ejército Popular de Liberación (EPL), 70
elders, 139
El Quiché, 139
El Porvenir, 143
El Rahad, 26
emancipation, 111. *See* empowerment
'embodied pain', 58
emergency, 12, 39. *See also* relief and
    development
    aid, 77
    acute phase, 168
    assistance and integrating
        development, 179
    and decapacitation of local

government, 173
and developmentalist approaches,
    170
'emergency development', 188
'package', 192
rationale of development, 182
relief, 169–77
as temporary disruption of
    development process, 169
undermining past development
    achievements, 168
empirical data, 21
employment, 91, 129, 194
advice, 129
opportunities, 29
restrictions, 91
empowerment, 54, 87, 95, 122–24
ambivalent, 11
concentration camps and
    disempowerment, 127
disempowering process, 133
through formal community
    association, 131
as guiding principle in social and
    community work, 122
as intention, 134
settlement project, 129
terms, 136
theory of (by Adams), 122
women, 104, 151, 157
women's economic, 3
women's political, 3
women's social, 3
engagement, vs. neutrality, 191–200
enrolment, 34
entrepreneurial spirit, 103
Episcopal Conference, 77
equity, 13, 185, 188, 200
Eravur, 44–45, 48, 50, 51
farmers, 51
Mukuvar caste, 50, 51
offerings, 51
Eritrea, 19–30
Esquipulas II agreement, 142
Esquipulas process
right to participate in, 142
Es Suki, 26
ethics, 63
dilemma's, 65
ethnic abuse, 49
ethnic boundaries, 51
'ethnic cleansing', 121, 154, 188, 193.
    See also rape

ethnic minority community, 123–24,
130
ethnic tensions, 186, 188
ethnicisation
of politics, 132
process, 198
ethnicity, 40, 77, 109, 110, 111, 124, 199
abolishment, 188
articulation, 132
evacuation
convoys, 121
vehicles, 128
'evaluation committee', 195
'evils of social decay', 98
exceptional leave to remain, 130
exclusion, 4, 192, 200
from benefits of development and
globalisation, 192
social, 70, 110, 118
exploitation of natural resources, 170
exploratory visit, 127
extortion, 69–70, 170

F
factionalism, 131
family fragmentation, 152, 160
favouritism, 128
female leadership, 72
femininity, 2, 15
in Dutch society, 110
feudal dynamics, 51
fishing, 38
flexibility, 100
flexible interpretation, 63
flight, 6–7, 10, 14, 16, 42, 53, 59, 70, 90,
136, 147, 200
experiences, 20
and massacre, 139, 143
story, 58
transformative potential, 12
by violence, 78
from war in Angola, 38
food aid, 26, 35
targetted, 40
food-for-work programmes, 169
food security, 174–75
forced labour, 33
foreign investment, 141
forewarning, lack of, 73
forging of documents, 23
France, 129, 146
freedom
of association, 37

of movement, 26
of residence, 27
of self-determination, 55
*Fuerzas Armadas Revolucionarias de
Colombia* (FARC), 70
funding practices, 178
future research, 15

G
game animals, 38
game parks, 38
García, Lucas, 139
garment assembly, 137
Gash Barka region, 28
Gedaref region, 26
gender, 20, 34, 61, 69, 91, 103, 109–111
and application for refugee status,
58
balance, 80
changing relations, 88
characteristics, 12
configurations, 10
construction of roles, 104
differences, 8, 71, 76, 192, 194
in aid, 175
different tasks, 161
equality as threat to patriarchy, 98,
104
forms of violence, 153
hierarchy, 152
identities, 2, 71–74
identity trajectories, 79
ideology, 11, 26, 97, 99, 104
as a major interpretative scheme,
104
perceptions, 2
practices, 11, 152
cultural analysis of, 159
programmes, 159
relations, 94, 104, 155–56
breakdown in, 97
in refugee camps, 95
unequal, 91
representations, 72, 78
restrictions, 5
roles, 25, 151
non-traditional, 152
traditional, 155
status quo, 152, 156–57, 160, 162–63
genocide, 172, 179, 180, 182, 187–88
survivors, 183
Germany, 56, 116, 128
Ghandi, Indira, 84

Ginda, 28
Gisenyi, 184–86
   and equity, 185, 188
   and non-discrimination, 188
   as politically neutral programme,
      184–86
globalisation, 4, 192, 200
   antithesis of, 4
   benefits of, 192
Goluj, 28–29
governmentality, 95, 103
grassroots movements, 77
'great transformation', 3
group loyalties, 71
Guatemala, 12, 103, 135–50
   army, 140
   City, 146–47
      national welcome in, 147
      occupation of consulate in Mexico,
         146
      return of civilian government (in
         1986), 141
guerrillas, 69, 78, 137–39, 141
   incursions by, 146
'guest labourers', 109
guilt, feeling of, 22, 160
Gulf States, 23

H
habitual residence, 32
Habyarimana, 181
Hagaz, 28
Haikota, 29
Haiti, 137
Halfa, 26
hammock making, 147
harmony, 28
harassment, 35
harvest, 185
hawashas (plots), 26
Hazari (transit camp), 84, 87, 90
health, 141
health (care), 54, 59–64, 141, 149, 158,
   194
   civil disobedience, 60
   ethical dilemma's, 60
   individual response, 63
   in Meheba refugee settlement, 37
   medical evacuees, 127
   medical exclusion, 59
   medical facilities, 196
   medical insurance, 62
   for people without legal status,

59–64
   practitioners, 12
   pre- and post-natal care, 59
   professional ethics, 12
   promoters, 144, 147–48
   'Refugees, Citizenship and
      Healthcare: Ethical Dilemmas and
      Solutions' project, 62
   relation between client and
      professional, 61
   risks,and life in illegality, 62
   services, job opportunities in, 38
   tolerance of service to illegal
      patients, 63
hierarchic harmony, 104
hierarchy, 95–99
Hindu(s), 8, 22, 50, 80–93
   Bengali-speaking, 81–82
   caste structure, 155
   cultural ethos, 155
   goddesses, 155
   service castes, 50
   temples, 51
   and widowhood, 160
horrific treatment, 127
house
   building, 38
   raids, 44
   household resettlement packs, 40
housing
   acutu problem, 180
   lack of, 79
   needs, 179, 185–86
   policy in cluster areas, 129
Huehuetenango, 139
human capital, 149
humanitarian aid, 168, 190
   abuse, 168
   agencies, 152
   artificiality of distinguishing with
      development aid, 192
   bureaucratic and organisational
      boundaries, 169
   'cleansed' from development
      activities, 199
   conditionalities, 171
   debate on the nature of, 191
   diversion, 168
   manipulation, 168
   narrow concept, 192
   negative side effects, 168
   participatory manner, 198
   short-term, 190

taking neutral stand, 192
top-down manner, 198
humanitarian convoy, 125
human rights, 53–65, 136, 138
    abuses/violations, 141, 144, 171
    international, 151
    international groups/organisations,
        136, 140, 145
    international promotion of women's
        rights as, 151
    international standards of, 199
    monitors, 148
    Universal Declaration, 53, 55
    violation, 55
    weak spots, 65
hunger strikes, 198
hurricane, 141
Hutu, 94–105, 185–86
    customs, 104
    timidity, 102
    'virtues', 100
    See also Parti
hypergamy, 46–47

I
identification
    differential structure of, 113
    exclusive form, 116–17
    inclusive form, 116
    with Muslims, 132
    of needs, 132
    process of, 52
    as refugee, 88, 90
identities, 9, 10, 74, 133, 140
    based on age, 92
    based on caste, 92
    based on class, 92
    construction, 106–107
    cultural, 113
    discursively constructed, 51
    as dynamic processes, 71
    economic, 8
    ethnic, 25, 49; politics, 193–94
    formation, 106
    gender, 71–74
    genuine Dutch or European, 112
    hybrid, 118
    imaginary notion of, 118
    masculine, 10, 103
    Maya, 149
    Muslim, 48, 112
    Muslim Bosnian, 132
    national, 25, 41, 69

negotiation of, 69
and non-exclusion, 118
personal, 35
political, 8, 69, 73
postcolonial discourse, 49
processes, 73
reconstruction of, 79
social, 8, 74, 77–79
    negation of, 71
typically Dutch, 113
identity checks, 35
illegality, 7
    as complex urban problem, 65
    concept of, 53
    'manufacture of', 58
illiteracy, 90, 145. *See also* literacy
Imidugudu villagisation project, 13,
    179–89
    as 'antipolitics roller-coaster', 188
    consultation and participation, 186
    effectiveness, 188
    feasibility, 188
    implementation, 180–81, 186–88
    and local knowledge, 189
    and municipal authorities, 185
    political implications, 188
    as politically neutral project, 184
    and reconciliation and reintegration,
        184–86
    top-down character, 180–86, 188
    See also villigisation
immigrant policy
    and moral behaviour, 54
immigrants
    Dutch, 55
    European, 55
    Mexican, 114
    undocumented, 53
immigration
    authorities, 44
    controls, 45
    procedures, 32
    regulations in the West, 46
Immigration and Asylum Act 1999
    (U.K.), 134
Immigration and Naturalisation
    Service (Netherlands), 58
income-generating, 21
    project, 76
    skills, 194
India, 8, 22, 23, 43, 193, 196
    British withdrawal (1947), 81
Indian(s), 139

Indian community property, 137
Indian resistance, 143
Indian Union, 82
indigenous, 138
  culture, 140
  values, 143
industrialisation, 3, 60
infectious diseases, 59. *See also* health
infiltration, 185
infrastructure, 37, 39, 169
  destruction, 168
  rehabilitation, 40
inheritance, 158
  male, 158
  virilocal forms, 158
innovative change, openness to, 24
institutional dependency, 76
insurgency, 137–38. *See also*
  counterinsurgency
integrated rural development, 187
interfaces, 177
  concept of, 177
  of cultivators and authorities, 186
  discontinuities, 178
  discrepancies, 178
intermarriage. *See* marriage
internal conflicts, 190–91
internally displaced persons, 27, 39,
  40, 193
  outnumbering refugees, 190
international accompaniment, 143
International Nursing Association, 60
International Red Cross, 76
intrastate conflicts, 4, 190
Iran, 9, 106
  prerevolutionary, 115
  revolution (1979), 106–108, 110,
    114
  'spring of freedom', 107
Irangeles, 114–18
Iranian-American, 116
irrigation schemes, 26
Islam, 132
  practice of, 133
Islamism, 107
Islamists, 107
isolation, 73
Italy, 57, 109
Ixcán, 138–39, 141, 146, 150
Ixmucané, 145

J
Jaffna, 43, 46–48, 156–57, 193, 195

job-oriented courses, 108
'Judgement of Solomon', 185. *See also*
  Gisenyi
'juggernaut of modernity', 97

K
kale-siyah (blackheads), 112
Kanaki, 161
Kandy, 49
Kandyan Sinhalese law, 158
kangas, 96, 98
Kanjobal, 147
Kanongesha, 34–36
Kanzenze (commune), 183–87
Katanga, 33
katchcheri (Government Agent's office),
  48
Kattankudy, 44–45
  Hussainiya mosque, 44
  Meera Jumma mosque, 44
Kerala, 158
Khartoum, 23
Khomeini, 111
Kibungo (Prefecture), 184
kidnap, 69–70, 138, 142
kinship, 7, 38, 71, 156, 158
  change, 88
  classificatory, 46
  Dravidian, 46, 156, 158
  group, 161
  matrilineal, 38, 47
  networks, 124
  ties, 46–47
kitchen sets, 40
Koppelingswet (Netherlands), 59
Kumaratunga, 44
Kutali, 47
kutis, 50

L
labelling, 15, 36, 83, 88, 112, 182
  derogatory, 186
  self-, 88, 92
labour
  bonds, 75
  contracts, 109
  forced, 33
  local, 35
  market, 20, 26, 75, 79, 86, 129
  migrants, 56, 124, 131, 137
  permanent, 137
  power, 34
ladinos, 139

land
  allocation of plots of, 36
  distribution, 11, 185, 187
  distribution patterns, 137
  distribution schemes, 158
  needs, 185
  owners, 70
  reform, 139
  restitution, 142
  rights, 156
  scarcity argument, 181
  tenure, 137
  use, 183–84
landing strips, 138
language
  Arab, 49
  classes, 130
  Dutch, 108
  English, 100, 103, 130
  French, 100
  Kirundi, 100
  linguistic groups, 147
  mastering foreign, 100
  problems, 62
  Spanish, 148
  Swahili, 100
latrines, 140
legal residence, 45
liberation theology, 138
Liberation Tigers of Tamil Eelam
    (LTTE), 43–44, 48–49, 153–54,
    185–87
'liberatory policy', 92
'life projects', 10
  reconstruction of, 74
liminality, 25, 26, 99, 103
'limits', 56
line ministries, 36
linking relief and development, 13
literacy, femal, 158. *See also* illiteracy
'little Iran' (Los Angeles), 10
London, 48
Los Angeles, 10, 106, 114–8
loss
  experience of, 185
  feeling of, 97–98
  making-up for, 29
  of morality, 78
  national citizenship, 19
  nonmaterial, 19
  (social) relationships, 19, 20
  sense of, 75
Lukole Refugee Camp, 94–105

Lunda (people), 32, 39
Lusaka peace process, 32
Lutheran World Federation (LWF),
    36/7, 185

M
macro-economic stabilisation, 169
Madhari, 161
Madhya Pradesh, 82
Madre Tierra, 145
malaria, 90
male dominance, 50
Mam, 138, 147
Mamá Maquín, 145, 147–48
Mana Camp, 90
mandates, 182
  of donor agencies, 172
Mannar, 153, 195
marginalisation, 25, 113, 117–18,
    199
marriage, 7, 34, 47–48
  arranged, 46, 111
  and children, 34
  cross-cousin, 46
  dowered, 46
  inter, 34
  inter-caste, 89, 157
  inter-communal, 51
  monetarisation of, 48
  remarriage, 157
Marxism, 107
Marxist organisations, 106–107
masculinity, 2, 10, 15, 103, 163
masonry, 196
matriclan system, 47
matrilineal societies, 158
matrilineal tendencies in Tamil society,
    155
Maya, 136–43
  area, 138
  associations, 149
  cultural needs, 149
  identity, 149
  mediation, 146
Meghalaya, 82
mercenaries, 70
message transfer, 100
Mexico, 8, 9, 136–150
Middle East, 48, 111
migrants
  economic, 39, 40, 78, 80
  as guests, 109
  as 'other', 109

migration,
chain, 46, 124, 131
choice, 51
internal, 51
research, 51
for short-term work, 48
unwanted, 56
voluntary, 32
military, 137, 172
military training, 102
mines, 23
mistrust, 71–73
'mobile lives', 73
mobility, 72, 100
experiences of, 79
patterns, 157
physical, 91
traditions of, 74
'model villages', 140
modernisation, 3, 136
Moneragala, 47
moral choices, 198
'moral community', 78
morality, 198–99
Morocco, 109
mosques, destruction of, 49
Mothers and Daughters of Lanka, 153
Mothers' Front, 153
Mothers of the Disappeared, 153
motivation, 7
MPLA, 33
mugorigori (beer made from maize),
    101
Mukkuvar society, 51
Muslim Bosnians, 132
Muslim-Croat Federation (Bosnia), 130
Muslims, 42, 81, 131
British, 132–33
elite self-representation, 49
as harbingers of peace and order, 50
identity, 112
as land-owning town people, 51
localising strategy, 48
national identity, 48
personal law, 158
prosecution by Croats in Bosnia,
    131, 133
settlements, 48, 50
Sri Lanka, 43–50, 193–94
withdrawal into its own defended
    territory, 52
muzungu, 100, 103
Mwanta Yavwa, kingdom of (Congo-

Kinshasa), 33
Mwinulunga District (Zambia), 32, 38

N
Nahal, 26
Nairobi, 101
narratives, 15, 107, 118, 182, 188
acceptance of, 188
auto-, 9
broadening historical, 143
explanatory, 187
of life, 106
master, 8, 139
of the past, 92
self-, 106
of violence, 71
widow's, 84, 91
nation-state formation, 4
national antagonism, 132
national bourgeoisie, 137
'National Dialogue', 145
National Institute of Agrarian
    Transformation (INTA), 139
nationalism
Sinhala, 49
Tamil, 49
national reconstruction, 135, 149
National Registration Card (Zambia),
    35
green, 35
nationalist leaders, 130
nationalist mobilisation, 152
nationality, 6, 32, 35, 113, 117
attachment to, 35
change, 32
of the groom, 46
papers, 38
Zambian, 39, 40
natural resources, 38. *See also*
    exploitation
Nayars, 158
Nehru, Jawaharlal, 85
neoliberal development strategy, 137
neoliberal ideology, 136
neophytes in rites de passage, 99
Netherlands, 9, 56, 106–114, 116–18,
    192, 199
Advisory Council on International
    Affairs, 192, 199
Minister of Development
    Cooperation, 174, 192
neutral aid, 192
neutrality, 13, 60

concept of, 15
versus engagement, 191–200
Newcastle, 125
news distribution, 48
NGOs, 95–96, 100, 101, 136, 159, 169,
    181–82, 184, 194, 199
consortium, 194
embezzlement, 101
funding cornmill project, 148
'incentives', 100
as intermediaries, 101
international, 149, 187
local, 172, 194, 196
relief, 182
staff for workshops, 144
UNHCR-funded, 196–97
non-agency, 84
non-interference, principle of, 55
normative standards, 55
North America, 193
Northern Red Sea region, 28
Norway, 42, 46, 154, 193
nostalgia, 78, 80, 118
    ambiguous, 78
feelings, 110
Nuevo Huíxtan, 144
nutritional indicators, 169

O
observers, 149
Ombudsman, 76
openness, 65
oral histories, 50. *See also* narratives
'ordinary criminality', 70
'organic intellectuals' (Gramsci), 144
organisational cultures, 176
Organisation of American States
    (OAS), 137
Organisation of Economic Cooperation
    and Development (OECD),   175
Orientalism, 111
Orissa, 82
'orphan camps', 85
orphans, 138
Orwell's 1984, 131
Oslo, 48
'othering'
    process of, 9, 27, 109, 113, 116, 118
'otherness', 12
    Iranian women in the Netherlands,
        108–109
    Iranian women in the United States,
        114–18

racial aspect of, 112
OXFAM, 97, 198
Sanitation Information Team, 96

P
paisanos, 74–76
Pahlevi regime, 107
Pakistan, 50, 81
West, 81
East, 81–82, 84, 88
paramilitary groups, 70, 136, 154
state-sponsored, 136
parcelas, 138
partiality, explicit, 192
participation, 13
institutionalised forms of, 73
participatory development theory, 198
Parti pour la Libération du Peuple Hutu
    (Palipetehu), 102
partition, 92
'Partition' (India/Pakistan – 1947), 81,
    90
pass, 195
system, 196
three months-, 196
passivity, 15
passports, 101
pastoralists, 26
Pathan
men, 51
warriors, 50
Paththini, 161
patriarchy, 11, 95, 155
breakdown of authority, 104
British Victorian, 156
cultures, 155, 162
and gender equality, 98
society, 90–93
system, 92
patrilineal descent, 155
patrilineal group, 158
patronising attitudes, 15
patterns of movement, 40
paysannat, 189
peasant
economy, 143
organisations, 72, 149
peer group
evaluation, 101
loyalty, 12
pension, 89, 91
People's Liberation Organisation of
    Tamil Eelam (PLOTE), 154

Permanent Commissions of
    Guatemalan Refugees In Mexico,
    136, 142, 144–46, 149
    and participation in Esquipulas
        process, 142
permanent liability camps, 8, 81–93
    Darbhanga, 83
    Deoghar, 83, 85, 88, 90
    Gaya, 83
    Khanjarpur, 83, 91
    Monghyr, 83
    Ranchi (Brambey), 83, 85, 88, 90
permit to stay, 57
Petén, 139, 141, 145
petitions, 90
philanthropic philosophies, 13
physical safety, 19
placidity, 28
planned development interventions,
    187
planned mobility, 45
plantation
    building, 137
    labourers, 137
    workforce, 194
plunder, 170
pocket money, 196
polarisation, 4
police stations, 43, 100
    Kalmunai, 44
policy discourses, 14
political activism, 106, 108–109, 151
political affiliation, 77
political aid, 149
political constraints, 148
political deprivation, 186
political imagery, 48
political involvement, 107, 149
politically 'cleansed' space, 102
politically vulnerable people, 199
political mobilisation, 152
political motivation, of local officials,
    186
political persecution, 59
    fear of, 78
    protection against, 55
    refuge from, 58
political representation
    at local level, 123
'politics of the belly', 102
pollution, 148
Polonnaruwa, 45
Popol Wuh, 143

population
    community-oriented nature, 9
    growth (Rwanda), 180
    density, 40, 180
    increase, 31
    regrouping, 183
Portuguese colonial regime, 33
post-conflict societies, 174
potable water system, 147
pottu, 160
poultry, 34
poverty, as a motive force, 23–24
poverty line, 137
power
    distribution, 123
    and knowledge, 123
preservation of rivers, 148
Presidential Solidarity Network, 76
priests, 139–40
privacy, 143
procession, 146
PROFERI programme, 29
professional 'agents', 46
'progressive policy', 92
protest actions, 76
public sector, 45
Punjab, 22
purana (villagers), 156

Q
Qala, 26
Quetzal Edzná, 141
Quezada Toruno, Monsignor Rodolfo,
    142
quick impact projects (QIPs), 37
Quintana Roo, 138, 150

R
racism, 143
raids, 70
rape, 11, 58
    established as 'war crime', 151
    as systematic policy of ethnic
        cleansing, 154
Rasik group, 154
ration card, 91
reception centres, 124
    length of stay, 125
refugee(s)
    access to business licences, 21
    adaptability, 21, 100
    as assets rather than a liability to
        society, 134

as babies in the arms of UNHCR, 102
as benefits to society, 123
as burden to host society, 32, 36, 82, 86, 123
boosting local production, 36
categorisation of, 36
credit facilities, 21
criminalisation of, 54
distorted images of, 16
economic, 5
'fake', 7, 12,
feeling of 'in-betweenness', 99
'genuine', 12, 39, 57
as helpless women and children, 103
human dignity, 195
human rights, 12
inability to help themselves, 24
income-generating activities, 22, 25,
income-generating opportunities, 21
integration, 37–8
internal, 190–200
as a legal concept, 45
and literacy, 100
loneliness, 128
mode of definition for, 124
motivation, 39
as objects of pity, 123
participation, 95
passivity, 176
passivity and dependency through aid, 195
perception as burden, 21
perception as deskilled, 21
perception as immobilised, 21
perception as liabilities, 83
perception as passive and dependent, 15, 16
perception as people with initiative and talent, 9
perception as a resource, 21, 29,
perception as traumatised, 21
permanent, 82
political, 5, 114
protection in Western countries, 45–46,
'pure', 7, 65
'real', 56
registration, 36–37
relationship with support staff, 133
and restrictions, 37
of rural origin, 20
self-confidence, 195

self organisations, 194
self-settled, 36, 39, 41
social interaction, 37
static view of, 40
stories, 57
timidity, 100
training opportunities, 21
treated like patients, 24
treated as strangers, 108
'underclass', 195
and Universal Declaration on Human Rights, 53
urban, 20, 21
'voting with their feet', 32
working as businessmen, 100, 101, 103
working for relief agencies, 100
refugee concept
'demasculinisation' of, 91
Refugee Convention (1951). *See* UN
'refugee crisis', 192
Refugee (Control) Act 1970 (Zambia), 36
refugee cycle, 31
Refugee Identity Card (Zambia), 35
'refugee issue', 4
'refugeeness', 3
'refugee problem', 39, 41
refugee research, 42
relief and development
and chronology, 173
compartmentalisation as self-inflicted restriction, 175
conceptual differences, 172, 175–76
constraints, 176
continuum, 14, 167–68, 173–75, 177
coordination, 168
costs, 173
debate on linking, 167–79
donor's political judgement, 172
discontinuity, 167
fundamental differences, 170
gap, 174
institutional differences, 172, 175–76
integrated approach, 14, 188–89, 191
international recognition, 172
multitrack approach, 173
and population's vulnerability shocks, 169
rehabilitation as logical junction, 169
strict separation, 191
religious activities, 149
religious councils, 123

religious services, 140
remarriage. *See* marriage
repatriation, 135–36, 144, 148–50, 178
  development and successful, 135
  discourse, 27
  'events of', 6
  full-scale, 141
  Meheba settlement, 37
  orderly and effective, 136
  programmes, 40
  not a straightforward or problem-
    free solution, 27
  studies, 32
  and tension, 28
  voluntary, 27, 31, 32
  from Zambia to Angola, 39
repression, 135–50, 199
resettlement projects, perception as
  'cannon fodder', 197
resilience, 74
  emotional, 75
resistance, culture of, 82
respect
  for 'big men', 98
  lack of, 97–98
  for politicians, 103
restitutio ad integrum, 28
retainment of culture, 144
retaliation, 185
retaliatory killings, 44
return
  assumption of, 159
  collective, 136, 142, 146
  desire to, 109
  expectation of, 129–33
  link between migration and, 109
  myth of, 9, 109
    the waning of, 114
  negotiation of terms, 136
  'to reconstruct the country', 149
  and structural reform, 135
  voluntary, 142
  working concept, 146
returnees
  New Case, 180, 184–86, 189
  Old Case, 180–181, 185–86, 189
'rightful struggle', 103
riots, 81, 91, 193, 197
risk
  -aversion, 22
  -spreading, 25
  -taking, 9, 22–23
ritual sanctions, 91

road building, 35
Roche, Barbara (British MP), 123
RPF, 183
rubber tapping, 148
rude behaviour, 102
Rugby, 125
Rwanda, 13, 101–102, 151, 174, 179–89,
  191

S
sabotage, 138
Said, Edward, 111
Salmin, 27
sanitation, 175
schools, 33–37, 39
  fees, 37
  local secondary, 34
  teachers, 72, 75
scientific objectivity, 60
'scorched-earth' campaign, 8, 136–37
Scottish Refugee Council, 121
sedentarisation, 26
segmentation, 131
self-confidence, 8, 9, 91
self-enrichment, 101
self-initiatives, 5, 7,
self-interest, concept of, 60
self-reliance, 13
self-repatriates, 28
self-representation, right of, 142
self-sufficiency, 36, 137
selfishness, 95
Semsem, 26
Serbs, 131
Serb republic (Bosnia), 130
service availability, 29
service providers, united front against,
  133
settlement papers, 46
sexual service industry, 154
sexual vulnerability, 154
Shah, 114
shambas (fields), 94
Sharia law, 22
Siddambarapuram, 156–60
Sikhs, 22, 81
Sillapaddikaram, 161
Sinhalese, 43, 154–55, 158, 193, 197
  chauvinism, 49
slave trade, 33
solidarity
  bonds of, 46, 71
  eroded, 73

Solwezi, 35, 37
'social breakdown', phenomenon of, 20
social change, 187
social consciousness, 136, 139
social decay, 104
social equality, 95
social history, 144
social inclusion in American society, 118
social mobility, 46
social networks, 24, 46
social organisations, 24
social reality, description of, 140
social relations, spatial dimension, 47
social security, 75
social segregation, 157
social skills, 103
social tension, 186
social transformation
    as a dialectic process, 4
    dimensions, 5
social values, emergence of new, 99
solar-powered radio, 148
solidarity aid, 149
solidarity tour to the United States, 148
Solihull, 125
'soup-kitchen' mentality, 194
South Asia, 133, 158
Spain, 109
Spanish conquest, 143
Srebrenica, 191
Sri Lanka, 13, 42–52, 77, 105, 151–63, 190–200
    Airforce, 153
    Army, 153
    Freedom Party, 49
    independence from United Kingdom, 193–94
    Muslim Congress (SLMC), 49, 50
state-imposed restrictions, 3
state fragmentation, 69
state officials, 36
state power, exertion of, 92
state sovereignty, 197
status, 41
    change of, 40
    refugee, 130
    social, 47, 50
    socio-economic, 25
    temporary, 122
stereotypes

characteristics, 113
of Middle Eastern women, 111
perceptions, 110
Stettler, Karl (German priest), 139
stigmatisation, 78–79
street leaders, 99, 100, 102, 104
    election of, 95
street selling/sellers, 75, 79
strong state, 29
structural adjustment programmes, 197
structural discontinuity, concept of, 177
submission, 70
subsistence, 76
    (in)security, 22, 26
    needs, 149
    peasantry, 136
Sudan, 22, 24
suicide, 51
    tendencies, 163
sumankali, 160
Supreme Court (India), 90
surveillance, 181
survival
    daily activities, 74, 76
    guarantee of, 79
    physical, 170, 176
    responsibilities, 77, 80
    stories, 140
    strategies, 24, 74
svartskallar (blackheads in Swedish), 112
Sweden, 146
Swedes, 112

T
taboo, 62
    purity pollution, 157
    sexuality, 92
Taliban, 162, 192
Tamil, 11, 42–52
    Batticaloa, 194
    diaspora, 48
    Jaffna, 194
    Indian, 43, 194
    mythology, 161
    settlements, 51
    Plantation, 194–97
    Sri-Lanka, 43, 194
    as 'state enemies', 197
    'Tamil homeland', 197
Tamil Nadu, 197

Tanzania, 10, 94–105, 180, 185
target groups, 175
taxes, 33, 88, 102, 154
teaching certificates, 144
Teheran, 108
Telata Asher, 29
temples, 193
temporary protection, 129–30
temporary residence, 32, 110
terror, 70, 71, 154
Tessenei, 23, 28, 29
testimonies, 97
Thailand, 154, 193
Thali, 51
Thesawalamai law, 155, 158
'time-space strategies', 52
top-down
    attitudes, 15
    development, 187
    governance, 188
    implementation, 180
    procedures, 3
    programme, 13, 187
torture, 108, 154
tourist visa, 53
tractor, 51
    use, 27
transformation, 25, 27
transit camp, 196
trauma, 13, 27, 28, 75, 152, 154, 160
    experiences, 15
    and memories, 78
    psychological, 22, 159
    recovery from, 161
traumatised people, 58–59
trading, 38
transport papers, 46
Tripura, 82
trucking industry, 23
tuberculosis, 59
Turbo, 70
Turkey, 109
Tutsi, 104, 180–83, 186
    authorities, 186
Twa, 94

U
Uganda, 124, 129
Um Hajer, 29
urbanisation, 97–98
United Nations, 149, 181–82, 191
    Development Programme (UNDP),
        174–75

humanitarian coordinators, 175
'neutral' military protection, 191
Refugee Convention (1951), 32,
    57–58, 140, 190
    Protocol (1967), 140
Special Rapporteur on Violence
    Against Women, 151
unemployment, 75, 79. *See also*
    employment
unfair treatment, 102
UNHCR, 11, 135, 140, 145–46, 156, 182,
    194–95
    in Angola, 32–3, 36–7, 39, 40
    as a 'better husband', 11, 94, 98
    in Bosnia, 121
    ideology and practice of equality,
        103
    'laws', 96
    in Tanzania, 95–96, 100, 102–103
UNICEF, 194
UNITA, 33
    conscription, 35
United Kingdom, 121–34, 193
United Nations, 100
United States, 9, 106–107, 112, 114–18,
    148
Universal Declaration of Human
    Rights (1948). *See* Human Rights
upper Zambezi, 33
uprooting, 28, 70–74, 108
    economic, 21
    feelings, 118
    link with social change, 22
    sense of – in the Netherlands, 113
    social, 21
    within own community, 190
urgency, 182
uxorilocal practice, 48

V
Vakarai, 50
Vanni region, 156, 193
Vavuniya, 153, 156–58, 160, 194–97
Veedu attavargal, 154
veils, wearing of, 111
velinatu (foreign land), 45
vengeance, 69
victim, 72
    discourse, 1
    ideology, 11, 14, 161
    passive, 9, 111
    of violence, 78
victimisation, 49, 84, 91

Vietnamese refugees, 129, 132
  isolation, 126
  refugee programme, 125–6
  secondary migration, 126
village headmen, 35
village leaders, 98, 100, 102
  elections, 95
villigisation
  contribution to reconciliation and
    reintegration, 184, 186
  implementation, 180–81
  involvement of donor
    representatives, 182
  political objectives for, 181
  sites, 180
  See also Imidigudu
violence
  counterrevolutionary, 137
  domestic, 58–9, 154, 163
  genocidal, 136
  inter-ethnic, 199
  physical, 22
  political, 199
  sexual, 11, 153
  state, 58
  suddenness, 75
  traumatic, 162
  upsurges, 190
  victims of, 78
La Violencia, 70
visa document, 130
voluntary groups, 128, 134
voluntary sector, 124
Voluntary Services Unit (U.K. Home
  Office), 123/4
volunteers, 64
  'silent network', 64
  teams, delegation to, 140
voting rights, 86
vulnerability, 22, 95, 170, 173, 200
'Vulnerability and Capacity
  Assessments', 175

W
warlords, 168
war zones, 195–96
wazungu (white men), 94
weaving, 147
'webs of relationships', 20
welfare benefits, 126, 129
  for asylum seekers, 134
'Welfare centres', 153, 193, 196
welfare state, the declining, 65

well-functioning state, 29
West Bengal, 81–82, 85, 91
Western Europe, 23, 193
'whiteness', 112
  construction of, 114
  neutrality of, 112
widowhood, 11
  culturally prescribed role, 160
  Hindu, 160
  in India, 91
  as polluting and inauspicious state
    of being, 160
women
  agency in post-conflict situations,
    152–53
  as breadwinner, 96
  and burden of social stigma, 155
  cadres, 153
  committees, 95
  'double burden', 11, 153, 155, 161
  employment, 156
  empowerment, 151, 159, 161
  and guilt, 160–61
  as head of household, 152, 155–57
  health needs, 198
  high status in society, 156–57, 162
  as housemaids, 196
  lack of male support, 161
  land rights, 158
  life stories, 91, 106–107, 110, 113
  militants, 155
  mobility, 153, 156–57, 159, 162
  negative images of Middle Eastern,
    112
  organisations, 115
  participation, 95
  as principal decision-maker, 157
  as principal income-generator, 152,
    155
  promiscuity, 105
  prostitution, 96, 154
  protest, 87–88
  rape, 151–55
  recruitment in armed liberation
    army, 47
  rights, 107
  sanitation needs, 198
  and secondary victimisation, 155,
    161
  self-esteem, 162
  sexual services, 91
  sexual vulnerability, 154
  shame, 58–59

single – and sexuality, 92
transformed roles, 152, 160
'unattached', 82–83
as (helpless/passive) victims, 95,
    111, 152–53
as victims of war, 151–56
Women for Peace, 153
Women's Coalition for Peace, 153
Woods, William (Maryknoll priest),
    139
workshops, 144

Xamán, 147

Yucatan, 138
Yugoslavia, 130, 132, 151, 191

Zaire, 180
Zambia, 6, 31–41
    Government Commissioner for
        Refugees, 36
    law, 40